Law, Art and the Common

The concept of the cultural commons has become increasingly important for legal studies. Within this field, however, it is a contested concept: a sphere for creativity, democratic access and freedom of speech, but one that denies property rights and misappropriates the public domain. In this book, Merima Bruncevic takes up the cultural commons not merely as an abstract notion, but in its connection to physical spaces such as museums and libraries. A legal cultural commons can, she argues, be envisioned as a *lawscape* that can quite literally be entered and engaged with. Focusing largely on art in the context of the copyright regime, but also addressing a number of cultural heritage issues, the book draws on the work of Deleuze and Guattari in order to examine the realm of the commons as a potential space for overcoming the dichotomy between the owner and the consumer of culture. Challenging this dichotomy, it is the productive and creative potential of law itself that is elicited through the book's approach to the commons as the empirical basis for a new legal framework, which is able to accommodate a multitude of interests and values.

Merima Bruncevic is Senior Lecturer and Research Fellow based in the Department of Law, Gothenburg University.

Space, Materiality and the Normative

Series Editors: Andreas Philippopoulos-Mihalopoulos and Christian Borch

Space, Materiality and the Normative presents new ways of thinking about the connections between space and materiality from a normative perspective. At the interface of law, social theory, politics, architecture, geography and urban studies, the series is concerned with addressing the use, regulation and experience of space and materiality, broadly understood, and in particular with exploring their links and the challenges they raise for law, politics and normativity.

Books in this series:

Spaces of Justice
Peripheries, Passages, Appropriations
Chris Butler and Edward Mussawir

Spacing Law and Politics
The Constitution and Representation of the Juridical
Leif Dahlberg

A Jurisprudence of Movement
Common Law, Walking, Unsettling Place
Olivia Barr

Animals, Biopolitics, Law
Lively Legalities
Irus Braverman

Spatial Justice
Body, Lawscape, Atmosphere
Andreas Philippopoulos-Mihalopoulos

Urban Commons
Rethinking the City
Christian Borch and Martin Kornberger

www.routledge.com/Space-Materiality-and-the-Normative/book-series/SMNORM

Law, Art and the Commons

Merima Bruncevic

Routledge
Taylor & Francis Group
LONDON AND NEW YORK

First published 2018 by Routledge

2 Park Square, Milton Park, Abingdon, Oxfordshire OX14 4RN
52 Vanderbilt Avenue, New York, NY 10017

a GlassHouse book

Routledge is an imprint of the Taylor & Francis Group, an informa business

First issued in paperback 2019

British Library Cataloguing in Publication Data
A catalogue record for this book is available from the British Library

Library of Congress Cataloging in Publication Data
Names: Bruncevic, Merima, author.
Title: Law, art and the commons / Merima Bruncevic.
Description: Space, materiality and the normative. | Abingdon, Oxon ; New York, NY : Routledge, 2018. | Based on author's thesis (doctoral - Gèoteborgs universitet, 2014) issued under title: Fixing the shadows : access to art and the legal concept of the cultural commons. | Includes bibliographical references and index.
Identifiers: LCCN 2017023443 | ISBN 9781138697546 (hardback)
Subjects: LCSH: Culture and law. | Law and art. | Intellectual property. | Deleuze, Gilles, 1925-1995--Influence. | Guattari, Fâelix, 1930-1992--Influence.
Classification: LCC K487.C8 B78 2018 | DDC 344/.097--dc23
LC record available at https://lccn.loc.gov/2017023443

ISBN: 978-1-138-69754-6 (hbk)
ISBN: 978-0-367-23249-8 (pbk)

Typeset in Baskerville
by Fish Books Ltd.

Contents

Acknowledgements

Thank you Colin Perrin, and Routledge, for giving me the opportunity to write this book the way I envisioned it.

Thank you Andreas Philippopoulos-Mihalopoulos, for seeing that it could be part of the Space, Materiality and the Normative series, and for all your work that has been so inspiring not just to me, but to so many of us.

Thank you Fiona Macmillan, for being a wonderful mentor and role model, and for inviting me to Rome and Roma Tre where most of this book was written.

Thank you Håkan Gustafsson, for opening up the world of legal philosophy to me, from that very first lecture on Frankfurt School, to your supervision during my doctoral studies, through to this day, without you, I would not be here.

Thank you Jannice Käll, for being my friend, colleague and collaborator that resolutely and always stands next to me.

Thank you Department of Law, Gothenburg University, for being such an encouraging academic environment.

Thank you students, for keeping me on my toes.

Thank you Gothenburg, Rome, Paris, for the spaces of existence.

Thank you art and culture for being entangled with me and for giving me reason to breathe.

Thank you friends, for walking with me.

Thank you family and loved ones, for being the stable foundation that even a nomad needs.

Götaplatsen, Gothenburg
7 April 2017

Preface

Drank the kool-aid?

The summer is withdrawing. We have just arrived in London. We have *four hours* here before we need to get to Heathrow to catch our flight that is taking us back to Gothenburg. We took the high-speed Southeastern train in the morning from Canterbury West to Charing Cross. The train was late, but incidentally we were on time. We have only four hours and the clock starts – now.

> *Atmosphere*
> *Change of seasons*
> *Affect*
> *Transportation and movement*
> *Across territories*
> *Time*

There are five of us. We have a plan, to go on a London walk, a walk that begins in Trafalgar Square and ends in front of Birkbeck College. We have just left the Critical Legal Conference held at Kent University (the year is 2016, it was the conference's 20th anniversary). Some of the "sights" on our planned walk include Westminster Law School on Little Titchfield St. and Birkbeck College (the Mecca of critical legal thinking in Europe as someone at the CLC had referred to it).

> *Familiar*
> *Uncanny*
> *Networks*

We begin by walking from Charing Cross to Trafalgar Square. From there, I thought, we will be able to see Nelson's Column, Big Ben, the Houses of Parliament and the National Gallery all at once. But what will it mean to *see*?[1] Besides, we can only stay five minutes if we want to make the full walk.

1 For a general view on law and senses see The Westminster Online Working Papers *Non Liquet*: https://nonliquetlaw.wordpress.com/

So we walk briskly and reach Trafalgar Square rather quickly. When strategically placed we can indeed see all sights, simultaneously. Standing on the steps in front of the National Gallery we become *entangled* with the *atmosphere* of the place, with the London traffic, with the noises of buses, the excitement of tourists, the concentration of the street performers, the frustration of Londoners trying to get on with their Sunday plans... It is intoxicating. To *see* turns out to mean to enter this open space and to *become* entangled with the *bodies* that are there, to become *other*, to see means engaging all our sensorial perceptions at once. We take some photos, we point to some landmarks, we catch some Pokémons on the go. Then we leave. Did I mention? We are in a hurry. Three and a half hours left.

Landmarks
Spaces of culture
Museums
Entanglement
Bodies
Digital platforms

We walk up Charing Cross Road, through China Town (where Jannice quips: "This almost feels like Singapore, with the British and the Asian blended!"), we cross Shaftsbury Avenue, walk across Soho (we walk past those gentrified sex shops and commercial massage parlours that are more boring than they are subversive). As we are walking I am telling whomever happens to be walking next to me about my own memories from living in London: "I used to work in this shoe shop when I was a student," "Curzon Soho is one of my favourite cinemas in the world." Three hours left.

Hybrid spaces
Sexuality
Identity
Memory

We reach Carnaby Street, and the discussion inevitably turns to the Swinging 60s. The era that once defined London still seems to be an indispensable part of the London *brand* or perhaps more so of its *heritage*. Then we walk to Piccadilly Circus – a circus, but not one in a traditional sense – a circular view and a focal point of traffic, information, sounds, smells, people, vehicles and spaces. We walk up Regent Street towards Oxford Circus. Kristina is not feeling well, it has been a long week, she has delivered her first conference presentation. The paper she presented was entitled "The court as the narrator: narrative strategies in the construction of children as legal subjects". The presentation was a success, but now, as with most of us after a significant conference presentation, her energy levels are wearing thin, she is breathless, she needs to sit down, rest, breathe, eat. Two hours and three quarters.

Heritage
Brands
Lack
Energy
Will to power

We cross Oxford Circus diagonally (they did not believe me that it was possible!) and walk to my alma mater, the University of Westminster. Of course we cannot enter the building, because we are not students or staff. Andreas Philippopoulos-Mihalopoulos, Andrea Pavoni and Danilo Mandic will be organising a conference here in November, we will be back soon.[2] We are hungry. The restaurant on the corner of Little Titchfield St. is full, *no room* for us, so we have to keep walking. We find another place somewhere off Goodge Street. Two and a half hours left.

During our lunch we inventory what is left to do: a run through the British Museum, only to see the Rosetta Stone and the Elgin Marbles. We do not have time for anything else, but I would have loved to see the exhibition "Sunken cities, Egypt's lost worlds"[3] because I have been doing some work on the 2001 UNESCO Convention on the Protection of the Underwater Cultural Heritage at Roma Tre. Then we plan on going to Store Street Espresso (best coffee in London?), Waterstones on Gower Street (best bookshop in London – no question mark), then the School of Law at Birkbeck and then back to the train station. Can we make it? I doubt it, I know too many people that have missed their flights like this, underestimating the congestion and inertia of the London traffic. We have to get back to Charing Cross, get our luggage, get to Paddington, take the Heathrow Express. There may be delays. But we, or they, my friends, decide to roll the dice, give it a try anyway. I, as they say in memes with cute cats, "sweatz profusely". The lunch also took longer than we thought. I tell them that if we want to do all of this in the time frame that we have left we will have to walk even quicker – and no complaints. They don't listen. One hour 45 minutes.

2 Law and the Senses Conference II, held 17–18 November 2016 at the University of Westminster.

3 I did return two months later and see the exhibition. While it was impressive in many ways, the irony of an exhibition on sunken cities being corporately financed by British Petroleum was impossible to ignore, keeping in mind the Deepwater Horizon oil spill that the very same company was responsible for a couple of years before the exhibition itself. Was this meant to appease something? On oil spills as hyperobjects, see Morton, 2013.

Barred entry
Enclosure
No room
Cultural heritage
Aleatory points
Speed

We cross Tottenham Court Road and half run towards the British Museum. A group of women cut in before us on the street and we have to *slow* down. Erik says: "This is *spatial justice* for you," I give him an annoyed look. When we finally arrive at the courtyard in front of the British Museum we realise that we are being diverted to a tent on the left-hand side for security checks. There is a queue there. We look at the clock.

Once through the museum security, we run. We run past that Tennyson quote: *and let thy feet millenniums hence be set in the midst of knowledge.*[4] Then we run to Gallery 4 where we find the Rosetta Stone at the very entrance (Oh I had it all wrong – it was discovered by the French and not the British! I mutter, half to myself), we run past the Elgin Marbles. My friends all love the female statues, with the delicate *folds* in the stone, that still to this day seem to be fluttering in the Mediterranean summer breeze. I love the male statute, the one whose head is still preserved, albeit battered. I think about the bodies, past and present, more or less living,[5] at the shores[6] and in the waters[7] of the Mediterranean. Somebody remarks on the centaurs – half men, half animals, so beyond the anthropocentric glance, *posthuman*. One hour.

Borders
Spatial justice
Cultural entanglement
Slowness of time
Imperialism/colonialism
Posthuman

When we walk out of the British Museum, we are all a little bit sweaty, increasingly exhausted, but also inspired, moved, still determined to manage to visit the sights that are left. David walks next to me and remarks in passing and a little bit absentmindedly: "I still think the friezes should be returned to Greece, where they rightfully belong." "It is not that easy," I reply. "There is some form of legal title, a *firman*, and the British Museum

4 The excerpt from the "Two Voices" poem by Tennyson famously inscribed on the floor at the entrance of the British Museum.

5 Bennett, 2009.

6 A child's body, washed up at the shores of Turkey.

7 Drowned people, sunken ships, is that too dark heritage?

is a type of *commons*, but then the imperial aspect of it…" I run out of breath.[8] We round the British Museum and we find ourselves in front of Senate House. We stand still for a moment. Somebody once told me that they say that Hitler wanted this building to be his headquarters, if ever he took over London. We laugh. "He would choose this building, wouldn't he?" Jannice remarks, "It looks Argentinian to me," David says. Erik takes a photo. Kristina is adding me on Instagram. Fifty minutes left.

Digital platforms
War machine

Then we go through the gates and enter the courtyard. We stand in front of Birkbeck School of Law. Suddenly there is a quiet silence that is flowing between us, somehow binding us together, connecting us to the building in front of us. None of us says a word. But we all know that something is being formed right then and there that will *stick* to us, some call it memory, others call it *hyperobjects*. Then we run again. We take the side entrance to Waterstones. "How much time do we have?" somebody asks. "Five minutes," I reply sarcastically. They all laugh again.

The philosophy section is on the third floor of the bookshop. We run up the stairs. We tear down books by Deleuze, Guattari, Haraway, Husserl, Nietzsche. We run to the tills. There is a 10p surcharge for the plastic bags.[9] *Nature. Oil. Plastic. Global warming*. We think about the *Earth* for a second as we look outside.[10] The London *air*[11] is thick as usual. Is our time up?

Environment
Air
Resources

Undulation of time: we have to head back. Still time for a coffee? Maybe. Two matcha lattes, and three cappuccinos in take away cups later, and we are running towards Tottenham Court Road tube station. I am in front of the pack with David, manoeuvring through the bodies in front of us. At this point David is the only one who is even trying to keep up the pace. We are still talking, discussing human rights and Nancy's concepts of singular-plural[12] as we scurry. The others are lagging behind and we keep losing sight of them. In the end we all gather at the *underground* station, the subterranean web of transport that will allow us to escape the congestion on the ground and take us to the airport. On time. If we are lucky.

8 Waxman, 2010; Bring, 2015.
9 Purdy, 2015.
10 Bring, 2015.
11 Hyde, 2012.
12 Nancy, 2000.

The Northern Line takes us back to Charing Cross. We collect our luggage and head back to the underground, to the Bakerloo Line. At Paddington, the Heathrow Express is on time. We are on time. Terminal 5 looks like a *mirage* once we get to the arrival hall. We made it.

Taste
Underground
Rhizome
Singular/plural
Flight – lines of flight

Volume I

(Re)Imaginations

Part 1

Law

Chapter 1

Enter

From landscape to lawscape

1.1 A walk in the commons

Much like the title gives away, this book is, simply put, about law, art and commons. The four hours in London can be the framework for it. It recounts very much true events, or as true as I remember them now as I am writing them down, a couple of months after they took place. It occurred to me that the four hours in London encapsulate what this book tries to show, that these four hours may perfectly depict what I am trying to discuss and advance here. Dear reader, this book is a walk, sometimes quicker, sometimes slower, sometimes full speed ahead, through museums, cityscapes, cultural landscapes, through subterranean webs, into the world of law, art and commons. It is a human story as much as it is a story of something well beyond the human, dare I say *post*human. I do not mean any of these as metaphors either as you will shortly see. To read this book means to enter into the cultural commons through the lawscape, to walk in it, to displace ourselves in it. Literally. Sometimes I walk alone, sometimes we walk together, at times I am in the more or less reassuring company of others, as we traverse these spheres. In this book I will be presenting something that may at times seem like abstract, ephemeral, imaginary concepts. Sometimes they will seem material, concrete, menacing, real, *all too real.* I want you to think about the four hours in London when those feelings overwhelm you, and know that they are at the same time true as they are constructed figments of (my? our collective?) imagination. Rest assured. You are in a safe environment. This is only a drill. A simulation.

To express it more plainly and bluntly. This book explores the possibility of constructing a legal concept of the cultural commons. In order to do that law, art and the commons need to be expressly connected. Or better yet, the connections that are already there, binding the three together, already entangling them, forming a space, an object, a *hyperobject*, will be revealed here. I will attempt to do precisely that by setting in motion the so called *rhizome theory* developed by Gilles Deleuze and Félix Guattari. I will then fold their theory within the writings of Andreas Philippopoulos-

Mihalopoulos on spatial justice, concentrating mainly on the notion of *lawscape*.

This book discusses how to advance legal pathways that facilitate access, ownership, control and production of art through a cultural commons. The idea of the *legal concept of the cultural commons* is introduced and towards the end of the book given a platform in law. In order to arrive there, firstly, the commons needed to be *conceived of* in jurisprudence. The book therefore begins with a rather traditional legal approach analysing the impediments that jurisprudence seems to face in conceiving of such a concept as the cultural commons. Through a theoretical exercise that opens up the possibility of so called rhizomatic jurisprudence, the first part of the book, Volume I (Re)Imaginations, studies various perceived legal obstacles that stand between law and a concept of the commons. Volume I aims to get at the potential of law in imaging, reimaging, seeing or even remembering, the commons. The second volume is called (Re)Constructions and it (de and re)constructs the concept of the commons, both how it has been described in previous research and how it may be taken forward today. Volume II aims to analyse the potential of a cultural commons concept and its interaction with law. The overall aim of the book is of course to arrive at a legal concept of cultural commons in the end.

The book focuses on questions such as what does law *do*, what could it *do*, other than settle conflicts and answer the questions: *who* the legal owner of the artwork is or who owns the intellectual property right. Is it at all possible for law to do something other than that? Can law be a productive, creative force and envision as well as create the concept of the commons?

In order to answer those questions, I use the theory developed by the French philosopher Gilles Deleuze (1925-1995) and the French psychoanalyst Félix Guattari (1930-1992), particularly in dealing with law. I develop a critique of dogmatic legal reasoning and study particular obstacles to commons created by e.g. traditional divisions in law, for instance the private and the public, property and personhood, inside and outside. This is done by leaning on the philosophy of Gilles Deleuze (henceforward "Deleuzian") as well as the philosophy which Deleuze developed together with Félix Guattari (henceforward "Deleuzeoguattarian"). Finally, I arrive at a discussion concerning a legal concept of cultural commons. I do so by way of a rhizomatic legal reasoning that can conceive of a conception of a cultural commons by means of avoiding, for instance, common legal dichotomies (open–closed, public–private, right–heritage) and, hopefully, overcoming them. Therein lie the theoretical and methodological commitments of this book.

For a reader of Deleuze, and Deleuze and Guattari, these types of questions and approaches are obvious when using their theory. Addressing a similar issue Deleuze once wrote in a letter:

> You either see it as a box with something inside and start looking for what it signifies, and then if you're even more perverse and depraved you set off after signifiers. And you treat the next *law* as a box contained in the first or containing it. And you annotate and interpret and question and write a book about the *law*, and so on and on. Or there's another way: you see the *law* as a little non-signifying machine, and the only question is 'Does it work, and how does it work?' How does it work for you?... This second way of reading's intensive: something comes through or it doesn't. There is nothing to explain, nothing to understand, nothing to interpret. It's like plugging into an electric circuit... It relates a *law* directly to what is Outside...[1]

In that vein, this book seeks not to see law as a "box" but instead it attempts to get beyond this proverbial box that seems to regard law either as a cognitive creation or as an ontological metaphor. Within this context, it does not help to approach law as a set of boxes placed inside one another not connected to the "outside". It only leads to a dead-end. What I instead aim to do is to show that by connecting law to its "outside" rhizomatically, a lawscape is created, and here the potential for a cultural commons in law is revealed. The theoretical approach shall be developed in detail in Chapter 2.

1.2 Landscape/lawscape

However, it is worth pointing out already here that we must refrain from being too theoretical. A strong connection to the material and empirical is required. As I now start to discuss the commons I want to discuss it as a concrete phenomenon, a space, in existence from the beginning. This is not necessarily how commons studies are usually undertaken.

So, when we refer to the *commons*, what do we usually mean? Often, "the commons" seems to refer to the so called "physical" or "natural" commons – i.e. nature, urban spaces, fields, pastures, fisheries, rivers... Connected to this physical or natural commons are the resources tied to it namely, natural resources, commercial spaces, irrigation water, clean and fresh air, fish, berries. In this context commons, it is often assumed, has to do with the distribution and allocation of (natural, or at least physical) recourses. Other times, when we talk about the commons we talk about certain, often digital, initiatives or platforms like for instance the "Creative Commons", and the content and information shared there. Previous research on the concept of the commons is now typically divided in these two strands, natural and intellectual/digital commons. This is a direct consequence of

1 My emphasis, quote modified. The words in italics have been changed from the word "book" in the original quote, to the word "law". Quote taken from Stivale, 2005:73.

how we usually see the commons, namely either as *natural* consisting of nature and the resources in nature; or *human* or *intellectual commons* consisting of the man-made, intellectual and cultural resources.[2] Thus, these two types of commons are usually mentioned in research and in discussions: the natural commons and more so lately the human made, intellectual or cultural commons. Instead, both have to do with management of resources, it is often claimed.

I will try to move beyond these assumptions. Firstly, I will try to move beyond the nature–culture dichotomy, by raising the impossibility of disentangling the natural from the cultural. Secondly, I will try to move beyond the idea of the commons as management of resources, and I will move towards the question of being-in-the-commons, i.e. becoming entangled with the commons as part of ourselves.[3]

But before I do that, let me give a Swedish example. This book does not directly have a jurisdiction that it addresses, but it certainly has a number of contexts, the Scandinavian being one of them. In Swedish law there is a legal principle, which can be described as a "right to roam", called *allemansrätten.* It is relevant in this setting.[4] Various versions of this principle exist in most Scandinavian jurisdictions.[5] *Allemansrätten* has for a long time been acknowledged by for instance the Swedish Supreme Court (*Högsta Domstolen*) and is today also inscribed in the Swedish constitutional law[6] as well as in the Swedish Environmental Code (*Miljöbalken*).[7] In broad terms the principle grants the public a right to access and roam in nature, which means, generally speaking, that everybody may, for a limited time and on certain terms and conditions,[8] dwell in nature, hike, camp, swim in the lakes, pick berries, and so on.

The right to roam in and access nature has in Scandinavia traditionally been considered to be of particular significance since it is directly connected to public health and wellbeing. The wellness produced by continuous and frequent access to nature ought to be, it is argued, secured

2 Hardt, 2010. See also Bertacchini, Bravo, Marrelli and Santagata, 2012.

3 See e.g. Kapczynski and Krikorian, 2010.

4 This principle also exists in similar forms in the other Scandinavian jurisdictions, e.g. in Norway where it is called *allemannsrett* and codified in the Norwegian Outdoor Recreation Act (*Friluftsloven*). A similar principle exits in Finish customary law, *jokamiehenoikeus*, but while it is not directly codified it is mentioned in the Finish Nature Conservation Act (*Luonnonsuojelulaki*) and Criminal Code (*Rikoslaki*).

5 It can be compared to the Anglo-Saxon "right of way".

6 Swedish Constitutional Law (*Regeringsformen*), 2:15.

7 Mainly in Chapters 2 and 7.

8 While the term *allemansrätten* is not defined in law, initially being a customary legal principle, it is usually interpreted in the following manner: Short-term stay usually means a 24-hour stay. The public is allowed to pick berries, flowers, mushrooms, cycle, hike, swim, etc. The public may not do any harm to the nature, land, crops, animals, and so on. The public may not disturb the private residences.

and safeguarded. This wellness that access to nature gives rise to has thus been given a legal status and transformed into a public right. *Allemansrätten* as a legal construct thus connotes a reasonable and limited access to nature. This access, however, must happen under certain terms and conditions, and has never been of such legal character that it encroaches on the underlying ownership of e.g. the land. The limitations to *allemansrätten* are often described in the following manner: the public may roam in the woods but may never enter the fenced off private garden or the family home on the land. The public may dwell in nature but this comes with the obligation not to disturb private life, not to litter or damage the land, nature, animals or crops.

However, within this book I need to reach even further. The phenomenon that I call *the commons* is a complex concept and not always, or only, connected to the rights to access or rights to roam such as *allemansrätten*. It can also be connected to a space or a realm where resources and people are entangled. I will devote some time to explore what that means, particularly being entangled with artwork as a hyperobject (Chapter 3) or being entangled with the commons itself (Chapter 5).

A further layer to the commons discussion is the economical aspect, where the commons as a concept in economy theory is often presented within a "prisoner's dilemma" setting, that is, as a paradox where property that is somehow owned or shared in common also produces free riders and as a consequence may result in over-use and eventual peril of the underlying resource, create depreciation of value, and that it therefore can undermine individual ownership and private rights on the one hand, and the resource itself on the other hand. This tendency can then lead, it is argued, to the now very well established *tragedy of the commons*.[9] This is part of a larger (liberal, or neo-liberal) argument that makes the claim that resources will always be best managed in private, by virtue of the incentives bestowed on the individual owner by the private property rights as a legal and economical construction. This was at least the dominant view until Elinor Ostrom, the 2009 Nobel laureate in Economy, managed to show in her pioneering work *Governing the Commons: The Evolution of Institutions for Collective Action*,[10] how this is not necessarily always the case and how the concept of the commons as a tool for management and governance, on the contrary, can mean an optimal management of resources, particularly when it comes to finite resources in nature. Building on, and moving beyond the results found by Ostrom, I ask how a legal concept of the cultural commons could deal with and overcome these "tragedy of overuse" and "prisoner's dilemma" issues?

9 The much discussed and nowadays legendary essay by Garrett Hardin, "The Tragedy of the Commons". Hardin, 2009, see Chapter 5.

10 Ostrom, 1990.

In the 1972 UNESCO Convention Concerning the Protection of the World Cultural and Natural Heritage the heritage of the world is divided into two categories: natural and cultural. That is, it relies on a similar, not to say the same, divide as presented so far. So I ask here, if natural heritage, *landscapes* or *cityscapes*, can be envisioned as physical commons that partly can be governed by legal principles such as the various forms of rights to roam in nature or rights to the city[11] formulated as e.g. the Scandinavian *allemansrätten*, without causing tragedies or resource extinctions, it begs the question whether this rationality can somehow be transposed to the cultural landscapes? It then opens up the subsequent question; whether the same type of legal reasoning could be applied to also govern the *cultural* commons that comprises the common cultural heritage that is (constantly being) created by the human intellect: knowledge, skill, ingenuity and those things connected to it such as cultural expressions and works of art. In order to provide an answer to these broader questions we must now start talking about the legal concept of the cultural commons more theoretically first, and then add materiality to the discussion, constantly asking whether a cultural commons can be conceived of legally. And could cultural commons regimes, as with e.g. *allemansrätten*, be inscribed in law?

I will throughout the course of this book propose that it is possible, provided that some (dogmatic) legal constructions are reimagined in order to reach beyond certain obstacles that have so far hindered the construction of an in law formulated (cultural) commons. Such obstacles are for instance the (false?) dichotomies of e.g. the notion of the public and the private as opposites, or that ownership of cultural works can either be governed by a legal concept that is conceptually closed (e.g. individual intellectual property rights) or open (i.e. a reduction or removal of the intellectual property rights for the benefit of for instance the public domain, freedom of expression, open access, and so on).

In the Scandinavian legal traditions, we are quite accustomed to legal constellations such as *allemansrätten* as a right to roam or right to *access*. Similar traditions exist in other jurisdictions both in civil law and common law. The Swedish Environmental Code is for instance based on principles and conceptions that are able to handle various seemingly different interests simultaneously (e.g. conservation of nature and the biospheres, as well as the interests of the land owners, the state, the public, future generations, etc.), in an, at least theoretically, economically and democratically sustainable manner. Could the same be conceived of for the *cultural* environment?

I will argue that today the natural and cultural commons can and must be equated as a first step. The public has an equal claim on the right to access the natural and the cultural commons, a claim on both the natural

11 More about that in Chapter 4.

and cultural spheres; a claim on equitable access to vital resources needed in order to feel well, partake in the community, or simply lead a (perhaps Aristotelian?) *good life*. As opposed to the natural resources, the cultural resources are not, necessarily or at all, dwindling. It means that Ostrom's conclusions may possibly be transferrable to the cultural sphere.[12] And more importantly, it also means that we can potentially even reach beyond them.

And then I will go even further still. I will question whether such a clean cut between the natural and the cultural commons at all can even be made by adding on the layer of e.g. "subversive property" where the spatial, personal and property are entangled, as well as the concept of "being-in-commons" where the commons is an ecology. My approach to the commons will be based on the constellation of a number of interests by employing the rhizome theory and connecting it to various bodies that exist in a space. The concept of lawscape as developed by Andreas Philippopoulos-Mihalopoulos will clarify this argument. This is my theoretical commitment used here in order to reach beyond dichotomistic reasoning and arrive at a spatial, entangled, relational commons. This will help me resolve the great paradox of the commons.

This paradox has to do with the claim that management of e.g. art can only be governed in two opposing manners: *either* within a regime where the artworks are legally conceived of as privately closed off though e.g. intellectual property law and where access is granted on a case-by-case basis, often in a commercial setting. In such a case one or several individuals own the artwork and the person who can afford access is the one who is granted access: the artwork is seen as a commodity or capital. *Or* the artwork is legally conceived as completely open, as e.g. a heritage, or a free expression or as part of the public domain, and as such it is un-owned or "owned" by a community, or everybody. In the cases where artworks are legally constructed as fully open or in the public domain the incentive to create and exploit one's intellectual works diminishes it is argued, as this approach restricts or removes the individual ownership right, and this can lead to fewer works, less diversity and *ipso facto* become a *cultural* tragedy of the commons. Therein lies the paradox, the two approaches are incommensurable, and as such mutually exclusive. The rhizome theory applied here might provide an alternative to this conundrum.

The core idea of the rhizome theory in law as employed here may be that it appears to be able to transcend these, admittedly false, dichotomies between public and private, open and closed, as it stresses not the hostile opposites, but rather interlinkage, the and... and... and...[13] and the potential of constructing legal concepts based on alliances rather than

12 See also Ostrom and Hess, 2007.

13 Deleuze and Guattari, 2011:27.

oppositions. Which means that commons as a concept can be envisioned legally, with e.g. some inspiration from the Scandinavian *allemansrätten*. In this manner when put into play, the principles of the rhizome do not *dissolve* but rather *resolve* the dichotomies of law, enabling a constellation-based concept to be formulated legally, one that can tend to several different interests at the same time. I will return to this claim many times during the course of this book.

I am also putting forward that jurisprudence may already have, or indeed has, rhizomatic qualities. The concept of the commons may be a perfect way of exploring the rhizomatics of law, a concept where the idea of the public and the private are allowed to co-exist and not necessarily form a hostile opposite pairing or a dichotomy. The commons can thus be moved away from the prisoner's dilemma setting, from the tragedy of the commons, from being understood as paradoxical in terms of the private and public, or as only belonging to the extra-legal, political, sociological, or economical realms.

As we have seen already, *allemansrätten* in nature comes with responsibilities in terms of privacy and ownership rights; and the person who is given the right to access nature is also simultaneously given an obligation not to harm, disturb, litter, nor to damage the land, its resources, biospheres, the animals or the crops. When we arrive at *allemansrätten* in culture, it too must come with similar set of limitations, obligations and responsibilities, i.e. to not harm the underlying personal rights and the property connected to them. I will also return to the personhood and property divide many times, and claim that within the approach employed here, the commons is produced in the space that is opened up by the entanglement of the person and the property.

Commons, as a cultural sphere formulated through a legal construct that allows the public to, for a short term and under certain conditions, legally access the cultural landscapes and roam there, is the result I am trying to find in this book. The rhizomatic approach to legal reasoning opens up the possibility to conceive of such concepts that can handle the public and the private together, as an alliance in law. A lot of inspiration for the arguments raised in this book has been drawn from e.g. *allemansrätten* as well as the institutions that are already somehow managed and governed as cultural commons such as museums, libraries, archives, open access platforms, sharing initiatives…

A cultural commons as discussed here is thus imagined as the equivalent of the hiking, cycling, camping and the picking of berries in the cultural environment. The notion of "environment", or more accurately ecology, is also what further enables the connection with the concept of lawscape as well as with the comparison to the natural commons and *allemansrätten*. This ecology of law has to do with spaces where the public's (cultural) health and wellbeing is allowed to thrive. It certainly does have to do with democracy and resource allocation. But, as I hope to be able to show, it also has to do with formation of identity, bodies and spatial justice. The rationale of this book is therefore to engage in this discussion and in the end present the possibilities of creating a concept of the commons that is given a platform in law.

1.3 Atmosphere

Before we end this introductory chapter and move on to look at the theoretical framework of this book I need to make one more short point about its structure, a cartography of it if you like, or to paraphrase Boaventura de Sousa Santos, a map for your (mis)reading.[14] The atmosphere[15] that is created here, and I will have reason to return to the concept of atmosphere later on, is a rhizomatic journey.

I have already introduced that the book is divided in two volumes: Volume I (Re)Imaginations, and Volume II (Re)Constructions. The two volumes have in their turn been divided into four subparts: Law, Art, Commons and Legal Commons. The first subpart maps out the *law*, the legal problem and the theory that underpins the conception of the commons. The second focuses on *artworks* with an approach that centres on placing the artwork within the context of this project by approaching it as a hyperobject. The third subpart opens Volume II and develops the concept of the *commons* by applying commons-related theories. The fourth and final subpart fuses all three previous subparts, all the theoretical approaches and the presented case studies, in order to arrive at a *legal commons*.

The book is also divided in eight chapters. Chapters 1 and 8 provide the entrance to and the exit from the study respectively. The remaining chapters form a serpentine journey that has been undertaken and the reader is invited to follow, in order to travel between Chapters 1 to 8. Each of the chapters in the middle (namely Chapters 2 through 7) have a mirroring chapter, so for instance Chapter 2 and Chapter 5 mirror each other (theory), as do Chapters 3 and 6 (the artwork), and 4 and 7 (the issues of possession). The eight chapters can be summarised in the following manner.

Volume I: *Chapter 1* provides the entrance to the study through an introduction, description of the problem and the contextualisation of the study. *Chapter 2* introduces the main Deleuzian concepts such as rhizome, line of flight, plateaus, (re/de)territorialisation. It connects them to the lawscape. A critique of dogmatic legal reasoning is developed to create a space for the conception of the commons. This chapter is structured as a critical exercise, analysing certain jurisprudential assumptions such as the unity of

14 De Sousa Santos, 1987.

15 And as we now know, all lawscape wants to become atmosphere. Philippopoulos-Mihalopoulos, 2014:4.

law, foundations of law, coherence, structure, etc. particularly in terms of how these are presented and envisioned within dogmatic jurisprudence. The critique is conducted by and through Deleuze and Guattari's theory. In *Chapter 3* the artwork as hyperobject is presented. Adding on the notions of the rhizome and the lawscape, this chapter develops the five traits of the hyperobject as presented by Timothy Morton. The chapter argues that by applying an object oriented ontology (OOO) and by approaching artworks as hyperobjects a shared space is revealed which opens up for the construction of the commons. *Chapter 4* then presents the three empirically-based case studies that I return to throughout the book. Case 1 deals with the mural of Bruno Schulz. It studies how a dispute concerning the belonging of this lost work of cultural heritage forms part of both the artistic subjectivity as well as a communal identity. The aspects of viscosity and nonlocality in the hyperobjects in particular are discussed further. Case 2 is the so-called Wikimedia Commons case from the Swedish courts and it deals with artworks in the public sphere. This case shows how the works of art that exist in public spaces and in the urban commons are entangled with the digital sphere when they are photographed and uploaded on a digital platform. Connecting this tendency to the "right to the city" I argue that the dichotomy between the physical and the intellectual commons is flawed. The aspect of interobjectivity of the hyperobjects is discussed. Finally case 3 deals with the *New Portrait Series* by the artist Richard Prince and the platform of Instagram. This case shows how the concept of the "author" in the digital spheres is being dissolved. Discussing the spectra between that which is traditionally seen as personhood and that which is seen is property, the argument that is advanced is that this dichotomy between personhood and property has now collapsed giving rise to the so called *inforg* (information carrying organism). The aspect of subjectivity as lawscape is discussed.

Volume II: *Chapter 5* presents and defines the commons as a phenomenon. The chapter is divided in three sections: ownership, space and commons. The ownership section moves topographically from immovable property thought to immaterial property in order to find openings in the ownership concepts that can enable the construction of the commons. The space section moves from "public space" to "subversive property-space" in order to show that the idea of the commons requires more than a Habermasian public sphere. The commons section then in the end traces the genealogy of the commons constructions from resource management (Ostrom), a relational type of network that includes affects (Hardt/Negri), and finally arrives at the posthuman definition of the commons as ecology (Burdon/Morton).

Chapter 6 confronts the concept of the commons with current intellectual property laws. It demonstrates that the dichotomies of intellectual property law such as right–privilege, content–carrier, invention–information must be rethought. The chapter approaches the global market and the advanced capitalism as deterritorialising forces that are able to understand the lines of flight of the artwork, while intellectual property law seems to struggle to do the same. This chapter also provides a critique of the underlying dichotomies in intellectual property law particularly in light of the fact that the artworks as hyperobjects are difficult to frame in a binary manner.

Chapter 7 discusses commons initiatives, mainly focusing on the "Creative Commons" (contract-based solutions/licences). It also addresses other types of contracts that create commons solutions and focuses particularly on the settlement agreements that came out of the Bruno Schulz case. This chapter presents the legal concept of the cultural commons.

Finally, *Chapter 8* concludes the study in three parts, first "Visualising the lawscape: cultural commons as an e-scape", where it is argued that the commons needs not to be created, it needs to be made visible or seen. Second, in "Cultural Commons in times of crisis: an ecology" it is argued that commons as a concept must always be understood as an ecological concept. And finally in "Not one but several ecologies: on an apocalyptic note", I argue that commons is not a ready-made ethical concept but one that must constantly be fought for.

Chapter 2

Rhizomatic jurisprudence

Terra firma and terra incognita

Almost every book or article ever written on Deleuze and law, or Deleuze and the philosophy of law, begins by quoting the, by now legendary, utterance that Deleuze made in an interview with Claire Parnet: "Si je n'avais pas fait de philosophie, j'aurais fait du droit".[1] Paradoxically, Deleuze never wrote a book on law or jurisprudence, and while it appears that law and jurisprudence are only ever marginally mentioned in his other works or *en passant*, there still appears to be a strong connection that links Deleuze to law. In this chapter I explore the Deleuzian, or more accurately, Deleuzeoguattarian, connections with law and jurisprudence. As I have already outlined in the introductory chapter, this theoretical exercise is done in order to open up the legal imagination towards first a conception of the cultural commons, and later on a construction of that very concept within a legal platform. This chapter mainly aims at shortly and topographically introducing the Deleuzeoguattarian theory, as it is employed here. Some might say, this can also function as a general introduction to these two thinkers, even though it is not intended as such.

2.1 Deleuze and Guattari

Gilles Deleuze, it is often claimed, is one of the twentieth century's most important thinkers. Contemporary of Michel Foucault and Jacques Derrida, he belongs to what is sometimes referred to as the post-structuralist tradition. He was born in 1925 and chose to end his own life in a dramatic manner by jumping from his balcony at the age of 70 in 1995, after enduring a long illness.

Deleuze studied philosophy at the Sorbonne in the 1940s and finished his doctoral thesis in the, certainly for Paris, iconic year of 1968. It was in fact during the events of 1968 that Deleuze met his friend and lifetime

1 [Eng.] "If I hadn't become a philosopher, I would have studied law". Original French quote taken from Deleuze, 1994. The English translation taken from de Sutter and McGee, 2012.

collaborator, the psychoanalyst, Félix Guattari. The spirit of a revolutionary *soixante-huitard* was therefore always present in Deleuze's thinking, even if some internauts seem to be warning us about making such brazen and rash connections: "Danger warning! Deleuzian ethics are unconventional in ways that tend to piss people off, especially Marxists!"[2] Very well, you have been warned.

That Deleuze is difficult to place in any one philosophical tradition is undisputed. But it is precisely that which produces the potential in his philosophy. Deleuze became a professor at the University of Paris VIII Vincennes/St. Denis, an experimental institution that had been founded by, among others, Michel Foucault. The Parisian and international activists, anarchists and other intellectuals frequently visited the Tuesday seminars held there during the 1970s.[3] This formed Deleuze's philosophical trajectory and maturity. He has written books on Hume, Kant, Spinoza, Nietzsche, Bergson, Leibniz and Foucault. From his, albeit often peculiar and perhaps wayward, approach to the history of philosophy, he developed firstly a critical approach that then morphed into a constructivist approach to philosophy. Later on in his career he wrote books on topics other than "pure" philosophy such as: art,[4] cinema,[5] literature,[6] etc.

Félix Guattari was one of the French psychoanalyst Jacques Lacan's first students. He was a practising psychoanalyst. Guattari was born in 1930. Other than being a trained psychoanalyst, he was also a philosopher, political activist, and some even give him the epithet, *militant*. He edited the Trotskyist newspaper *La Voie Communiste* (*The Communist Way*) and he was involved in various anti-governmental movements during the events of 1968. Some of Guattari's more influential works are *Chaosmosis: An Ethico-Aesthetic Paradigm*,[7] *Psychanalyse et transversalité*,[8] and *La révolution moléculaire*.[9] He co-authored with Suely Rolnik *Molecular Revolution in Brazil*[10] and with Antonio Negri *Communists Like Us*.[11]

Guattari worked his entire life at the *La Borde* clinic that was run by another Lacanian student, Jean Oury. The work at La Borde gave Guattari certain insights in terms of therapy, as well as theory. His experimental approach to psychoanalysis as well as his critique of Lacan worked its way into the work he would later conduct with Deleuze.

2 See e.g. Bauman, 2011.
3 See e.g. Hjelm, in Wallenstein, 1998:31.
4 Deleuze, 2003.
5 Deleuze, 2009; Deleuze, 2010.
6 Deleuze, 1999; Deleuze, 2000; Deleuze and Guattari, 1986.
7 Guattari, 1995.
8 Guattari, 2003.
9 Guattari, 2012.
10 Guattari and Rolnik, 2008.
11 Guattari and Negri, 1990.

Deleuze and Guattari developed their joint thought experiment mostly in their work *Capitalism and Schizophrenia* that consists of two volumes: *Anti-Oedipus*[12] and *A Thousand Plateaus*.[13] Within the *Capitalism and Schizophrenia* project they particularly expanded the critique of psychoanalysis in *Anti-Oedipus* (or as Foucault dubbed the book, "Introduction to the Non-Fascist Life", in his introduction to the American edition) as well as their other tenets of nomadism and multiplicity in *A Thousand Plateaus*. In *Anti-Oedipus* and *A Thousand Plateaus* Deleuze and Guattari develop concepts such as "rhizome", "nomadology", "bodies without organs", "territorialisation" ("de/re/territorialisation"), "plateaus", "lines of flight", "assemblages", "machines", "smooth and striated spaces", etc.

It is almost impossible to tell the two thinkers apart in their collaborative works, or to claim that the one contributed to this aspect while the other contributed to the other. Deleuze and Guattari contaminated, to use their own turn of phrase, each other's thoughts, and this very contamination symbolised for instance their experimental style of writing, making it, as Paul Fry once put it in one of his lectures, "versatile" for the ones who like it, and "murky" for the ones who do not. I am without a doubt inclined towards the former, rather than the latter. What makes the Deleuzeo-guattarian philosophy so *versatile* and intriguing for me then, and what I will try to develop throughout this book, is their unique way of relating to traditional philosophical concepts and then putting them into play with for instance societal challenges and struggles. As such, their philosophy is always an event, a becoming, where philosophy and philosophical concepts are not created, but happen and affect one another, contaminate one another, through the various meetings, clashes, entanglements and interlinkages with the "real" that are constantly taking place.

It is well known that both Deleuze and Guattari abhorred categorisation or being classified in any one philosophical or psychoanalytical tradition. As a matter of fact, they always remained derisive of the terms "post-modern" and "postmodernity", particularly when it came to their own work. However, there are aspects tying their work to the postmodern project, especially their critique of e.g. holistic, hierarchical reasoning, the unified self, as well as their focus on the inhuman or the dehumanised processes that affect the subject. I will be picking up on precisely the inhuman and the dehumanising processes in developing the posthuman, as we shall shortly see. There were also other influences from postmodern thinkers such as Jean-François Lyotard, whose ideas were incorporated and developed in Deleuze and Guattari's work. The same can be said about their placement in the psychoanalytical tradition. While neither Deleuze or

12 Deleuze and Guattari, 2004.
13 Deleuze and Guattari, 2011.

Guattari alone, nor together, ever fully distanced themselves from the Lacanian psychoanalytic tradition, their critical approach to both Lacan and Freud formed the backbone of their collaborative works. That they explored the realms and existed within the *in-betweens* of science and philosophy gradually became quite apparent during the course of their collaboration.

Their philosophy has since moved on, evolved, creating its own lines of flight, to employ another one of their terms, becoming a life of its own, away from postmodernism and poststructuralism, moving into and giving raise to new movements and schools of thought for instance *new materialism*, *object oriented ontology* (OOO), and *posthumanism*. Their ideas have been picked up and developed by other philosophers, one of the more prominent ones being Deleuze's own student, Rosi Braidotti,[14] whose writings on posthumanism are particularly important. One of the more prominent legal philosophers inspired by Deleuze and Guattari is of course Andreas Philippopoulos-Mihalopoulos with whom I engage extensively throughout this book.

One quick note before I move on. For some, to me still unexplained reasons, even the works that were written in collaboration with Guattari, are often referred to as Deleuzian. Here, I have tried, as far as that has been possible, to designate works and concepts as "Deleuzian" if they were created by Deleuze alone in his own writing; "Deleuzeoguattarian" if they were developed in their joint writing (even if initially the concept in question may have stemmed from the one or the other such as e.g. the "rhizome"); "Deleuze/Guattari" where I refer to them as joint authors, and, finally I use "Deleuze and Guattari" to designate where I generally refer to them as collaborators or when they jointly relate to issues outside their own philosophy.

2.2 Resolving the opposites: ... and law

Let us now begin properly by going back to the Deleuzian claim that if he had not become a philosopher he would have studied jurisprudence. This chapter takes up Deleuze on that very utterance, and plays along. What would Deleuzian and Deleuzeoguattarian jurisprudence have looked liked, had they done it? This is in no way an intentionality study, nor do I claim that this is how they would have used their body of work on jurisprudence. Instead I connect my own machine to theirs and I ponder about that question by setting into motion most of the abovementioned Deleuzian and Deleuzeoguattarian concepts within a jurisprudential setting.

Even though it still might be somewhat unusual to use this particular philosophy in conjunction with legal theory, it is certainly not the first time

14 See e.g. Braidotti, 2011; Braidotti, 2013; Braidotti, 2013b, etc.

it has been attempted. On the contrary, many interesting works on Deleuze and Deleuze/Guattari and jurisprudence have been presented in the last couple of years. Several books and many articles juxtaposing Deleuze and Deleuze/Guattari place their philosophy in the setting of jurisprudence.[15] I try to inscribe myself in this tradition. The vast body of secondary literature outside jurisprudence that comments on Deleuze, Guattari and Deleuze/Guattari, is far too extensive to list here. Therefore, I will attempt to position myself in the many discussions concerning these philosophers and jurisprudence, borrowing some concepts, commenting on others. Throughout the book I will attempt to develop my own reading and application of the Deleuzian and Deleuzeoguattarian philosophy, as well as discuss it under the banner of "rhizomatic jurisprudence".

In my view, the two most significant works in the field of jurisprudence are Alexandre Lefebvre's *The Image of Law: Deleuze, Bergson, Spinoza* and Edward Mussawir's *Jurisdiction in Deleuze: The Expression and Representation of Law*. Both of these books discuss concepts of *territorialisation* and *deterritorialisation,* as well as *smooth* and *striated spaces,* (Chapters 5–7) and *nomadic* and *sedentary forms of possession* (Chapter 7). The other research that fuses Deleuze and law has so far been presented mostly in articles or in anthologies, and as such it will not be addressed as actively, but that type of research has also been tremendously important for this book, even when used obliquely. I will attempt to engage with as many of these as possible.

Duly, in accordance with Alexandre Lefebvre and his preface to *The Image of Law*,[16] when using Deleuze and his concepts in jurisprudence and in legal research, a study of Deleuze and jurisprudence does not so much have to do with "applying" the Deleuzian concepts, but rather using the thoughts and ideas "in coordination with law toward the creation of new problems and new concepts."[17] The same is true of Deleuze and Guattari and the Deleuzeoguattarian concepts. One of the overall aims here is to argue that Deleuze, and Deleuze/Guattari, can indeed be very beneficial to jurisprudence and legal reasoning, as well as provide a new type of explanatory values, and add to the study of law as well as the philosophy of law. Their philosophical concepts such as "territorialisation", "deterritorialisation", "reterritorialisation", "rhizome", "plateaus", "lines of flight", etc. shall be used, applied and discussed here as well as placed within a jurisprudential framework in order to demonstrate how valuable such ideas may be in the sphere of law, and particularly within the context of law, art

15 For some of the key works addressing the relation of jurisprudence in Deleuze's work, see e.g. Moore, 2000; Moore, 2004; Lefebvre, A. 2005; Lefebvre, A. 2006a; Lefebvre, A. 2006b; Lefebvre, A. 2007; Moore, 2007; Murray, 2007; Lefebvre, A. 2008; Braidotti, Colebrook and Hanafin, 2009; Mussawir, 2011a; Mussawir, 2011b, de Sutter and McGee, 2012; Murray, 2013.

16 Lefebvre, A. 2008: preface.

17 Ibid, p. xi.

and the commons. Ultimately these instruments will be the very tools that shall be used in Volume II for arguing more concretely how a concept of the cultural commons can be envisioned and introduced in law.

So why employ the Deleuzeoguattarian theory, particularly the rhizome, in order to discuss the connections between law, art and the commons? Because, a rhizomatic understanding of law does not create closed boundaries like many other systematic approaches do. The theory is simply very useful in a discussion like this precisely because it is open-ended. Challenging for instance Luhmannian and Kelsian notions of closed systems and hierarchies, Deleuze and Guattari's theory and the manner of thinking that they propose opens up alternative paths (in)to or through law. In other, perhaps more familiar academic words, it signifies a multi/pluri- and interdisciplinary approach to law. But in more provocative words, it signifies a monistic, radically immanent approach to law, but one where law becomes much more than law, much more than we assume it to be, one where law is always becoming a *lawscape*, as we shall soon see.

For a long time critical legal research has generated studies devoted to the plurality, multiplicity, and indeed pluricentricity of law challenging the notions of systems, unity and singular origins in law ontologically. Here I shall be stressing the significance, in line with the Deleuzeoguattarian reasoning as I employ it, of understanding law not as a static, vertical, hierarchical body of coherent regulation but rather as rhizomatic, fluent, horizontal, open-ended network, a space consisting of dynamic sets of plateaus, each with its own concepts and themes that can be interlinked or function interdependently. For instance, instead of focusing on how law might or might not be hierarchically ordered, I instead focus on the connectedness between various themes that it interacts with. More exactly for the matter at hand, instead of approaching e.g. private laws such as intellectual property law and public laws such as cultural heritage law, as two different, often opposing legal occurrences or fields, that have to be balanced against one another and that have two different hierarchal positions – I am interested in how they can be connected, particularly within a commons setting. Or even broader, instead of seeing law, art and commons as three different spheres, to instead approach them all as connected, folded into one another. Such an approach acknowledges the deterritorialising lines of flight that challenge all assumed territoriality (inside/outside) of law and its concepts. Instead, I am on a quest to find out whether law can be approached as a nomadic rhizome, always unfinished, in process, moving, connectable, as opposed to territorialised, hierarchical, systemic, closed off. Spoiler alert. I find that the answer is yes.

So if there is no outside to law, and if it is always already connected to everything, then the ontological question, very much in line with the Deleuzeoguattarian theory becomes perhaps unnecessary. What is law? It is, always already, everything. But another far more pertinent, equally

Deleuzeoguattarian question, then comes to the fore, namely if it is always already everything then what does it do? How does it function? This is what will take us into the lawscape, allow us to see that we are quite literally already inside law, inside its all-encompassing scape. However, this is not always a comfortable insight. From here on we explore it, walk in it, using rhizomatic jurisprudence as a map, in order to see how law-art-and-commons interact within this sphere.

2.2.1 Deterritorialising jurisprudence

Many argue that *A Thousand Plateaus*, where Deleuze and Guattari fully develop the rhizome theory, may be one of the strangest philosophy books ever written. Deleuze and Guattari guide the reader through a "thousand plateaus" as it were – where each chapter of the book forms what they call a plateau. Each plateau is then marked with a date that represents something in the chapter, for instance year 1914 for the chapter "1914: One or several wolves?". It addresses Freud's famous Wolfman case. In the year 1914 the patient known as Wolfman finished his therapy with Freud. The year 1914 was the year when Freud wrote *From the History of an Infantile Neurosis* in which he described the treatment of this patient. Deleuze and Guattari were critical of the conclusions that Freud drew in the Wolfman case. No wonder then that they chose the very date that marked the end of his therapy sessions, the year in which Freud wrote the thesis based on this patient. Of course it is a date which also signifies other things, like its own backdrop, the violent, changing world of that year. Obviously, the year 1914 marks the beginning of the Great War. Another example is the date 1227 – the year when Genghis Khan died. This year is the signifying date placed on one of the mostly read and mostly quoted chapters in *A Thousand Plateaus* "1227: Treatise on nomadology" where Deleuze and Guattari develop what would later become one of their more significant concepts namely "nomadology" and "nomadic space". There, they introduce the concept of the *nomad*. The nomad is a figure quite unknown to Marxism, an agent who runs counter to the state. The nomad is constantly in progress, moving, creating, inventing. The state machine always aims to capture the nomadic movement, to ground it, territorialise it, govern it… In accordance with their philosophical style, Deleuze and Guattari do not provide the reader with a definition of the nomad, but they put the word into play in different contexts, and as such it never acquires a definite meaning, but is rather intended to serve as a conceptual tool: an agent in an unfinished philosophical, political, artistic, legal field.[18]

As a matter of fact, Deleuze and Deleuze/Guattari almost never come

18 Marcussen, n.d.

up with any definitions or engage in defining any of their concepts at all, at least not in a traditional manner. The traditional definition of concepts in their understanding seems to embody the very act of grounding a concept, of territorialising it, stripping it of its inherent potential. Instead, they put into play their concepts in various different registers, and as such, the concepts employed by Deleuze and Guattari always constitute events, they are performative, open-ended, unfinished, continuous. This mode of writing is both helpful and obstructive for anyone attempting to apply or use the Deleuzeoguattarian concepts. On the one hand, the Deleuzeoguattarian tools provide a set of concepts that are open, imaginative, and lend themselves to a number of different purposes, such as the conception of the commons in law. At the same time, their concepts are difficult and obstructive in the sense that any attempt to use them, due to their fluidity, challenges the user, the user is never fully provided with any real definitions or any leads as to how (and how not) to use or apply their tools.

Another challenge when employing a Deleuzeoguattarian theory is to decide where to begin or which concept to present first, as they so often come entangled and in networks, constantly intertwined, ever so tightly connected. Deleuzeoguattarian concepts must therefore here be presented as assemblages or as local interventions – always unfinished, always in progress, never fully defined.[19]

The "thousand" plateaus in *A Thousand Plateaus* are divided into 15 chapters, and can be read in any order according to Deleuze/Guattari, which is what makes the chapters nomadic. The authors suggest however that the first and the last chapter be read first and last respectively, as a type of entry and exit to the book. Each plateau treats and employs a number of different subjects and theoretical fields such as philosophy, psychoanalysis, biology, music, literature, economy, mathematics, and so on. This is probably why the book is considered both strange and fascinating at the same time, showcasing the particular manner of writing that Deleuze/Guattari employ, experimental, not necessarily dependent on defining the concepts ontologically but rather guiding the reader's journey through their plateaus.

There is one principle that binds the plateaus together, and it is the fact that in each chapter the authors are also composing a so-called plane of consistency – i.e. a field where a resonance between various concepts is created. This is the philosophical matrix Deleuze/Guattari use, one that does not give rise to a closed circle, an "en-cyclopaedia" (with an absolute centre point) of knowledge but rather these planes of consistency remain open to all manners of connections. This approach is referred to as *experi-*

19 Wallenstein, 1998: 182.

mental constructivism.[20]

But let us begin somewhere, if not from the beginning then in the middle with some of the Deleuzeoguattarian concepts that will be most frequently used here. The concepts of *territorialisation, deterritorialisation* as well as *reterritorialisation* were developed in *Capitalism and Schizophrenia*, firstly in *Anti-Oedipus* and then in *A Thousand Plateaus*. They "provide an alternative to thinking of territories as bounded entities, and thus, to thinking of border as frontiers or as the boundaries of an entity."[21] A territory for Deleuze and Guattari could in this sense be anything that we conceive has borders, it can be geographical, political, conceptual, or what ever else, and here I am exploring the legal, that which could be called the *legal territory*, law's space – the lawscape. As will soon hopefully be apparent, this is much more than jurisdiction.

A Deleuzeoguattarian territory is constantly and continuously subject to change, there are always occurrences that flee the territory and its (more or less temporary) orders and structures, making the assumed borders unstable and changing. This moment of destabilisation and change is referred to as *deterritorialisation*, another concept developed in *Anti-Oedipus* as a comment (or an attack) on psychoanalysis.[22] Deleuze and Guattari show how societal, political and psychological movements constantly produce *lines of flight*, occurrences that defy any fencing off and always flee any given or assumed territorial order, *deterritorialising* a static territory, forcing ruptures from within, forming new *assemblages*, new territories. A deterritorialisation is thus the act of breaking away with an established configuration through rupturing occurrences dubbed lines of flight. Such movements give rise to new assemblages, while at the same time being open to *reterritorialisation*. Reterritorialisation hegemonises the newly created assemblage that has sprung up out of a deterritorialisation. Reterritorialisation thus stabilises, albeit often only temporarily, a new alignment. The alignments, or assemblages, that are created form new constellations from traits deduced out of flows from lines of flight and deterritorialisation. The singularities and traits are (again, temporarily) selected, organised and stratified – artificially or naturally – to form new constellations, new assemblages.[23] And so in perpetuity. Assemblages can therefore be both small and large, they can constitute "cultures" or "ages" or any other constellation. The territory is always the first assemblage, the first

20 Wallenstein, 1998: 179.

21 Engel, 2009.

22 Deleuze and Guattari opposed the Lacanian understanding of desire in terms of negativity, lack and castration, and instead, by fusing Marx and Nietzsche, presented desire as production of new realities. When the concept of lack is abolished, they argue, a productive aspect is introduced in its place.

23 Deleuze and Guattari, 2011: 448.

thing that constitutes an assemblage. Therefore the notion of assemblage is fundamentally territorial,[24] spatial, *spherical*. Law's territory is where we begin.

Already at this point we see how the Deleuzeoguattarian concepts are connected, and in order to present one, others are put into play. Therefore, here territory is a space – it may refer to a physical territory, e.g. a national territory, a jurisdiction, as well as a conceptual territory such as for instance the legal system, the field of intellectual property law, a cultural commons, etc. Lines of flight that emerge from the territorialised orders challenge the previous constellation of the territories. Let me give you a legal example to illustrate precisely this. With the emergence of EU law (line of flight) national sovereignty (territory) was challenged, the traditional physical territoriality and jurisdictions were called into question (deterritorialisation). However, EU law was pronounced as a "new order" (reterritorialisation) stabilising, at least until 23 June 2016, the line of flight. Or take another example involving the technological and digital progress which challenged the concepts of intellectual property law with e.g. peer-to-peer distribution (lines of flight), the boundaries of the territory considered as traditional intellectual property law (territory) were challenged in the digital era (deterritorialisation). With for instance new legal acts such as the *Infosoc*[25] directive or a technological solution such as e.g. Digital Rights Management, stronger enforcement rights were achieved and this change was stabilised, more or less temporarily (reterritorialisation). The technological advancements thus forced intellectual property law to move, to be reconceptualised, deterritorialised and then reterritorialised again within a slightly different order or territory. The technological lines of flight induced further deterritorialisation, through e.g. illegal downloading, or aggregates of Big Data, forming nomadic movements that confronted the territory of intellectual property law and its underlying systems and orders with non-systemic challenges. The lines of flight can therefore be said to be the force that makes the system re-invent itself, rethink some of its founding assumptions and elements such as jurisdictions or, as we shall see further below, core concepts, such as e.g. individuality or subjectivity. We will of course look at this much more closely during the entire course of this book.

When the lines of flight assemble under a new order and under different forms, a new assemblage is thus formed – i.e. new forms of more or less temporary constellations appear such as, if we are following the above examples, the EU-law which requires harmonisation, and further reterritorialisations takes place, e.g. the Member States sign and

24 Deleuze and Guattari, 2011: 356.

25 Directive 2001/29/EC of the European Parliament and of the Council of 22 May 2001 on the harmonisation of certain aspects of copyright and related rights in the information society, "Infosoc".

implement directives such as *Infosoc* or the *Copyright Term Directive.*[26] A deterritorialisation is always temporarily appeased. Lines of flight are thus movements that flee a territoriality (physical as well as conceptual, if we are for a moment to stick with such a heavy handed dichotomy) of a given system. At the same time there are reterritorialising forces, such as the legal or capitalist forces, that move along with the lines of flight, following them, forcing them into new assemblages, attempting to once again reincorporate that which once fled, to once again reign in that what has fled within its own (given, already territorialised or territorialising) systems. This is the nomadic movement that is produced by lines of flight forming new assemblages with constant de/re-territorialisation. What makes lines of flights happen, and what force moves constellations into the one rather than the other direction is that which Philippopoulos-Mihalopoulos refers to as *spatial justice.* I will return to the concept of spatial justice frequently but it is enough here to just introduce the concept, namely the struggle of various bodies, human, natural, non-organic, technological, etc. to occupy a certain space at a certain time. This struggle gives rise to lines of flight and the nomadic movement. This very struggle also sets deterritorialisation in motion.

The creation of an assemblage therefore happens when a line of flight breaks away from a territory. In "Treatise on Nomadology" Deleuze/Guattari argue that capitalism is one of the more powerful deterritorialising forces, which challenges previous territorialising notions of identity, traditions, symbolic orders, etc. At the same time capitalism gives rise to its own reterritorialising instruments that create new territories that instead are there to hold together not the territory but the capitalist machine itself, which may very well appear as stateless, global, deterritorialised.[27] This is something that Félix Guattari in his own writing has also grappled with, particularly perhaps in what today almost seems like a prophetic essay, "The Three Ecologies".[28] Written in 1989 Guattari is already able to foretell the ecological crisis, the migration crisis, the tensions in the EU, but also the struggle concerning access to aesthetic and immaterial content. As such, Deleuze and Guattari established the schizophrenic nature of capitalism, showing that it both produces lines of flight, deterritorialisation, as well as reterritorialisation, and hence the title of their joint two volumes, *Capitalism and Schizophrenia.* I will be exploring this particularly in Chapters 6 and 7 in conjunction with intellectual property law and then with the Deleuzeoguattarian models of possession.

26 Directive 93/98/EEC of 29 October 1993 harmonizing the term of protection of copyright and certain related rights, "Copyright Term Directive".

27 Wallenstein, 1998: 181.

28 Guattari, 2005.

2.2.2 Rhizomatic nomos

Since territories, assemblages and nomadism have been introduced let us now move to the even more pivotal concept, namely the *rhizome*. Deleuze/Guattari address the concept of the rhizome in *A Thousand Plateaus* in the following manner: "The rhizome is reducible neither to the One nor the multiple." they write in probably the most quoted passage of the book, which then goes on:

> It is not the One that becomes Two or even directly three, four, five, etc. It is not a multiple derived from the One, or to which One is added (n+1). It is composed *not of units but of dimensions*, or rather directions in motion. It has *neither beginning nor end*, but always a *middle* (milieu) from which it grows and which it overspills. [...] *Unlike a structure*, which is defined by a set of points and positions, with *binary* relations between the points and biunivocal relationships between positions, *the rhizome is made only of lines...*[29]

Deleuze/Guattari call into question the notion of so called "arborescent" knowledge, or the *tree metaphor*, which is often employed in order to describe a body of knowledge: at least in Occidental reasoning knowledge is often conceived of as linear, rising from a clearly defined, singular origin, with a central trunk that with time develops branches, leaves and shoots. Their theory of the rhizome is created in opposition to such descriptions that presume singular origins, often illustrated by a root or a deep structure, where knowledge stems from a certain point and then spreads upwards, chronologically, and thereby the image of knowledge is presented as having one single, or singular, unifying, constituting source.[30] The tree metaphor is used when describing the production of knowledge and it creates a sense and an idea of unity and continuity, homogeneity, a dependence on coherence. It is a hegemonising force. Such an understanding of knowledge calls for a systematic approach and the epistemology becomes systemised, exclusory. This is where Deleuze/Guattari propose an alternative understanding of knowledge, and as such knowledge gains a new, experimental, strange, status in their work:

> They do not seek an encyclopaedic knowledge of the processes present in all situations and events, from a universal, dispassionate perspective, according to which one could take practical decisions leading to chosen ends. Nor do they seek a critical knowledge of social processes from a moral and superior perspective, so that a programme of

29 (My emphases throughout), Deleuze and Guattari, 2011: 23.
30 Dyrk, 2013.

> transformation towards a better society can be ventured. Knowledge is no longer a question of being able to repeat the main points of as many books as possible in a library, nor is it a question of being able to criticize their weaknesses and failings *knowledge is more like the capacity to direct oneself, through encounters with others*, towards the most interesting and profound books in that library.[31]

I wrote already in the introduction that the rhizome is difficult to outline. But here is my attempt to explain it. Deleuze/Guattari use the concept in order to imagine the production of knowledge differently, in a non-arborescent, non-encyclopaedic way. But interestingly neither is it critical. At least not in the traditional sense of critique. The argument they are advancing is this. When a body of knowledge is understood in an arborescent way knowledge becomes territorialised and grounded. Such territorialised knowledge is dependent on being fitted within the encyclopaedic structure and as such it can never imagine anything new. Or, the arborescent way can be criticised from a different moral or superior perspective. Regardless, the dichotomical reasoning remains.

Here, my aim is to read law in the same way as Deleuze/Guattari have approached rhizomatic knowledge. What I shall be arguing is that law is often automatically, habitually, approached in an arborescent way – a reflex that grounds it, stratifies it, systemises it, places it in a static order. Or, it is criticised, in one way or another, but where the underlying assumptions remain unchanged. This approach oversees the potentiality of law, and the rhizomatic nature of law. As such dichotomic reasoning is not able to incorporate certain productive encounters and lines of flight that deterritorialise law, make it move, giving rise to an unending and constantly unfinished project, a process, the constant *becoming of law*. It is this becoming of law that will eventually lead to a becoming of commons in law further down.

We could take a moment here to briefly address the use of this (or any other) metaphor. Philippopoulos-Mihalopoulos has commented on the potentially problematic use of metaphors in legal philosophy and that the very use of metaphors can become territorialising or as he refers to it too comfortable, moving away the material use of the concept towards the abstract concepts "behind" the metaphor.[32] He writes:

> Of course, metaphors are not inferior to whatever the thing behind the metaphor might be. Metaphors are often the only means of overcoming the problem of disciplinary boundaries, thereby mutually revealing the other side. At the same time, however, metaphors can

31 (My emphasis), Goodchild, 1996: 4–5.
32 Philippopoulos-Mihalopoulos, 2014: 12.

> become too comfortable. They start working against the objective of confluence, facilitating instead a distance between, in this case, law and space, by appeasing the discourse with small chunks of meaty allusions. Metaphors remain a part of the legal discourse, which is far too integrated to allow law to exceed its boundaries and connect with the radical opportunities of space.[33]

Philippopoulos-Mihalopoulos refers to "fleshy metaphors", namely metaphors used in this sense, as part of the legal discourse that can envision radical opportunities in connecting law to space. The idea that he presents is thus the need to move beyond metaphors as abstractions – turning the metaphors into non-metaphorical material (fleshy!) concepts that become less allegorical and fully material. If not, the metaphors, he argues further, tend to frieze, or territorialise, what lies before their emergence. The rhizome here must be understood in such a spatial, fleshy, meaty way: not as a metaphor but as a material tool and a local intervention in jurisprudence in order to eventually construct a legal concept of the cultural commons, that too is spatial. Here, it ought to be stressed from the outset, there will be nothing metaphorical, in the sense of abstract or allegorical, about the rhizome. But before we reach that stage where rhizomatic jurisprudence becomes a material tool – let us examine the rhizome in more detail.

How does rhizomatic jurisprudence function then? The term rhizome itself has been borrowed from botany. Rhizomatic roots are in biological terms roots that are able to give rise to new plants. Even if such a root is broken or cut off from its stem it can start up anew. When separated, fragmented or cut into pieces the rhizomatic roots give rise to new plants. Rhizomes are, so to speak, reproducible even when fragmentised, they can give birth to themselves, they are auto-poietic. The Greek term *rhizoma* means root but it often infers a genealogy and/or race – to stem from someone, within an infinite lineage. However, such genealogical use of the term is something that Deleuze/Guattari refute. For them, the rhizome cannot be approached as a system or a structure – the rhizome is rather something connectable. Deleuze/Guattari argue, that the rhizome can only be described as flows on deterritorialised plateaus that connect and link concepts together.

Deleuzeoguattarian plateaus are as we already saw above clusters of intercrossed themes and concepts that span both over each other and over "disciplines". A plateau can include for instance philosophy, psychoanalysis, economics, literary theory, separately, and together, and within the plateau all aspects of the themes resonate, i.e. form a cluster. A plateau creates a plane of consistency where a resonance between the concepts is

33 Ibid. p. 25.

achieved, but not one that is closed off in a circular manner, meaning producing an encyclopaedic knowledge, a bordered off territory, but one that always remains open and connectable to other fields and themes. The clusters of themes in the plateaus are the different aspects that make up the rhizome.

Even though each plateau has its own theme, Deleuze/Guattari make a point of demonstrating that the plateaus interact and communicate *inter se*, but never establishing a vertical structure. Instead, there is a horizontal flatness that enables connectedness. It means that there is "a multiplicity that cannot be understood in terms of the traditional of the One and the Many, of origins and genesis, or of deep structures in which any point can be connected with any other point, and any sequence of elements broken at any juncture."[34] In *A Thousand Plateaus* Deleuze/Guattari apply this very manner of thinking in their writing; they assemble, put together, juxtapose, in order to show as well as test the nature of the rhizome, but they do not rank, coordinate, impose structures nor, as it were, draw conclusions, they write in another very commonly quoted passage:

> A rhizome has no beginning or end; it is always in the middle, between things, interbeing, intermezzo. The tree is filiation, but the rhizome is alliance, uniquely alliance. The tree imposes the verb 'to be', but the fabric of the rhizome is the conjunction, 'and… and… and…'[35]

I am proposing here that in the discussion of law, art and commons, the part that is so called *law* be approached less as a closed system, and more seen for its rhizomatic qualities, as an environment, as a sphere. *A lawscape*. Somewhere, where we quite literally dwell. The traditional dogmatic legal reasoning does not function like this. There, law, jurisprudence or however one may be referring to it is seen as an abstract, closed system or, in a more realist vein, as an institution. Both of these approaches to law always force the question upon jurisprudence that it must answer, namely "What is law?" and in turn "What is jurisprudence?", and in e.g. intellectual property law this question goes even further: "What is the artwork?", "Who is an author?", "What is a copyright?" etc. Such an approach automatically requires a closed, arborescent idea of concepts, binary- and dichotomy-based reasoning (it is *either* this *or* that), and a method that constantly reterritorialises the lines of flight that with time appear and challenge the territoriality of law and the dogmatic reasoning we know as various legal fields – law's smaller components, boxes – its building blocks, so to speak. But of course as we know now there is matter before boxes, even before atoms, there are waves, there is resonance, there is movement.

34 Bogue, 1989: 125.
35 Deleuze and Guattari, 2011: 27.

Therefore, we must imagine Niels Bohr when we are approaching law in this way, searching for its "vibrant matter",[36] looking for its rhizomatic qualities in this sense. But, even if this is difficult, even if our tools for studying law become entangled with the very object of our study itself there is an upside to this. In this way, certain traditionally difficult concepts that jurisprudence has never really been able to conceive of (properly) will start appearing before our eyes such as e.g. the concept of the cultural commons. It is like looking at those paintings that when you look long enough at them and then start distancing yourself from them the object of the painting becomes three dimensional, jumping up or away from its surface, moving up and away, freeing itself from the paper's two dimensionality. The cultural commons as a legal construct becomes precisely in that vein a three dimensional *possibility*, a space, but one that already exists within law, we have just not looked at it long enough, nor have we distanced ourselves far enough from the dogmatic image of law. Applying this approach makes the concept of the commons move away from being understood as a collection of impossible, paradoxical, political or economical concepts that can only be formulated "outside" law in e.g. economic or sociologic terms – two dimensionally. Relying on the rhizome theory, the legal concept of the commons will in fact become the natural concept in law that needs not be formulated from the outside, because it is already there, immanently, three dimensionally. This is not a metaphor.

More specifically for the argument at hand, the Deleuzeoguattarian theory will enable us to reach beyond what usually appears as paradoxes in law when it comes to access and ownership of art, e.g. the copyright wars, the tugs of war between ownership and access, high-brow and low-brow art, intellectual and mass produced art, private and public art, open and closed access, and so on. The rhizome theory attracts attention as it disrupts the need for these kinds of opposites that often create legal mazes impossible to logically exit from. Usually, artworks can legally only ever be conceived of as *either* closed off, owned as private property by one or more individuals *or* be completely open, un-owned, as non-property or heritage, or publicly owned as public property and as such accessible to all. We have to choose one – both cannot do! The two dimensional reasoning. The core idea of the rhizome on the other hand may be that it appears to be able to transcend this as it is stressing not the hostile opposites, but rather immanent interlinkage, more or less temporary alliances, the eternal and… and… and…[37] with an infinite number of potential formations inter se, alliances not oppositions. Rhizomatic theory thus allows for all these various formations to operate all at once – in a network – together, and as

36 Bennett, 2009.
37 Deleuze and Guattari, 2011: 27.

we shall soon see it resolves (rather than *dissolves*) hostile opposites created by arborescent reasoning. Three dimensional thinking – space – lawscape.

2.2.3 Assembling, dismembering and re-morphing the rhizome

In order to show this more clearly and manage the concept of the rhizome and apply it in law we must take a short detour from the description of the rhizome and look briefly at some other Deleuzeoguattarian concepts namely "assemblages", "machines", and "bodies without organs" (BwO). Assemblage for Deleuze/Guattari can be illustrated by an example: literature. Literature, they write, is an assemblage, a literary *machine*, something that can be plugged into and interlinked with any other assemblage in order to function. An assemblage always exists in connection with other "machines". A simple example is that a reader brings his own machine into reading, and adds a dimension to the text that s/he reads.

> Everywhere *it* is machines – real ones, not figurative ones: machines driving other machines, machines being driven by other machines, with all the necessary couplings and connections. An organ-machine is plugged into an energy-source-machine: the one produces a flow the other interrupts. The breast is a machine that produces milk, and the mouth is a machine coupled to it. [...] Hence we are all handymen: each with his little machine.[38]

A reader's own body machine is thus both his/her specific physical predispositions and his/her intellectual predispositions, as well as everything it is connected to. As an assemblage the individual is a machine, a hybrid, a cyborg,[39] a mutant, a zombie, a more-than-human, a posthuman. Deleuze/Guattari argue that a literary machine can both appear as an organism and as a signifying totality (e.g. a novel), with a determination attributable to a subject (e.g. the reader), but it does not have to have a subject in order to exist (a book exists even if it is not read). It is at the same time subject to lines of flight that constantly challenge its totality. We saw above that lines of flight are instances of encounters – where a static territory, something that is perceived as a totality, is challenged fundamentally by a development, let us say, in any given society. In law we saw how for instance lines of flight stemming from e.g. EU-law or technical or digital development can deterritorialise the territorialised legal order. This means that new assemblages have to be formed (EU law, directives that harmonise laws, stronger enforcement possibilities, etc.). In this way legal

38 (Emphasis in original), Deleuze and Guattari, 2004: 1.
39 Haraway, 1991.

concepts are transformed in a multiplying manner, constantly acquiring new territorial dimensions. I will for instance show the multiplication of the notion of the artist as a legal subject in Chapter 4, p. 98 in the Richard Prince case. This is relevant, as it not only introduces multiplicity in law required for the conception of the commons, it is also a critique of dogmatic methods that territorialise e.g. intellectual property law and the legal concepts on which it rests.

Another concept relevant to briefly mention here is body without organs, BwO. BwO is something that is continually and constantly dismantling the totality, the assemblage, or the appearance of the totality. Such dismantling is continuous, relentless, perpetual, it goes on until it leaves nothing more than an empty name. A BwO is both a state prior to or after existence, claim Deleuze/Guattari. If we continue with the example of literature – a book can thus simultaneously be seen as an existing corporeal totality, as well as being nothing more than a BwO, *a non-totality*. Literary assemblages have not one but several BwOs that they can face and interact with – for instance the genre, the theme, the geographical context, the author's background, all of those are various BwOs connected to the literary machine. This is what Deleuze/Guattari have deemed as "quantifying of writing" – seen in this way a book is always understood as an on-going event, as something continuous, unfinished, always able to be connected to other BwOs, constantly fleeing its totality, *becoming* something else. Therefore, Deleuze and Guattari conclude, the book, as a literary assemblage, can be said to neither have an object nor a subject.[40]

The term BwO itself is borrowed from the French playwright Antonin Artaud who in a radio play wrote that a person becomes truly free when s/he has become a body without organs, that is, when all automatic reactions and body apparitions have been stripped from the person and when s/he can experience affect and reason freely. Deleuze/Guattari develop the concept further and in detail[41] in *Anti-Oedipus*.[42] The concept of BwO was first introduced in Deleuze's *The Logic of Sense* where two fundamental intuitions of the body were presented "as a collection of dissociated body parts, dismembered, interpenetrating and mutually devouring; and as a miraculously solidified 'body without organs' [...] catatonic body 'without parts which does everything through insufflation, inspiration, evaporation, fluidic transmission'".[43]

This on the one hand dissociated, and on the other hand catatonic phenomenon, creates a struggle, a movement, a constant becoming, which is continuous, without limit.

40 Deleuze and Guattari, 2011: 4.

41 Deleuze had himself already introduced it in 1969 in *The Logic of Sense*, but had not developed it any further in that book.

42 Deleuze and Guattari, 2004.

43 Bogue, 1989: 74-75, Deleuze, 1990: 108.

> We come to the gradual realization that the BwO is not at all the opposite of the organs. The organs are not its enemies. The enemy is the organism. The BwO is opposed not to the organs but to that *organization* of the organs called the organism.[44]

The concept BwO is thus a concept that aims to get beyond the systemic organisation.

So can we imagine a *Law without Organs*?[45] Law without Organs as a concept opens up the constant becoming of law and allows for a legal rhizosphere, a lawscape, to become visible and all its nomadic tendencies to be revealed. This opens up the commons as a territory that encompasses law and art as "a collection of dissociated body parts". It also, simultaneously, puts into play the dismantling forces that exist and constantly create lines of flight from any legal territory, forcing law to come face to face with its unending movement and non-totality, leaving it in a catatonic state – as a body – or law – without organs.

2.3 Lawscape: ... in law

Let us return to the rhizome then. In the introductory chapter of *A Thousand Plateaus* "Introduction: Rhizome" Deleuze and Guattari propose that there are three types of literary machines: the root book, the radicle system/fascicular book, and finally the rhizome book.

With reference to the first one, *the root book*, they use, as I already started to introduce above, the image of a tree to describe it. The root book is as a tree in that it has a root e.g. the book's language, tradition, geographical context, historical place, author's background, etc. It relies on some sort of origin that acts as a root, a fixation, a substructure. The totality above the surface that we are able to see, grasp and examine is the book itself. In Freudian terms, the subconscious lies underneath the surface, the conscious on the surface, but both are nevertheless there in a vertical order. The root book signifies unity, coherence, organisation, territorialisation, and always has a(n assumed) singular origin. It is based on dialectical opposites and dependent on a dialectical and binary logic.[46] Deleuze/Guattari claim that traditional philosophical reflection is based on a root book-type thinking. Root books instil discipline, unity, chronology, and coherence within a singular, organised, solidified, territorialised, body.

44 (My emphasis), Deleuze and Guattari, 2011: 175.

45 Lefebvre, A. 2007: 179–201.

46 For a closer discussion regarding binary logic with a focus on Scandinavian legal philosophy, see e.g. Gustafsson, 2014.

The root book in itself is a process of perpetual deferral as one concept is defined by another in an infinite self-referential regress.[47] Such a self-referential regress in legal theory can for instance be found in certain modern legal theories like e.g. Kelsen's *Grundnorm* or Hart's *rule of recognition*. The root book, with its binary logic, dominates science and scientific reason, claim Deleuze and Guattari. Could it be argued that the root book type of reasoning is prevailing in jurisprudence too? In order to understand law and the legal system, we feel that we must organise it, we presume a unity, coherence, opposites, and a hierarchical order – we assume that it has been developed linearly, chronologically, that it really has become an organised body – enclosed and looking in, excluding its outside. A body WITH organs?

For Deleuze and Guattari the second type of book, *the radicle system/fascicular book,* emerged as an alternative to the root book with modernity. There, the root has been aborted, and an infinite number and multiplicity of secondary roots developed instead of the one root.[48] This idea rests on fragmentation as a method, for instance the cut-up techniques utilised in creative production or writing. Still, Deleuze/Guattari continue to argue, even though multiplicity had been introduced with modernity, and regardless of the infinite number of fragments that may have been created using modern fragmentising methods, there still exists a secret, albeit not directly discernable, unity even here. This is so to speak critique of critique. The mode of reasoning has here merely moved away from the basic binary, linear logic to a "circular or cyclic dimension".[49] As examples of such literary machines Deleuze/Guattari mention James Joyce's writing or Nietzschean philosophy. Joyce shattered the linear unity of words and showed how words do not have one, but multiple roots. Nietzsche, in his theoretical constructions, even went one step further than Joyce and shattered the linear unity of knowledge itself, they claim. Even further still, these kinds of fragmentations are not satisfactory, or radical, enough for Deleuze/Guattari. They maintain that such methods of fragmentation do not fully break and do away with dualisms, opposites, binary logic, and after all, there still remains a notion of unity, albeit fragmentised, shattered while it is circular, hermeneutic. It has just become a new type of unity, they write, or a mystification of unity, and it makes the fascicular type book "all the more total for being fragmented".[50]

If we assume that this is what postmodern approaches to jurisprudence have been doing, that is moving law away from a root-cosmos (dogmatism)

47 Bogue, 1989: 75.
48 Deleuze and Guattari, 2011: 6.
49 Ibid.
50 Deleuze and Guattari, 2011: 7.

towards a radicle-chaosmos (critique), in the words of Deleuze/Guattari, then we must assume that even postmodern jurisprudence has not gone far enough. It has not managed to truly break with the fictions of unity and coherence, invoking infinite numbers of plurality and multiplicity, but still helplessly presupposing a secret, opaque unity, an alternative unity, an *other* unity, a unity based on a higher moral ground, but a unity nonetheless.[51] Postmodernism can in such a view be seen as a mirror image of modernism, reproducing the tenets of modernism, without ever fully breaking free from it, or reaching beyond it.

2.3.1 The six principles of the rhizome

Deleuze/Guattari propose the rhizomatic book as an alternative to the two previous ones (root and fascicle books). In *A Thousand Plateaus* they define the rhizome by ascribing it six principles.

Principles 1 and 2: connection *and* heterogeneity

The first principle refers to the fact that a rhizome can be connected to anything, and in that sense it differs from a tree or a root that has a fixed point and a hierarchical order. They write:

> A rhizome ceaselessly establishes connections between semiotic chains, organisations of power, and circumstances relative to the arts, sciences, and social struggles.[52]

The idea of connection stresses the constantly changing nature, the temporality, the movements, the lines of flight, the constellations. In that way the fictional ideals of e.g. unity, with an assumed ideal speaker and listener, or signifier and signified, are circumvented. Binary reasoning that is marked by homogeneity can be subverted and immanent heterogeneity (principle 2) introduced with the rhizome, as constant interlinkage happens between components that are connected to one another. A centre, a core, a single origin becomes futile as the connectivity manages to create heterogeneous dimensions and unexpected connections from within.

The significant trait of the rhizome theory that may be interesting is that reasoning becomes a matter of making connections: a sphere where law is

51 See e.g. Panu Minkkinen's critique of the CLS movement and so called postmodern jurisprudence in general and Costas Douzinas and Ronnie Warringdon's *Postmodern Jurisprudence* in particular, developed in "Law, Science and Truth", in Hirvonen, 1998 See also Gustafsson, 2003.

52 Deleuze and Guattari, 2011: 8.

enabled to become a BwO, where law is not seen as a static, single, unified body[53] but as a radically immanent assemblage of inter-connectable norms, that are not dependent of a binary logic. Simply put, a lawscape – a sphere where we quite literally can enter and that we are part of. We walk in it and it sticks to us as a hyperobject as Timothy Morton has so excellently put it, as we shall further see in Chapter 3.[54]

The rhizomatic law is always already plural law and allows for alliances, and resolves opposites. A rhizomatic jurisprudence becomes a collection of potentialities. "Law without organs" thus becomes a lawscape and as such immanent, it sticks to bodies (more or less organised or unorganised) such as market, society, art, commons, etc. These types of connections are referred to by Deleuze/Guattari as "becomings", and it is through the becomings that the potentiality in a rhizome is actualised. In *A Thousand Plateaus* Deleuze/Guattari for instance mention the becoming-animal, becoming-woman, becoming-child, etc. in order to show the processes of multiplicity and what happens when "bodies" are (more or less temporarily) interlinked in a becoming. Here it is a becoming of the lawscape that we are witnessing.

However, the Deleuzeoguattarian becoming is *not* juridification in e.g. a Habermasian sense – where a societal issue or conflict is transformed into law – "the tendency towards an increase in formal (or positive, written) law",[55] that which Habermas calls colonisation of the "lifeworld".[56] No. Juridification assumes an outside and an inside of law. Becoming in the strict Deleuzeoguattarian sense is a much more radical concept. A becoming refers to becoming something *else*, becoming other, but from within. In Blanchotian terms it can be described as the move from the first to the third person, a becoming is a movement from No-one to a third person. It is a question of simultaneous appearance and disappearance, for instance the becoming imperceptible of the author, while at the same time appearing omnipresent, as we shall see in the Prince case in Chapter 4, p. 98. The concept of becoming is a concept of withdrawal and constitution at once. It is performative as it eludes e.g. identity or subjectivity as narrated by the territorialised legal order. The Deleuzeoguattarian becoming thus refers to production of an immanent counter-narrative of something that previously seemed unimaginable. In the refusal to be narrated and as such constructed by an outside force, the becoming acts as

53 On law's unity from a Scandinavian legal theory point of view see Gustafsson, 2014, or Peczenik, 1995.

54 Morton, 2013.

55 Habermas, 1985: 359.

56 Ibid. pp. 356–363.

a counter strategy. It is a refusal to produce an account of one self – to be *sub-jected*. It is law lived in third person.[57] I will explain.

In order to understand what that means in a material sense let us firstly look at how Deleuze/Guattari describe the concept of becoming.

> A becoming is not a correspondence between relations. But neither is it a resemblance, an imitation, or, at the limit, an identification. [...] To become is not to progress or regress along a series. [...] Finally, becoming is not an evolution, at least not an evolution by descent and filiation. Becoming produces nothing by filiation; all filiation is imagination. Becoming is always of a different order than filiation. It concerns *alliance*.[58]

Here it is a matter of the becoming of law, or becoming legal subject, of putting into play various BwOs connected in the lawscape. It is precisely this space that can conceive of a legal concept such as the cultural commons, where law and art are connected, entangled, part of the same sphere, an alliance. The legal concept of the cultural commons might have been difficult to conceive of in dogmatic jurisprudence, where it is presented either as an economical concept (it is a social dilemma), or as a political concept (it is allocation of resources), or as destroying individual rights (it gives rise to the tragedy of the commons), as undermining ownership, or as promoting the public over private, etc. A commons, as a space, where law and art are allowed to be connected and to resonate on the same plane of immanence, as a becoming per Deleuze/Guattari, then has to do with achieving heterogeneity, where concepts such as economics, politics, art, need not be opposites to law, or exclusory or seen as coming from the outside. A concept of the commons in law, it will be argued in the forthcoming chapters, manages to sustain fundamental (individual/private) interests as well as to provide alliances to natural and cultural resources (as opposed to allocation or co-ownership of resources), and much more. A commons is a relational space. As such it is not a question of pragmatism, it is a question of becoming. The concept of becoming, that stems from the first two principles of the rhizome, *connection* and *heterogeneity*, is what allows this heterogeneous immanence and formation of alliances to happen.

Principle 3: multiplicities

The third principle of the rhizome is the principle of multiplicity, or rather *multiplicities*, a double plural. We have already touched upon the notion of

57 Hanafin, 2014.

58 (My emphasis), Deleuze and Guattari, 2011: 262–263.

multiplicity more than once within the course of this chapter.

> Multiplicities are rhizomatic and expose arborescent pseudo multiplicities for what they are. There is no unity to serve as a pivot in the object, or to divide in the subject.[59]

This may seem a radical idea. Deleuze/Guattari explain multiplicities by using the example of a puppet on a string: multiplicities can be likened to an artist or puppeteer who forms one dimension and the puppet the other. However, the puppeteer is not a single dimension, there is also the artist's nerve fibres which form a dimension of their own. An additional dimension is then the artist's physical body, and then his mental abilities, and then his geographical place, etc. All of these constantly form new *nth*-number of dimensions that are connected to the first and the second, and so on. This is how an assemblage is created by multiplicities. Deleuze/Guattari explain, that it is the "increase in the dimensions of a multiplicity that necessarily changes in nature as it expands connections. There are no points or positions in a rhizome, such as those found in a structure, tree or root. There are only lines."[60] It is this very multiplicity of dimensions that is particularly interesting here. And, the increase in multiplicities does not require hierarchical structures according to Deleuze/Guattari, as:

> [a]ll multiplicities are flat, in the sense that they fill or occupy all of their dimensions: we will therefore speak of a *plane of consistency* of multiplicities, even though the dimensions of this 'plane' increase with the number of connections that are made on it. Multiplicities are defined by the outside: by the abstract line, the line of flight or deterritorialisation according to which they change in nature and connect with other multiplicities.[61]

Philippopoulos-Mihalopoulos suggests further that law becomes a plane of immanence precisely by reaching beyond traditional boundaries in this sense:

> The law becomes a plane of immanence, namely the term that Deleuze & Guattari reserve for the all-embracing sum of folds and falls and connections, where all causality is immanently contained within its boundaries. The plane of immanence is infinite. Its boundaries are virtually everywhere and actually including everything – not unlike a system whose boundaries are the world as the system knows it,

59 Deleuze and Guattari, 2011: 8.
60 Deleuze and Guattari, 2011: 9.
61 (Emphasis in original), Ibid.

> potentially expanding to ingest more and more environment. The crucial point is that the law as a plane of immanence contains all there is to be contained. Its exteriority is always internalised but always powerfully appearing as a movement that pushes the boundaries ever further.[62]

Postmodern jurisprudence has challenged the inside and the outside of legal boundaries already. By adopting this Deleuzeoguattarian reasoning and focusing on the immanent reflexivity which produces inner ruptures and lines of flight, the problems with exclusions from the legal sphere could if not be overcome then at least resolved. The legal dimensions will always be multiplied on an *nth*-level, be connectable to another plateau e.g. a new technological or digital development, new market developments and new business models, globalisation – but also conversely, to new exploitations, new injustices, new discriminatory practices etc. This is spatial justice where the plane of immanence might be flat, but it is as Philippopoulos-Mihalopoulos rightly points out also tilted, where certain bodies weigh more than others. And as such the constantly moving law-scape can be connected to anything, that is folded within it, immanently contained. This is what the legal rhizomatics opens up for, immanent multiplicities. And whenever a line of flight occurs, we do not leave the lawscape, we just move onto another plateau. Why we move in one direction, instead of another, again, depends on how much our bodies weigh. This is ethics, and I will arrive there eventually towards the end of the book.

Principle 4: asignifying rupture

Each time the rhizome is broken the fourth principle, *asignifying rupture*, occurs – the rhizome starts up anew on a new or on an old line of flight. The rhizome has a recuperative nature in that sense, as it allows movements and flows to be re-routed or diverted. Deleuze/Guattari do not use genes but rather viruses as an example of how rhizomes are broken, spread, contaminate and are contaminated, and how they multiply, moving from body to body.[63] The rhizome, they write, is antigenealogy.[64]

While arborescent reasoning based on binary logic has to appear to be mimicking the world, the rhizome does not have to mimic anything. Law has traditionally been obsessed with mimicry, of having to imitate reality, in order to bring the "real" into the "legal".[65] The rhizome, however, allows for

62 (Emphasis in original), Philippopuolos-Mihalopoulos, 2009: 55.
63 Deleuze and Guattari, 2011: 11.
64 Ibid. p. 12.
65 See e.g. Björling, 2017.

the real instead to *colour* or *contaminate* the legal in the lawscape,[66] and vice versa, for them to be interlinked and communicate with one another.

Principles 5 and 6: cartography and decalcomania

[A] rhizome is not amenable to any structural or generative model. It is a stranger to any idea of generic axis or deep structure.[67]

What would happen if legal philosophy was to stray from the dependence of (or the metaphor of) generic axis and deep structures? Deleuze/Guattari propose that such a structure-dependent reasoning can only achieve descriptions of some simplified and constructed status quo, and can only ever maintain a balance in the already given inter-subjective relations. It is a method that comes "ready-made", they argue. "The tree articulates and hierarchizes tracings; tracings are like leaves of a tree."[68] That means that territorialised law seen in this way can never really be fully in contact with the outside, with the real, when a structural approach and the method of tracing are applied because in such a case the real can only be understood if "translated" into the legal in order to fit within the legal system.[69] Through this act of translation, aspects of reality may be, or are in fact, lost. Here we are invited to make *maps*, as "[t]he map has to do with performance, whereas the tracing always involves an alleged 'competence'".[70]

Deleuze/Guattari make a distinction between maps produced by *tracing* and maps produced by *cartography*. *Tracing* assumes a notion of a closed off, structuralised, organised, totalised (legal) body where norms exist in a hierarchical, binary order. If this is presumed then we are only conducting a tracing when interacting with the "outside" of law. Tracing means mimicking – but it is only partial mimicking as some aspects of reality always have to remain outside the designated legal territory. The body of law is also (like the root book) often described by using the metaphor of a tree, it begins with a root below the surface (deep structure) and then spreads upwards with a trunk (legal culture), finally branching out and creating offshoots (legal surface).[71] Such reasoning rests upon an assumption that something will always have to fall inside or be translated to

66 "Pink Panther imitates nothing, it reproduces nothing, it paints the world its colour, pink on pink; this is its becoming-world, carried out in such a way that it becomes imperceptible itself, asignifying, makes its rupture, its own line of flight, it follows its 'aparallel evolution' through to the end." Deleuze and Guattari, 2011: 12.

67 Ibid. p. 13.

68 Ibid.

69 Björling, 2016.

70 Deleuze and Guattari, 2011: 14.

71 See e.g. Tuori, 2002.

fit within the inside of the legal system (even if it is within the deep structure) and conversely that something else will have to fall outside (even outside the deep structure). Deleuze/Guattari write:

> An assemblage has neither base nor superstructure, neither deep structure nor superficial structure; it flattens all of its dimensions onto a single plane of consistency upon which reciprocal presuppositions and mutual insertions play themselves out.[72]

We have to look closer at the contact with the "real" that a *mapping* then calls for. Mapping according to Deleuze and Guattari means that reasoning in general and here legal reasoning in particular always remains open and connectable to all other dimensions, like a map. Such connectivity does not depend on an inside and an outside. Boaventura de Sousa Santos of course also famously addressed the concept of legal cartography in the 1987 article "Law: A Map of Misreading. Toward a Postmodern Conception of Law" writing:

> [L]aw and society have been conceived in the conventional paradigm, *as two separate and distinct realities or entities* which are then juxtaposed in order to investigate the extent to which they correspond or do not correspond. The most important 'exemplars' of sociological research on law have been developed from this conception (the study of the relations between law in books and law in action and the study of the impact of society on law or, inversely, the study of the impact of law in society).[73]

De Sousa Santos challenges this "conventional paradigm", or what I here refer to as dogmatic legal reasoning. He argues for a legal cartography, where the concept of the map, even though it distorts "reality", is still convenient to use as it is able to become a *privileged way of imagining* reality.[74]

> In the modern era law has become the privileged way of imagining, representing, and distorting, that is to say, of mapping these social spaces and the capitals, the actions and symbolic universes that animate or activate them.[75]

While de Sousa Santos does not use or refer to Deleuze/Guattari per se, or the Deleuzeoguattarian mapping method explicitly, his article provides an

72 Deleuze and Guattari, 2011: 100.
73 (My emphasis), de Sousa Santos, 1987: 280.
74 Ibid p. 283.
75 Ibid. p. 286.

insight into the critique of the dogmatic legal reasoning where law and reality are approached as two separate or distinct entities and the need for spatial(ised) reasoning through cartography. This can help us in further understanding the Deleuzeoguattarian mapping method connected to the lawscape. The mapping method opens up law and places the changing reality, usually conceived to be outside law in dogmatic legal reasoning, immanently within law, thus allowing what may seem as opposing (legal) fields to be inter-connected, for instance private and public law, or civil and constitutional law, etc. Also, it allows for a connection with the "outside" as we have already seen. What is then the difference between mapping and tracing? Does not mapping also include a tracing aspect? Deleuze/Guattari write:

> The tracing has already translated the map into an image; it has already transformed the rhizome into roots and radicles. It has organised, stabilised, neutralised the multiplicities according to the axes of significance and subjectification belonging to it. It has generated, structuralised the rhizome, and when it thinks it is reproducing something else it is in fact only reproducing itself.[76]

That is, the act of stabilising and neutralising decreases the potential alternatives of actions, which in turn creates impasses, "bottlenecks" and blockages in the system. It means that the binary logic will perpetually be locked-in in a "One-Two" reasoning, a logic that can never be circumvented. The society of couples exists in a centre-based system, whereas the rhizome is a-centred (or multi-centred) and the "communication runs from any neighbour to any other, the stems or channels do no pre-exist, and all individuals are interchangeable, defined only by their *state* at a given moment – such that the local operations are coordinated and the final, global result synchronized without a central agency."[77]

The rhizome theory is at once a critique and a productive re-imagination of the dogmatic legal reasoning that rests and depends on the idea of a root-foundation, of a *Grund*.[78] Still, it is radically immanent. It is not sociology. In classic dogmatic reasoning law is understood as arborescent, as we have seen. In the rhizosphere, the lawscape is immanence, a becoming.

2.3.2 Through the lawscape

All this taken together makes up the rhizomatic jurisprudence that shall be used and developed as a tool throughout this book by connecting it to what

76 Deleuze and Guattari, 2011: 15.
77 (Emphasis in original), Ibid p. 19.
78 Cf. Kelsen's *Grundnorm* even if Gustafsson does not interpret it that way, see e.g. Gustafsson, 2010.

Philippopoulos-Mihalopoulos refers to as the lawscape, and towards the end, atmosphere and spatial justice. I want to particularly show how these concepts are imperative when it comes to theoretically putting into play law, art and the (cultural) commons, to resonate on a plane of immanence.

2.3.3 C'est quoi?

It is worth reiterating at this point – once we have moved through the basic tenets of the rhizome and the rhizomatic jurisprudence that these are not mere metaphors. While, as Philippopoulos-Mihalopoulos appropriately points out, some metaphors can be treacherous, not all of them are condemnable. The problem begins, he writes, "when metaphors occlude what has led to them and what is to be done on an ontological and even transformative level."[79] Before we can connect the rhizome to the lawscape in more detail, a reminder that the rhizome is an image of the structure of knowledge is warranted. But not just as an abstract metaphor, but as a material empirical occurrence, a "fleshy metaphor". In other words, it can be argued that while the arborescent image of thought, or the structure of knowledge, is a simplified territorialising image, the rhizome is a material ontological commitment, that is describing the assemblages and entanglements of knowledge, bodies, power, etc. As such it is space. Once again here, not space in its abstract metaphorical sense, but a genuine, material space, that we can quite literarily enter and that, conversely, can enter (into) us. An obvious example in the context at hand is a museum as a lawscape, but it could also be Palmyra, or Spotify, or the archive, or the bank vault, where law, art and space converge rhizomatically into a lawscape. Jane Bennett writes for instance in the opening paragraph to the preface of *Vibrant Matter* that the "idea of matter as passive stuff, as raw, brute or inert" is a habit of thinking, where "dull matter (it, things) and vibrant matter (us, beings)"[80] are divided into two opposites. Often then artworks are assumed to be dead matter (it, things) and artists or users are seen as vibrant matter (us, beings). In a spatial understanding of bodies, both the so called dull and vibrant, to continue Bennett's turn of phrase, are always entangled: we (beings) do not only enter a museum (it), the museum also enters us – forming a memory, knowledge, identity – it quite literally *sticks*[81] to us. The entanglement between the "us" beings and the "it" becomes vibrant matter, a hyperobject as we soon shall see, that can be addressed and captured in law through a rhizomatic approach to jurisprudence – forming a lawscape.

79 Philippopoulos-Mihalopoulos, 2014: 28–29.
80 Bennett 2009: vi.
81 Morton, 2013.

Before I develop this further in Chapter 3, let us first look very briefly at the notion of the lawscape.

Lawscape. As topographically introduced so far the term alludes to a fusion of the notions of law and (land)scape. It emerges from the two in a seamless manner forming a wor(l)d that sits comfortably with the reader, that sounds natural, even though it was only recently employed in this setting by Philippopoulos-Mihalopoulos. The merger of law and space is certainly nothing new, maybe that is why it comes so easily to us and why is feels confortable to take in. Its spatiality appears self-explanatory. This tendency of turning to the spatial in law, the so called *spatial turn*, has been going on for quite some time now and is fully established. Equally, it has been established to such an extent that the field of law and space is not purely, or only, even geographical any longer. Connecting law to, once again material, space is not just a matter of jurisdiction or territoriality. In this context space is rather seen as a multiplicity immanent to law, a rhizomatic multidimensional sphere that is constantly unfolded onto bodies and spaces – forming entanglements, assemblages. This concept enables us to see the spatial in law, art and the commons. The spatiality in turn opens up the legal concept of the commons.

The spatial turn in social sciences and humanities of course spans all the way back to the writings Henri Lefebvre,[82] Michel Foucault,[83] the Situationists,[84] and later on Edward Soja,[85] David Harvey,[86] Doreen Massey,[87] and so on. There have already been a number of studies that have devoted far more focused interest to the occurrence of the legal spatial turn than I am able to do here[88] so I need not engage in any detailed comment on it. Suffice it to say that the spatial turn is no doubt established as a tendency in law and it is from this tradition that the notion of lawscape has emanated. Therefore, I do not need to create a diversion here relating to the spatial turn in law. What I instead aim to do is to engage with the lawscape concept as developed by Philippopoulos-Mihalopoulos within the law and space tradition in order to connect the lawscape to the rhizomatic jurisprudence and later on to *hyperobjects*[89] or as Bennett refers to it "animate things and not passive objects".[90] This approach will employ rhizomatic jurisprudence and reach beyond the dichotomy of beings-things, exploring instead a legal concept of the commons.

82 Lefebvre. H., 1991.
83 Foucault, 1986.
84 Debord, 1956.
85 See e.g. Soja, 1996.
86 Harvey, 1973; Harvey, 2000; Harvey, 2001.
87 Massey, 2005; Massey, 2007.
88 See e.g. Borch and Kornberger, 2015.
89 Hyperobject is discussed throughout the book, but particularly in Chapter 3 below.
90 Bennett, 2009: vi.

What needs to be advanced is of course as Philippopoulos-Mihalopoulos points out, that within this context, the spatial in lawscape is material (as I have already pointed out a number of times), but it is important. That means, let me state it again, that lawscape as a concept is in no way metaphorical. Philippopoulos-Mihalopoulos writes that:

> [s]pace also brings an awareness of (other) spaces, both within and significantly beyond the reach of the law, which, in turning spatial, the law is progressively taking into consideration. Gendered labyrinths, sexualised basements, refugee camps, spaces of vulnerable bodies, postcolonial reterritorialisations, leaking spaces, graffiti-written cities, transboundary pollution flows, and so on.[91]

Before I move on then, a quick note on the notion of the "material" within this context. I mean to inscribe the use of the term material in the same tradition as Jane Bennett – following the Deleuzian, Nietzschean, Spinozian philosophies – namely material in the sense of *vital materialism*, "the idea of materiality that is itself heterogeneous [...] itself a life".[92] This approach of course eludes the dichotomies of material (tangible) and immaterial (non-tangible), as well as vital ("living" in a traditional sense) and non-vital (without life, in a traditional sense). Material is thus used to also refer to the so called in-organic (such as e.g. objects) but the intensity in the assemblages in which they exist exercise a vitality, a life. So rather than referring to beings and things, I am exploring the vibrant matter through *hyperobjects* as I will do more directly in the next chapter. There, I look at artworks as hyperobjects and their entanglement with humans and law: constantly forming new assemblages within the lawscape.

In Volume II, I will then connect hyperobjects to the notion of property, space, the distribution of resources, and the relationality between personhood and property, by adding on the dimension of the commons. What I am striving to achieve is to show how that which is considered to be inhuman (dull things: art, spaces where art is exhibited) always forms an entanglement with the human (vibrant things: artist, user, public). In more traditional terms – this will allow me to connect two traditionally opposing legal fields that govern art namely intellectual property law (mostly copyright law) and cultural heritage law. Copyright law, it will be argued, relies on the distinction between the human (e.g. artist) and the inhuman (e.g. the artwork). Cultural heritage law has a different approach where the artefact of heritage is entangled with community, identity, future generations, traditional knowledge, and so on. However, cultural heritage

91 Philippopoulos-Mihalopoulos, 2014: 34.
92 Bennett, 2009: 57.

law on the other hand tends to rely on static or definable communities and groups, and does not accommodate ownership in terms of individual rights. As such it does not rely on the same dichotomies as intellectual property law, but has its own territorialising aspects.

Suffice it to say, this is not a study of positive rules but rather a philosophical approach that forces law in general, and intellectual property and cultural heritage laws in particular, to reach beyond static or territorialising reasoning and *become* a commons. Or to become more (post) human. So we move from terra firma, the terrorised two-dimensional law, to terra incognita – three (or more) dimensional law. Welcome to the lawscape.

Part 2

Art

Chapter 3

Artwork

From object to hyperobject

In *Spatial Justice* Philippopoulos-Mihalopoulos places his study "in the register that comes from object oriented ontology".[1] I have only briefly mentioned OOO so far, and will not engage in describing the approach much further here, rather I will, as Deleuze and Guattari refer to it, put it into play by engaging with it and using it here. What is particularly interesting with object oriented ontology, it ought to be noted from the outset, is the conception of bodies, here in the Deleuzeoguattarian understanding of bodies, or even BwOs, as *objects*.[2] Within this study the "artwork" is understood as an object, but not object in a traditional manner, i.e. dead matter, separated from the human. Rather, I arrive at a radical understanding of objecthood in the sense of OOO through "hyperobjects" as described by Timothy Morton.[3]

In the early versions of this study I wrote in one of the first drafts that it can be presumptuous to attempt to define "artwork" in the context of a legal study. In subsequent versions of the text I removed that sentence – providing instead, if not a definition at least various rhizomatic approaches as to what an artwork *could* be. I moved from the Adornian divide (the artwork as either authentic or mass-produced commodity[4]), towards Bourdieuian understanding of art as capital[5] (the artwork as economical, social and cultural capital) ending up at the artwork as knowledge through a reading of Jamie Stapleton's concepts of rhetoric-based and semiotic/network-based artworks.[6] Within that context, I wanted to show that all these appearances of the artwork exist simultaneously in law as rhizomes, but that we may not always be able to see them, at least not all of them at once, as we are caught up in the binary dichotomies of inside-outside of law, open-closed concepts, public domain-private domain, etc.

1 Philippopoulos-Mihalopoulos 2014: 121.
2 Ibid.
3 Morton, 2013.
4 Adorno, 1998; Adorno and Horkheimer, 2007.
5 Bourdieu, 1991: Bourdieu, 1993.
6 Stapleton, 2002.

Now, I once again feel that I need to reiterate that it can be presumptuous to attempt to define "artwork" in the context of a legal study. But now I say that from a somewhat different, and let us hope, more scientifically mature stand point. When I first wrote that very sentence I probably understood law and art as two separate entities, and while the two sometimes inter-crossed (in e.g. copyright law) they nonetheless seemed to remain ontologically (as well as epistemologically), separate. I still feel that it is presumptuous to attempt to define the "artwork" in a study like this. So I write again, it would be presumptuous of me to attempt to define the "artwork" here. However, this time I am writing it for a vastly different reason. The idea of law and art separated, or separable, as the separation of scientific fields is traditionally understood,[7] has been dissolved or at least dissimulated at this point. In Chapter 2 I described the rhizomatic approach to law, going through a Deleuzian reading of law as *body*, as BwO, then a territory, moving towards the concept of the lawscape (and later still as we shall see in Volume II, *atmosphere*). Within that particular Deleuzian tradition within which Philippopoulos-Mihalopoulos' work also sits, the utterance that there is no outside of law – that we walk inside the law, we breathe it in – is now superfluous. We know that.

In this vein, art is always already immanent to law. And to make matters even more frustrating, the reverse is also true, namely that law is always already immanent to art. The two are folded within one another.[8] Therefore the rhizomatic jurisprudence, so to speak, *englobes,* to use a false English version of a French word, the artwork, they are always rhizomatically immanent to one another. I will explain this soon. But I want to keep on revealing more layers. Moving through the lawscape towards the hyperobject that emanates from the conception of object in OOO, the arrival of which I have already announced, I will start to unpack the approach to the artwork as hyperobject. It is not a definition per se, to stay true to the Deleuzeoguattarian method, rather it is an ethico-onto-epistemological commitment.[9] With that commitment in mind, and within the register of OOO then the artwork will be approached as *(hyper)object.* This fits neatly with the Deleuzeoguattarian approach and will later also be connected to rhizomatic jurisprudence more concretely. An example of this is e.g. as we saw on p. 32 when Deleuze/Guattari argue that a literary machine is a body that constantly appears both as an object (e.g. a novel), and as a subject (e.g. the reader). At the same time, this object/subject body produces an affective excess, the BwO. The notion of the BwO is something that is constantly dismantling this subject/object body, or the appearance of a totality, forcing it towards an open-ended and continuous

7 As inter or trans disciplinary – and see also David Bohm in Morton 2013: 41.

8 See e.g. Barr, 2016.

9 Barad, 2007.

non-totality. As such, following Deleuze/Guattari it was shown that a book is always an event, continuous, unfinished, constantly becoming something (or *someone* as we shall soon see) else. In reverse then, a literary assemblage, as I already discussed above, can be equally said to also neither have an object nor a subject as the two are constantly being dismantled through the BwO.[10] This discourse displaces the "subject", often the human being (the author, the reader), from its centrality as well as it displaces the "object" (the novel, the book) from being a closed in, external, totality, an object in the traditional sense. Thus, a posthuman understanding of the bodies is articulated – as something that is "neither subjects/objects nor human/nonhuman, but objects that assemble into objects and relate to other objects".[11]

That very approach is used here in terms of the artwork. The conception of the artwork is therefore not objectified in a traditional manner, or fetishised as something transcendental or sublime or *elsewhere*, but rather what I am trying to achieve is to resist such objectification or fetishisation through revealing the spaces that are produced between the (hyper)objects, making them *interobjective*.[12] When connecting this more explicitly to law, which I will do shortly, I will try to show how the assumed dichotomical divides that tend to be produced in (dogmatic) legal reasoning are always unable to engage with the hyperobjects as they are impossible to grasp in their entirety. This opens up for the connectability and the immanence of rhizomatic jurisprudence. But, first things first.

Morton developed the concept of hyperobjects and here I am engaging with his concept in approaching the notion of the artwork. Morton ascribes five traits to the hyperobjects. He writes that they are *viscous, nonlocal*, subject to *temporal undulation*, that they occupy a high-dimensional phase that he refers to as *phasing*, and finally that they are *interobjective*. Schematically and briefly the five traits can be outlined as follows. Hyperobjects are:

1 *Viscous* – in that they are fluid, they "stick" to objects that are involved with them, they become entangled with other objects.
2 *Nonlocal* – they span spatially, any local manifestation is not the hyperobject itself, it always produces an excess that is withdrawn.
3 Subject to *temporal undulation* – which means that they are subject to a different time scale than the human (e.g. cultural heritage, duration of copyright, Big Data, etc.) All of these exist beyond the human lifespan as well as the human intellectual conceptions.
4 *Phasing* – which means that they occupy a high-dimensional phase space that results in their always being invisible to humans in their

10 Deleuze and Guattari, 2011: 4.
11 Philippopoulos-Mihalopoulos 2014: 121.
12 Ibid.

entirety (e.g. traditional knowledge, indigenous heritage, intergenerational justice).

5 Subject to interrelationships between aesthetic properties of objects – they have *interobjectivity*. There is no meta language to describe the hyperobjects – only a shared space in which human meaning resonates in a small region of a much larger interobjective configuration of the space.

The main example that Morton provides of a hyperobject is global warming. Global warming is in this vein a hyperobject because it is viscous as it quite literarily sticks to bodies, affects them, reconfigures them on a biological or a cellular level. It is non-local as it is everywhere and any local manifestation (for instance the hot September we experienced in Sweden that was warmer than most Nordic summers we are normally used to), is not the hyperobject itself, it is just that, a local manifestation. It has a larger than human scale and it stretches over time. In its entirety it is always invisible to humans, we can only study its manifestations. And when attempting to describe or study it, it becomes entangled with the very tools used to study it, in a Nils Bohrian sense.[13] Here I want to take the same five traits of the hyperobject as developed by Morton and use them in connection to the artworks instead. So the first commitment then is to show that *the artwork, as a hyperobject, is like global warming.*

3.1 Rhizome 1: viscous

What does it mean to claim that a hyperobject is viscous? Let me briefly stay with the concept of *viscosity* itself before we move on to Morton's more specific use of it. First of all – viscosity is used to describe the state of liquid matter. Secondly, viscosity refers to the thickness of the liquid and how the liquid changes its properties as it collides with neighbouring objects, how in the moment of collision it deforms and how it *reacts* in the meetings or encounters with other objects. The Oxford Dictionary provides the following definition of viscosity: "The state of being thick, sticky, and semi-fluid in consistency, due to internal friction. 'Cooling the fluid raises its viscosity'". It thus has to do with fluidity, the internal frictions of fluids and how they resist the forces that cause them to flow. Wikipedia provides a more simple example: honey has a thicker viscosity than water, when honey collides into other objects it is deformed, it is reformed, it sticks. The image being conjured up here is that of a sticky fluid, say honey, or oil, being poured into some kind of container, or that interacts with another object.

13 Barad, 2007.

Here I am imagining the artwork as honey-like – as fluid, sticky, *viscous*. Morton describes this in the following manner:

> When I listen to My Bloody Valentine I do not reach out toward the sound – instead I am assaulted from the inside by a pulsation that is also sound, a physical force that almost lifts me off the floor. Kevin Shields's guitar sears into me like an x-ray, scanning me, strafing me. [...] I think that this music could liquefy my internal organs, make my ears bleed...[14]

At this point it is warranted to remind the reader, even if it sounds repetitive, that the viscosity of the artwork is not used as a metaphor either. Instead it is the revelation of the aesthetic experience through which the artwork and the "I", "we", "objects", "matter" meld when they collide. Or as Morton puts it, as it becomes a "sticky mesh of viscosity".[15] The first aspect of the viscosity in the artwork then reveals that becoming takes place where every-body is formed at the "expense of some viscous, slightly poisoned substance".[16] The first trait of the artwork as hyperobject is that when we encounter it, it is reshaped, at the same time as we are reshaped, it sticks to us, we mould it and it moulds us too. Morton describes his encounter with the music of My Bloody Valentine, and I will continue to explore this line of reasoning, later connecting it to the objects of cultural heritage in e.g. the Bruno Schulz case. In encountering cultural heritage we become (re)shaped, it forms us, simultaneously as we (de/re)form it. It becomes part of our identity, our subjectivity – it sticks to us as we become entangled.

3.1.1 *In law: subject (human, author, user) v. object (non-human, artwork, commodity)*

Now, I want to take the theoretical trait "viscosity" and place it in a legal setting. I will do so with all five traits here.

The idea of a (rights) creating individual as the subject, living matter, and an artistic work as the object, dead matter, produced by the artist's hand is prevalent in laws that regulate artworks, arguably most prominently in copyright law. This tendency in copyright law can generally be traced back all the way to the state privileges that regulated the printing industry of fifteenth-century Venice.[17] Current intellectual property rights are based on the ideas of "invention" and "originality". The underlying assumption is that the human artist "genius" is seen as an inventor of a work assumed to

14 Morton, 2013: 29–30.
15 Morton, 2013: 30.
16 Morton, 2013: 31.
17 Stapleton, 2002.

have been created *ex nihilo*. Secondly, the work is always seen as an object external to the human being, as non-human. The work is extractable, and movable as it is seen to be a (dead/non living) thing. This, still to this day, forms the basis for copyright law.

Through the legal construct of copyright the artwork is first given its worth when it is connected to or claimed by an individual artist and their labour, that in turn gives rise to individual rights, more precisely here copyrights. Artworks are thus given value by being ascribed to a human. Market value. As such, copyright, a private right, transforms human creativity into an artwork, which in turn becomes an individual fruit of (Lockean) labour[18] – and then in extension of course, profit. An example of this is for instance a painting, it is fairly easy to identify an individual creator, the originality in the creation made by the artist's hand by applying paint onto a surface. It is not difficult to claim that a painting has been invented by an artist, created *ex nihilo*, by fusing the paint and the surface, and the rights generated in such a creation thus belonging, at least initially, to the said artist. This is the traditional ontological approach to the artwork in copyright law and the grounds on which it ultimately rests. In other words, legally, in order to apply copyright to works, we must assume that they have been "invented" by a human being (not nature, not animals[19]) out of nothing.

To be very explicit. In order to understand the cultural commons, and regulations of art within it, we must first understand the artwork. If understood in this way, as a fruit of labour, as an object created by a human, as an (industrial, dead) thing outside of and separated from the (living, creating) human being – the possibilities to create and govern the commons can at best be done in the way that Ostrom suggests, namely to approach art in the commons as an external resource that is more or less exclusive and that is managed by a human collective, e.g. a local community.[20] I will return to Ostrom in Chapter 5. However, I can already state here that this type of governance is problematic in a number of ways. Firstly, as I am attempting to show here, clichéd as it may sound at first, the artwork is much more than just a dead object or a resource. Furthermore, as I will attempt to show in Chapter 5, the commons is much more than regulation for management or co-ownership of resources. Only when that is established can we start discussing regulation, law, jurisprudence, or whatever we decide to call it, surrounding the so called cultural commons.

By beginning in a critique of copyright law, which lies closest at hand, but is in no way the only "law" that is relevant here, I have now started to demonstrate the legal packagings that turn the artwork into a resource that

18 But do see Burdon, 2015.

19 See e.g. the case concerning the so called Monkey Selfie discussed in Chapter 5, p. 147.

20 Ostrom, 1990.

can then either be managed privately (as a copyright, a property) or publicly (as cultural heritage, a common pool resource). But when art is approached as a viscous hyperobject, when it is revealed how hyperobjects stick to us, how we cannot be divided from them, nor they from us, how they form us, how they enter us and how we enter them, this division obviously becomes fraught. What is revealed initially, using the concept of viscosity is this very matter. Art becomes constitutive of subjectivity and as such it reaches beyond the private law and stretches into public law too. If art forms us, and we form it, and this connection forms a Deleuzeo-guattarian assemblage, or a Baradian entanglement, and the underlying dichotomy between subject (human, author, user) and object (non-human, artwork, commodity), is revealed as flawed.

Let me give you a simple example. Copyright law seems to assume that the artwork, or more accurately the "ideal" work, is separated from the artist at the point of creation and then it becomes a commodity that can be traded. This is the example of a painting. However, as we saw in the beginning of this section, Morton himself provides another description with the wonderfully illustrative example of My Bloody Valentine music and his entanglement with it. He describes how the music quite literally enters his body, gives him seizures, makes his "ears bleed". It sticks to him. *Perhaps it could kill me,*[21] he writes. Morton analyses how the music, as a viscous hyperobject, thus forms him, enters him and morphs into him.

While Morton provides a personal account connected to his body's encounter with music, I can give a similar personal example on a community level. Take the films of Emir Kusturica for instance, the Serbian-Bosnian film maker whose oeuvre of films generally explores life in the Balkans. Set in the territories of the former Yugoslavia, they focus particularly on the everyday lives of people, very much including the ethnic tensions before and after the Yugoslav wars. The films are equally constitutive as they are ideologically problematic for various ethnic, religious and secular communities in former Yugoslavia. In this example, the Kusturica films form part of a general understanding or constitution of the (ex.) Yugoslavian identity, they are constitutive of the sense of self. However, for the different (ethnic, religious, etc.) communities his films' constitutive nature means different things. For some the community constituted and perpetuated through his films is understood as inclusive and the films as explanatory. For others, his films are seen as violent, as dissemination of ideology, as exclusory. For some they are empowering, for others violently abusive. So Kusturica's films are viscous both in a negative and a positive manner in the community sense. Or more theoretically correctly put, whether his films are good or bad constituents of a community subjectivity

21 Morton, 2013: 30.

is a question of situated justice, that is, depending on from where we stand. Let me explain.

Kusturica's own initially fluid and later very exclusively defined identity and community belonging also plays a part in how his films are perceived. When Kusturica converted from Islam to Orthodox Christianity he is to have said something in the vein of: "My father was an atheist and he always described himself as a Serb. OK, maybe we were Muslim for 250 years, but we were Orthodox before that and deep down we were always Serbs, religion cannot change that." When it comes to Kusturica's films then, for all former Yugoslavians (present company included, naturally), they have entered our individual and communal bodies, we have been entangled with them, they are always already stuck to us, they give us seizures, make our hearts bleed. They force us to define ourselves, make us choose a communal belonging, pick a side. Whether we like it or not. They form us either in that we identify with them, or conversely in that we take an express stand against them. As such, however we may view them, they form(ed) our history. *Perhaps they could, perhaps they already have, killed us.*

How do we then split the dichotomy between the subject (human, author, audience) and the object (non-human, song, film, commodity). Between the copyright of the authors (My Bloody Valentine, Emir Kusturica) and the personhood, ourselves, our communal belonging, our identity. How or where do we draw the line? Why do we draw a line? We cannot. Because, quite clearly, we are intrinsically entangled with the artworks, they are stuck to us, we carry them as part of our subjectivity.

3.2 Rhizome 2: nonlocal

Moving on to the second trait of the hyperobjects as described by Morton, namely nonlocality. Returning to the example of global warming, Morton writes:

> [...] I do not see global warming as such. I see this brilliant blade of sunlight, burning the top of my head as I watch it with half-closed eyes reflecting off the burnished, sapphire surface of the solar panels. The manifold that I witness is not merely a "subjective impression" but is rather just this collusion between sunlight, solar panels, roof, and eyes Yet global warming is not here. Hyperobjects are *nonlocal.*[22]

When it comes to law, art and the commons, nonlocality in Morton's sense may not be as counterintuitive as the notion of viscosity. Nonlocality here is almost the starting point, the folding of the global and the local, the manifold of regulations, objects, people, resources. Still it is worth lingering

22 Morton, 2013: 38.

there and discussing the nonlocality trait too, particularly demonstrating the nonlocality of artworks. What is interesting in terms of how Morton puts into play the notion of nonlocality is the idea that a hyperobject is never fully visible to humans, at least not in its entirety, and can only show itself through its local manifestations. This is worth exploring as usually we assume (in law and elsewhere) that artworks as objects can only be present at one place and one time. To add on nonlocality to this assumption we have to engage with movement, maybe even digitalisation, and definitely *dematerialisation.*

Within for instance the digital spheres, the artwork has a tendency to be dematerialised, at least initially to escape or be freed from its material form. Many works have become dematerialised/object-less. They are also de-subjectivised, i.e. no longer necessarily created by only one individual artist, or even by a human being. Instead, the artist is positioned inside contexts of practices and creations. The artwork is located in the *network* of the existing technology and within the (creative) community. Cinema for instance has dematerialised qualities – so does e.g. modern or performative art. These artworks consciously withdraw from the idea of materiality and physical representation. Dematerialised works, are seen, following e.g. Lippard, as works where "the *idea* is paramount and material form secondary, lightweight, ephemeral, cheap, unpretentious".[23] With dematerialised artworks the notion of "tangible object" or "the original" directly becomes less significant as the work exists everywhere, at the same time. It is nonlocal. We can never grasp it in its entirety. Material uniqueness more often than not serves a secondary (or no) purpose for dematerialised art such as e.g. cinematic works. The film, the "idea", the story, the narrative, the performance, is far more interesting than the tangible "copy", or carrier, onto which the work is shown or projected. When it comes to films, a print, a tape, a DVD or indeed any platform such as e.g. a cinema theatre (to mention a physical space) or Netflix (to mention a digital space) is irrelevant. However, as we will see later in Chapter 6, the content and the space are also entangled, which means that both the material and the dematerial have formed an assemblage.

When it comes to dematerialised artworks the carrier and the content converge in this manner. This shall be further discussed in Chapter 6 in conjunction with intellectual property law. However, the same cannot directly always be said of object centric, material, works such as for instance paintings or sculptures that are inherently interlinked with the object/carrier by necessity (even if they are not always one and the same thing, as will be apparent in the Wikimedia case in Chapter 4, p. 98). The impossibilities in terms of enclosure when it comes to dematerialised works are key to discussing how they are envisioned in law and it is particularly relevant

23 (My emphasis), Lippard, 1997: vii.

for modern artworks, performative art, and image-based works such as films because these works themselves are overwhelmingly dematerialised and thus, potentially, un-enclosable and as such, nonlocal.

3.2.1 In law: public spaces, private works

As we saw above many legal approaches to artworks (and conversely artists) have largely been founded upon the ideas of the "genius inventor" and the artistic creation. The creation of the artwork is always assumed to be happening *ex nihilo* or as James Boyle famously puts it: "Copyright is about sustaining the conditions of creativity that enable an individual to craft *out of thin air an Appalachian Spring, a Sun Also Rises,* a *Citizen Kane.*"[24] In law, exclusive rights, and the enabling of packaging and enclosure of works as commodities have been the necessary tools for the (industrial) economy and the commercial exploitation of creative works. Such tools for exploitation have been the same for both tangible and intangible works. In the digital era on the other hand, and particularly when it comes to dematerialised, nonlocal artworks, these processes are no longer necessarily desirable in the same way, nor are they easily described, grasped or applied as they are inherently based on an industrial logic. Come advanced capitalism, and we no longer know how to handle the nonlocal artwork, that flows as data or as capital, without any seeming containers or constraints.

The objectless nature of dematerialised works challenges some of the basic tenets of (copyright) law. It must be noted, however just because a work is dematerialised in a sense, does not mean that it does not have any material or spatial qualities as local manifestations. Once again let us look at an example of the dematerialized nature of works before connecting them to the trait nonlocality that Morton has developed.

One of the latest discussions in access to art has been whether or not to allow photography in general and selfies (and selfie-sticks!) in particular in museums. While on the one hand taking pictures has always in some ways been restricted in museums either because of the damaging nature of flash lights or because of copyright infringement, or both, it has recently been shown that with digital images taken on smartphones there are also additional interactive aspects that are not always understood. This tendency became apparent when Jay Z and Beyoncé were photographed in front of the Mona Lisa at the Louvre in Paris. This image was shared on their social media, and then it became viral. It led to a number of people that usually would not have visited the Louvre flocking to see the Mona Lisa, wanting to stand in the same place where Jay Z and Beyoncé had stood, to recreate their own version of that iconic image, of popular culture meeting classical culture, of pop icons meeting classical icons. The

24 (Emphasis in original), Boyle, 1997: 99.

question of whether or not to allow selfies in the Louvre reached its peak, when on the one hand there were reasons to keep restricting photography, but on the other these devises were seen as key in reaching younger, as well as in conjunction to this very case, also other types of audiences such as e.g. non-white audiences. The Louvre as an institution had with the Jay Z and Beyoncé visit managed unexpectedly to reach a segment of the public with the publicity created by the two pop stars, a segment of the public that traditionally had always been hard to attract. As such, the art exhibited in the Louvre became visited by more people and accessed by more diverse audiences. Subsequently, the new patrons themselves engaged with e.g. the Mona Lisa by uploading their own images in front of it on their own social media profiles, literally dislocating the painting from its physical location in central Paris into the multiverse of the virtual sphere and social media.

The museums have been following this trend and many of them have incorporated new social media aware policies particularly in terms of photography and sharing of images. Some museums have even developed free apps for visitors to use and share pictures, that often even come with a built in selfie-function.[25] Many museums also provide free Wi-Fi encouraging patrons to instantly share their experience using designated hashtags in order to connect to their online communities. The dematerialised image here becomes something more than merely an immaterial expression. Bandle and Phammatter argue for instance that while traditionally a camera-based image served as a memento for the person that took it, a memory, in these instances the images also become a form of communal *interaction* or as Iljadica refers to it *play*.[26] This communication of the experience, of engaging with others that are not physically present in the museum, is the very nonlocal quality that can be shown here. It has been established that this possibility of interaction and sharing attracts new audiences while dislocating the artworks that are in the museums. However, taking pictures of works in museums can also mean another thing: infringement. Because, any reproduction and distribution of works that are still in copyright (70 years after the death of the author which includes most current and modern art) will of course constitute an infringement of the author's or copyright owner's rights. We will see more direct repercussions of this in the Wikimedia case in Chapter 4, p. 88.

As already mentioned, many museums provide free Wi-Fi access for the patrons to use, encouraging interaction and communication further. Does this mean that they also potentially encourage copyright infringement too? Taking a selfie is a reproduction in the context of copyright, and as such it can constitute infringement if the works photographed are still within the copyright term. So, do museums in that case need additional rights

25 Bandle and Phammatter, 2015.
26 Iljadica, 2017.

clearances and licenses?[27] What is the role of the museum then? An enabler of public access, a public space, or a contributory infringer of private (copy? property?) rights?

And in reverse, with e.g. the Google Art Project,[28] a digital platform that provides high resolution images of art from a number of museums around the world, the nonlocality of artworks has been established even further. Artworks are everywhere, and constantly elsewhere, shared, communicated, dematerialised. With the slogan "The World's Art at Your Fingertips", the Google Art Project certainly engages with and encourages the nonlocality of art, it allows audiences around the world to go on (virtual) walks in some of the world's largest museums, without physically being there. In this sense, the experience is both material and dematerialised, both local and nonlocal, here and elsewhere. This is an interesting phenomenon, one that is hardly captured through current copyright law and its defences to infringement, such as e.g. the defence for private use. Morton writes:

> Cut your coat into a thousand pieces–you won't find capital in there. Now try pointing to the unconscious. Did you catch it? Hyperobjects compel us to think ecologically, and not the other way around.

So how to think of (e.g. copyright) law ecologically in this digital and digitised environment? As we have seen here dematerialised aspects of the artworks enable the audiences to engage with that which happens to take place outside the framework of e.g. a museum, or a gallery, or outside of the traditional, enclosed, concept of the artwork. Instead, the work can be seen to exist inside various contexts, shared and interacted with among individuals and within communities which practice and (re)create it. In the setting of nonlocality, the artwork is always *(dis)located* from the private sphere, pushed out into the public sphere, and back, it is constitutive of subjectivity and of communities. As such, the artwork is nonlocal as we can never capture all of it in its entirety, we can only see the local manifestation of it, whether it is in a museum, on a social media platform, or *walking among us* as part of us or other people around us. Therefore, as it is truly nonlocal, it means that legally we need to rethink the notions of the public and the private spheres in and through which artworks are accessed and shared.

3.3 Rhizome 3: temporal undulation

The third trait of the hyperobjects is temporal undulation. Morton writes that this means that "a hyperobject [is] massively distributed in time and

27 This was recently the case with the exhibition Picasso Images, at the Ara Pacis in Rome, where all photography was strictly forbidden.
28 www.google.com/culturalinstitute/about/artproject/

space in ways that baffle humans and make interacting with them fascinating, disturbing, problematic, and wondrous."[29] The relativity or *undulation* of the time/space aspect emerges from the third trait, where "space and time are the two things [...] like 'objects' in the OOO sense, autonomous quanta that can't be divided further".[30] In this sense, time and space are not seen as containers of entities, but are rather seen as objects themselves.[31] I will try to unpack this here, and bring out the materiality of this statement.

The first aspect that needs to be considered is therefore the object-ness of time and space. I write it hyphenated in order not to confuse the idea with "objectivity". Here time and space cannot be divided as two separate entities. That being said, let me briefly break with that and look at time first, for reasons of clarity. In the temporal undulation sense time encompasses the past and the future simultaneously. There is an introduction of the idea of vast timescales that supersede the human lifespan, both backwards and forwards, if we think linearly. Then there are ruptures between epochs "so that the time of one entire people can pass to the time of another".[32] I will give some examples of this soon. In this very much posthumanist sense the correlation between the human and the world as linearly perceived where the human is the measuring stock is thus challenged.

The second aspect is space. The temporal undulation spans beyond the human also in terms of space. This means that we are caught in the hyperobjects – already lost inside them as Morton puts it.[33] He writes:

> Space can no longer be construed as an absolute container, but rather should be thought of as a spacetime manifold that is radically *in* the universe, *of* it rather than ontologically outside it.[34]

These aspects of temporal undulation, both in terms of space and time, need to be understood in the context of the artwork. In law the correlation human-world as a dichotomy is taken for granted, and a human timescale with an exterior space outside the human is also assumed. When those assumptions are challenged the Mortonian spacetime emerges. The insight of such a spacetime will legitimise as well as allow for a construction of the commons. For that to be done we need to address the notions of duration in law, and particularly in intellectual property and cultural heritage law, in

29 Morton, 2013: 58
30 Morton, 2013: 63.
31 Morton, 2013: 65.
32 Morton, 2013: 66.
33 Morton, 2013: 55.
34 (Emphasis in original), Morton, 2013: 56.

order to formulate the clashes of time and space that have so far been assumed, or more accurately yet, been forcefully infused in law.

3.3.1 In law: duration

One of the main objectives here is to show the materiality of the hyperobjects and demonstrate how the very abstractness of the theory is not a metaphor but rather a situated expression of events that are not dependent on an essentialist understanding of law, art or as we shall see in Volume II, commons. The notion of temporal undulation is of course abstract and can be difficult to fully grasp. Allow me to briefly discuss two recent Swedish cases then in order to make this more material. The cases concerned two collections, the so called *Turkish collection* and *Skärfva collection.*

The *Turkish collection* comprised 93 paintings and etchings that came from a Swedish manor called Biby. These had been inherited by three siblings that were no longer Swedish residents and that sought to export and sell the collection abroad. In accordance with the 1970 UNESCO Convention on the Means of Prohibiting and Preventing the Illicit Import, Export and Transfer of Ownership of Cultural Property as well as the Swedish Historic Environment Act, *Kulturmiljölagen* (1988: 950) (KL), export of cultural artefacts must be approved by a state body when it is a question of items deemed to be cultural property (KL, 5th chapter). The relevant state body in this instance is the Swedish National Museum (NM) In the case of the Turkish collection NM declined export sought by the heirs, citing that the collection was made up by irreplaceable cultural property items, a direct testament to the close ties between Sweden and the Ottoman Empire. The items had been in the country ever since 1788, imported by the then Swedish ambassador to the Ottoman Empire and his family, and had since acquired a strong connection to Sweden. The decision by NM was appealed by the heirs, and the higher appellate court (*Kammarrätten*)[35] annulled the NM decision, allowing the artefacts to be exported, the collection to be split up and sold to buyer(s) abroad. In the decision, and by interpreting Swedish inheritance rules broadly, as well as stressing individual property rights connected to inheritance, the court argued that since it was a question of Turkish paintings with a Turkish/Ottoman motif that the collection in question did not directly fall within the definition of Swedish national cultural heritage. As such, the export and subsequent sale had to be allowed as this was part of exercising the property rights of the family. The argument by the NM that the Turkish collection was to be seen as national cultural heritage, that it had been in Sweden for over 200 years, and that it was a unique collection, testifying to the close relationship between Sweden and the Ottoman Empire, was thus

35 Kammarrätten in Stockholm, case number 2069–13, delivered on 29 May 2013.

overturned. The items have since been exported from Sweden, sold at auction by Sotheby's in London to international buyer(s). There is a rumour that the buyer in question might be a large Qatari museum. Some art historians have argued that the fact that the collection was taken out of Sweden is a tragedy for the entire Swedish cultural heritage.[36]

The second similar example is the so called *Skärfva collection*. This was a collection of Chinese gouache paintings imported to Sweden by the Swedish shipbuilder and navy officer Fredric Henric af Chapman. From his voyages to China he took back the gouaches in question that had been painted with an ancient Chinese technique but that were depicting Swedish local motifs. Since the end of the eighteenth century this collection has been kept at the Skärfva Manor in Karlskrona. These paintings were in a similar manner to the Turkish collection recently acquired by a foreign buyer, namely a Chinese woman based in London. The export of the items, through the same procedure as described above connected to the 1970 UNESCO convention, was denied by NM and the items were detained in Sweden, defined as irreplaceable cultural heritage that could not leave the country. However, this time the decision made by the NM was upheld in the appellate court (*Förvaltningsrätten*) and the export was not allowed. The items have since been kept in a storage room in Stockholm. The buyer has claimed that she is not likely to appeal the decision to the higher appellate court, however she has expressed a sadness that the paintings are being held away from the public, when they could have been shown to a large audience at a Chinese museum. Furthermore, she claimed that these items were of high significance for Chinese cultural history as they testify to the longstanding historical Chinese connections with the West and their mutual cultural, religious, political and economical communications that have occurred throughout history. The fact that the paintings are stuck, as she refers to it, in Sweden is further unfortunate, she claims, because paintings such as these have historically always been bought by westerners and do not exist in China anymore. In that sense they make up a missing piece of Chinese (cultural) history. The only thing that differed in this case from the case of the Turkish collection is of course the fact that there were no direct heirs to the paintings, they had been left to a museum, and that the motif for these paintings were distinctly Swedish. The paintings had been commissioned by a Swedish buyer for the purpose of being taken to Sweden on the sailing vessel *Ostinidiefararen* (The East Indiaman) that was sailing between Gothenburg and the Chinese ports at the end of the eighteenth century. The case remains unresolved at the time of writing.

The temporal undulation is quite obvious in these two cases. First – we have a timescale that surpasses the human lifespan. In other words, the hyperobjects encompass the past and the future simultaneously here. They

36 Wadstein MacLeod, 2016.

are spatial in that they are quite literally connected to territories of China, the Ottoman empire, modern Sweden, modern Europe, etc. all at once. As such their spatiotemporality cannot be distinguished from the cultural heritage of the people they are seen to belong to as they also contribute in constituting both the past and the present (as well as the future) of these communities. With these particular cases, deemed as trans-boundary, the people or communities that can claim the works are both Asian and European. They, their identities, their *bodies*, are already placed inside these objects, and the other way around the objects have equally entered these communities as constituting parts of the common identity. "[H]yperobjects seem to beckon us further into themselves, making us realize that we're already lost inside them", notes Morton.[37]

So what is duration? And how can we in that case put a time frame on a work?

3.4 Rhizome 4: phasing

Fourth trait. Phasing. Hyperobjects have a transdimensional quality – they inhabit a higher dimensionality than regular objects. I spoke of three dimensions in the previous chapter when connecting law to the lawscape. Now I am adding further dimensions still. Hyperobjects do not operate within the three dimensions, they are "*phasea:* they occupy a high-dimensional *phase space* that makes them impossible to see as a whole on a regular three-dimensional human-scale basis".[38] What does that mean? The fourth trait can be described as a critique of the division between the human and the object, or the human and its perceived, or assumed, outside such as nature or culture, e.g. the idea of nature or culture as something external, over there – something that has a quality of "over-yonder-ness".[39]

As we saw in the previous trait, temporal undulation, both space and time are seen to be inside the objects and not as free floating containers. This quality, among others, the radical immanence, means that the hyperobject exists *transdimensionally*, and always already reaches dimensions that are never fully available to the human perception. That is why a hyperobject can never be seen in its entirety at once, as it phases in and out of perception. Morton writes:

> Hyperobjects don't inhabit some conceptual behind in our heads or out there. They are real objects that affect other objects. Indeed the philosophical view behind thinking that objects are one thing and

37 Morton, 2013: 55.
38 Morton, 2013: 70.
39 Morton, 2013: 72.

> relations [...] are another positively inhibits our transition to an ecological age...[40]

We are closing in on the idea of an ecological, or rhizomatic, to stay consistent with the terminology from the previous chapter, approach to the artwork as a hyperobject. This very idea that hyperobjects are always in a way suspended from full access is particularly interesting when applied to the artwork. That they appear as sometimes closer, and sometimes further, phasing in and out of perception, but can never fully be grasped is a trait that is significant to notice. This must be revealed. The fact that they cannot ever be experienced directly and fully, also means that there is an aspect to them that forms the basis for the commons, something shared, something experienced, a togetherness. As such they also defy the description of "subjective" awareness versus "objective" (external) world.[41]

What emerges is a "between-ness" instead, a shared spacetime that seems to be pointing to an interaction between, not subjects and objects, but only between (hyper)objects. In the last trait, namely interobjectivity, I will develop this further. For the purposes of phasing right now it is imperative to establish that when it comes to hyperobjects we are always only seeing one side of the object, it is always withdrawn from us in its entirety – but that quality also means that that a shared between-ness is created, where the hyperobject exists in a common perception.

3.4.1 In law: original-copy

When describing mass produced (and digital) artworks Stapleton for instance writes that while before the artwork "stressed the training of individuals for particular creative tasks, the new model approached the view that creativity occurred not within individuals, but in the relational *spaces* between human (and non-human) 'actors'."[42] It is precisely these spaces, or the spacetime, phasing in and out of perception that is the fourth trait of hyperobjects. These are the spaces between objects that are produced relationally.

Thus, we are moving away from the ideology of "unique", physical, singular artworks, the idea of the original, and focusing instead on the aspect of the work that is created when human and non-human (machines! They are alive![43]) objects interact. This particular phenomenon is signifi - cant as the previously prevailing notions of "author/creator" within the old

40 Morton, 2013: 73.
41 Morton, 2013: 76.
42 (My emphasis), Stapleton, 2002: 83–84.
43 Haraway, 1991, Käll, 2017.

ideology of creativity are here being challenged. We can recall John Cage's "song" or rather audio piece called *4:33* that consists of 4 minutes and 33 seconds of silence. Other examples of this phenomenon of phasing could perhaps be user generated content (UGC) created digitally where the content creators are both users and consumers at once, in an interaction with the machines, co-creators at the same time as they are audience, or *prosumers.*[44]

It is this aspect of "automatic subjectivity" that is not only human but also automatic, connected to something a-human such as a machine, that challenges the dichotomy in e.g. copyright law of the original and the copy of an artwork. At this particular juncture, when moving away from traditional objecthood towards hyperobjecthood, we can add on the dematerialised and de-subjectivised aspect to the artwork, requiring participation and an active audience, or as we just saw, prosumers.

This brings us back to the first trait of the hyperobject namely its viscosity and the human–thing dichotomy addressed above. When we have realised that the dichotomy between the original and the copy now also has collapsed, we become aware that the creator-consumer, or prosumer, has emerged out of, or phased in from, that collapse. As such the prosumer can be connected to the viscosity of the hyperobject. In that sense the phasing brings us to that which Haraway refers to as "Copies without Originals".[45] This is a larger argument that needs to be developed further connecting the content that humans create to the very same content that is then becoming part of the extended human body. I will explore this in more detail in the Richard Prince case in Chapter 4, p. 98.

The collapse between an original and a copy does not only affect intellectual property law. The phasing aspect of the hyperobject and as such the dilution of the two concepts can also be seen with the regulation concerning e.g. indigenous cultural heritage. Morton gives precisely the example of an "Aboriginal hyperobject" in the phasing chapter.[46] Addressing the painting *Untitled 2011* by the Aboriginal artist Yukultji Napangati, Morton writes:

> The function of the painting emits spacetime, emits an aesthetic field. The painting is a unit, a quantum that executes a function. It is a device, not just a map but also a tool, like a shaman's rattle or a computer algorithm. The function of the painting seems to be to imprint me with the bright red shadow of a hyperobject, the Australian Outback, the Dreamtime, the long history of the Pintupi Nine, the Lost Tribe, some of the last Neolithic humans on Earth. We shall see when

44 The term "prosumer" was coined by Alvin Toffler already in 1980. See e.g. Toffler, 1980

45 Haraway, 1991, Käll, 2017.

46 Morton, 2013: 69.

> it comes to talking about art in the time of hyperobjects just how significant it is that Napangati somehow manages to combine *map* and *device*.[47]

Here we have an issue of both a work created by an "individual" artist that arguably is governed by copyright law, but also a work that appropriates and uses as a tool, map or device that which stems from the entire history of this Aboriginal tribe. What or who is the original or the copy here, and is this a piece of copyright work as property or a piece of cultural heritage as a communal identity? Which spacetime does this artwork occupy? What aspects of it are phasing in and what are phasing out?

Connecting the human in this way to objects and content means that suddenly, as many of us working in this field keep stating over and over again, then it appears as if there is no outside. No outside to the human, no outside to law, no outside to the artwork, no outside to the commons. And as such we could claim, as Morton does, that the "outer space" or just the "outside" is a figment of our imagination that we are always as he puts it, inside an object but sometimes it appears closer and sometimes further.[48] Or put differently, we are always relational with artworks even when they appear far away from us in space and time. As such we are interobjective.

3.5 Rhizome 5: interobjectivity

The four traits listed so far eventually converge in the final and fifth trait – namely *interobjectivity*. It is here that the truly posthuman aspect of the hyperobjects is brought to the fore as it moves beyond the more or mere anthropocentric inter*subjectivity*. Morton distinguishes the two by defining intersubjectivity as a shared space in which human meaning resonates, whereas interobjectivity on the other hand is far larger than that. In fact, interobjectivity encompasses intersubjectivity as it "is a small region of a much larger interobjective configuration space".[49] The idea of excluding that which is "dead" or "non-human" from the shared space, and dividing e.g. the artist from the artwork or the commons from the commoneers is something that I will develop further in Chapter 5. Before reaching the concept of the commons proper, let me just develop the interobjective trait of the hyperobject.

Particularly when it comes to transmitting and sharing information, this idea of interobjectivity is crucial. For instance, and Morton gives a similar example too, in order to write we do not only require a human mind but

47 (Emphasis in original), Morton, 2013: 75.
48 Morton, 2013: 17.
49 Morton, 2013: 81.

also a pen, a paper, a computer, internet, electricity, solar panels, oil, trees etc. This network of human and non-human objects, the *mesh*, as Morton refers to it, forms interobjectivity.[50] He writes:

> A mesh consists of relationships between crisscrossing strands of metal and gaps between the strands. Meshes are potent metaphors for the strange interconnectedness of things, an interconnectedness that does not allow for perfect, lossless transmission of information, but is instead full of gaps and absences. When an object is born it is instantly enmeshed into a relationship with other objects.[51]

It is precisely these relationships with their gaps, absences, between-ness and all, that now towards the end of this chapter need to be demonstrated and later on connected to the commons. For me to do that I want to re-enter the cultural landscape: one is a traditional museum namely the British Museum, that we already entered at the beginning of this book, and the other, that we now enter, may not initially be considered as a museum but more as a cultural site, namely the ancient site of Palmyra.

3.5.1 In law: the mesh and the commons

That the Rosetta Stone is probably one of the most important items of cultural heritage for our civilisation is an undisputed fact. Dating back to 196 B.C. it has provided scholars with a key to reading Egyptian hieroglyphs, which in turn has opened up a wealth of knowledge in terms of the ancient world, as well as to understanding our own society and its past and current structures. In the year of 2013 the British Museum, the establishment that currently houses it among thousands of other pieces of cultural heritage, attracted 6.8 million visitors. Since 2003 Egypt has been requesting the repatriation of the Rosetta Stone, claiming that it is part of the Egyptian cultural heritage and serves as an "icon of Egyptian identity" and must therefore be returned to Egypt, its source country. The British Museum, together with some other leading museums, have generally and as a matter of principle claimed that certain cultural heritage items such as the Rosetta Stone, the Elgin Marbles, the Nefertiti bust, etc. on the contrary are now part of our common global identity and as such these items can be attributed to humankind as a whole. The so called market country museums have even issued a joint statement claiming that "objects acquired in earlier times must be viewed in the light of different sensitivities and values reflective of that earlier era" and that "museums serve not just the citizens of one nation but the people of every nation". The

50 Morton, 2013: 83.
51 Morton, 2013: 83.

items of cultural heritage in the British Museum are thus claimed as belonging not to a specific community of people but to the entirety of human kind, not to, as the museums have put it, one specific nation or citizens but everybody. Of course, it is difficult to forget the imperial pasts connected to the acquisitions of these items, which naturally begs the question whether it means that in order to be seen as serving human kind the items must be kept in the West or in the market states, often former colonial or imperial powers?

To make this point even clearer, let us enter Palmyra.

Most people will by now have heard of the ancient cultural site of Palmyra. The ancient Greco-Roman site in Syria is currently in the middle of fierce battles between the Al-Assad forces and Isis rebels. It is in urgent danger. The site is equally culturally significant as e.g. Pompeii or Ephesus. These cultural sites, once significant trading cities, have throughout the course of history been battlegrounds in various senses. Palmyra in particular is a battleground in terms of ownership and control, where war is waged not just on who controls the actual territory where the site (still) stands, but also in terms of its symbolic, religious and political significance. The bloody battle is being, still as we speak, fought out and Palmyra is at least at the time of writing under Isis control. This site, that has been so culturally diverse through many a century, also provides us with an example of contested sites that embody issues of identity, community and belonging.

Both the discussions surrounding the British Museum and objects housed therein as well as the control of Palmyra concern the ownership of artefacts which are closely connected to the "identity issue". In these instances cultural heritage represents, constitutes and re-constitutes identity and heritage (national, regional, communal, local or conversely that of human kind as a whole).[52] Within cultural heritage discussions, a reccurring question is whether the former imperial countries should be allowed to keep items of cultural heritage that they acquired in the course of their colonial rule? The source countries, as mentioned, constantly demand cultural heritage back relying on various legal instruments e.g. the UNESCO legal framework.

And now. With a long history of contested ownership and belonging, with a number of legal regulations struggling to deal with these issues that have to do with repatriation and/or return, France's former president François Hollande issued a call to create so called safe havens or "refuges" for artefacts that are seen to be under threat of destruction or peril. He is particularly referring to artefacts from Syria, and especially looted items from Palmyra. The Louvre, it has been suggested, should act as one such safe haven. Treating cultural objects as "refugees" that require asylum-like

52 See e.g. 1972 UNESCO Convention Concerning the Protection of the World Cultural and Natural Heritage (World Heritage Convention).

safe havens in western countries has now brought us full circle – where what we previously assumed to be dead matter, has been given the status of a migrant, living matter – voluntarily seeking refuge in the West.

But, lest we forget, destroying cultural heritage is already considered to be a war crime according to the Convention for the Protection of Cultural Property in the Event of Armed Conflict (1954),[53] or Hague Convention for short. In September 2016 the International Criminal Court delivered for instance a verdict against Ahmad Al Faqi Al Mahdi, held responsible for intentionally directing attacks against historic monuments and/or buildings dedicated to religion, including nine mausoleums and one mosque in Timbuktu, Mali.[54] Usually, the destruction of cultural heritage in armed conflicts is sentenced together or in conjunction with other war crimes in accordance with the Geneva Conventions,[55] particularly Protocol II[56] which includes the crimes listed under the Hague Convention. We saw this in for instance the Balkan wars or the more recent Afghan war, where various war crimes also included deliberate acts of destruction of sites of cultural heritage.[57] The Al Mahdi case on the other hand was unprecedented in that somebody was for the first time convicted solely of this particular war crime, namely intentional destruction of cultural property. The Hague Convention expressly states that damage to the cultural property of any people means damage to (the cultural heritage of) all mankind.

So back to Palmyra. On 9 March 2017 The Guardian featured an article written by Ruth Maclean called "Desecrated but still majestic: inside Palmyra after second Isis occupation".[58] In that article a resident of Palmyra declares at one point, echoing the rhetoric of the war crime conventions, that he feels that the activities carried out by the Islamic State in Palmyra are equal to killing people, he says: "[d]estroying our heritage is the same as killing a child". The same article describes a piece of graffiti at the entrance to Palmyra that reads: "No entry without Isis permission – not even brothers." This of course connects the human (war crimes against humanity) with the spatial (Palmyra as a physical site occupied by the Islamic State, the British Museum, a site that houses items acquired during colonial rule). The British Museum or Palmyra as sites therefore become

53 1954 Protection of Cultural Property in the Event of Armed Conflict with Regulations for the Execution of the Convention (Hague Convention).

54 The Prosecutor v. Ahmad Al Faqi Al Mahdi. ICC-01/12–01/15, 27 September 2016.

55 Convention (I-IV) for the Amelioration of the Condition of the Wounded and Sick in Armed Forces in the Field. Geneva, 12 August 1949 and their Additional Protocols.

56 Convention (I-IV) for the Amelioration of the Condition of the Wounded and Sick in Armed Forces in the Field. Geneva, 12 August 1949, Additional Protocol, II.

57 See e.g. Prosecutor v. Dario Kordic & Mario Cerkez, IT-95-14/2-T, 26 February 2001, p. 206.

58 Maclean, 2017.

hyperobjects in their own right, or lawscapes, precisely in the entanglement between various other hyperobjects (works of cultural heritage, people, war machines, etc.).

And now France, a former colonial power, with a very conflicted history in terms of import of works of cultural heritage, wants to provide safe havens for these objects that are systematically being destroyed in Syria. Sure, it is a matter of aid that might save the items. It is possibly even the humanitarian thing to do. It is proposed that this should be done by elevating the artefacts at risk from being seen as objects to giving them a migrant status. For something to be protected it needs to be made human-esque. Or the other way around, in order to provide humanitarian help, the objects need to *become human.*

What this means must of course be discussed, whether this is a legitimate and ethical moral safeguarding of heritage of the entire human kind or a clandestine appropriation of heritage and a hidden act of imperialism. It remains to be seen. Legally speaking we can now, however, safely say that there is no longer any idea of dividing human beings (migrants, people) from non-human things (cultural sites, works of cultural heritage, migrants!), as we have all quite clearly entered into the mesh of the hyperobject, in constant relationship with other objects, interobjectively. The cultural heritage items have now *become* migrants in a Deleuzian sense. So who is the hyperobject? We all are, of course. We have become hyperobjects even in the eyes of the law with this latest turn that France is advancing, one that might lead to other countries following suit. This very turn opens up the shared space, a lawscape, required in order to conceive of the artwork in the commons.

Chapter 4

Case studies

The contested spaces

Before we reach the commons and the discussion surrounding it, let us first delve even deeper into the artwork as a hyperobject and how it as such becomes a legal battleground and a contested space. In this chapter I look closely at three case studies which will provide us with additional concrete aspects as to the spatiality and hyperobjectivity of the contested artworks.

4.1 Bruno Schulz and lost art

This chapter begins with a story. The story is about a man, an artist and a writer, called Bruno Schulz. This case is particularly about one of Schulz's artworks that was lost and then found, many years after his death and after the work's original inception. By opening with the Schulz case we begin with the first crucial aspect of the discussion, how physical artworks also constitute hyperobjects and as such how they too need to be connected to a cultural commons.

Bruno Schulz lived between 1892 and 1942. He was born in the town of Drohobych that during his lifetime belonged to Poland. Drohobych is today part of the Ukrainian territory. This case study is about one of the works that was initially one of his lesser known but which, in time, became probably one of his most talked about and disputed pieces, namely a mural painting. Painted in 1942, lost for nearly 60 years, rediscovered in 2001, subject to disputes and mystified, the pieces that once made up this mural are today scattered and divided between two countries. Some parts remain in Drohobych, while others are on exhibition in the Holocaust Memorial, Yad Vashem, in Israel.

The mural was created during WWII. As many other works of its time it embodies the terror of the era and it is a living testament to the horror, despair and suffering that plagued the lives of people. Its subject matter is a fairy-tale, yet it is impossible to disregard the anguish and despair also encapsulated within it. Mirroring its own time, while acting as a shared memory it is allowing us to gain a glimpse into our shared collective history. More significantly within this context, the work reflects apparent issues that can be connected to ownership, control and access to artworks. It is probably one of the most conflict-ridden lost artworks of the last decades. To consider this case is, for a study like this, inevitable, imperative. This is the story of the mural.

Born into a Jewish family, Schulz would have normally needed to wear the Star of David on his outer garments, whenever he exited outside. However, due to his artistic skills he avoided this. Everyone who, like Schulz, was deemed to be somehow a "necessary Jew" by the Gestapo evaded being branded with the Star of David because skilled workers were needed and as a consequence they were kept away from round-ups and transports. A Nazi officer in Drohobych called Felix Landau, who had a keen interest in the arts, took to Schulz and chose him to be his artist-protégé, his own "skilled Jew", and commissioned several works from him. One such commission that Landau assigned to Schulz was to paint the walls of his son's nursery.

Creating for a young boy, under what can only be described as duress and fear for his life, meant that Schulz had to depart from his own usual style, which was dark, mystical, and employed an extensive use of overtly sexual visual vocabulary. However, in order to stay true to his style, Schulz decided to employ certain symbolical imagery, include hidden messages so to speak, and still be able to tell the stories he wanted to, but that would remain unnoticed by Landau, and of course be appropriate for a child. The work kept him alive for some time, but then there was an increasing sense of fear in him as well as the rest of the Drohobych Jewish community.

On 19 November 1942, one of Landau's rivals within the Gestapo used a commotion that had erupted in the Jewish ghetto as cover and shot Schulz to death. A couple of days prior to that Landau had, so the story goes, killed the same rival's Jewish dentist. The rival, upon shooting Schulz, truthfully or not, is to have retorted to Landau by saying: "You killed my Jew – so I killed yours," as these people were seen as possessions, belonging to one Nazi officer each. After that day of the commotion when Schulz died, the mural in the nursery that he had been working on fell into oblivion. It was only rediscovered some 60 years later, in 2001, by a German documentary filmmaker, Benjamin Geissler.

Geissler had travelled to Drohobych specifically in order to locate the mural.[1] Astonishingly, even though there had been a number of other failed searches for it, Geissler managed to find it. As soon as he and his crew had discovered what seemed to be traces of the mural in the old Landau house they immediately alerted the Ukrainian authorities, as well as Polish and Israeli art preservationists and requested help with the excavation. However, before the entire work had been lifted from underneath the

1 Geissler, 2002.

layers of paint and wallpaper that covered it, some five recovered pieces that had already been somewhat restored by Polish conservationists, were taken away by Yad Vashem representatives. These five fragments had only been rudimentarily restored.

The removal of the five pieces resulted in international ire. It also eventually led to a full dispute. Questions such as: "Who does this work belong to?" sprung up. Was it truly Yad Vashem, because Schulz was a Holocaust victim and because it is an institution devoted to precisely their memory? It is an institution with the means and knowledge to preserve the work properly. Or was it Poland, because Schulz had been a Polish citizen and this was part of Polish history? Or was it the Ukraine, on whose territory it had been found, and where at the time there was a plan to open a Bruno Schulz museum in Drohobych?

The hyperobject at hand is thus a mural that makes up a significant work of art for the Jewish people as it is a part of their history and identity (viscous), while it at the same time appears equally significant for the Polish people too (nonlocal), especially when considering the fact that they are trying to deal with their pre-war Jewish heritage and its past and present relationship with its own Jewish population (phasing). Furthermore, it embodies a piece of European history and present identity (time undulation). A traditional object–subject approach to identity for example is problematic here as at the core of this issue undoubtedly lies a question of an artwork that resists any such separation (interobjective).

Having to weigh the fact that Schulz, influenced by Judaism, its teachings and traditional Jewish methods of storytelling, at the same time was a Polish citizen and that he was, essentially and culturally secular, is very illustrative, particularly in order to reveal the hyperobjectivity of this artwork that then needs to be fitted into the rhizomatic legal reasoning that will later connect it to the commons.

4.1.1 Identity, hyperobjects and law

There is an identity implication, a so called *haecceity* in Deleuze/Guattari that they discuss in *A Thousand Plateaus*. Deleuze and Guattari write about haecceity:

> A degree, an intensity is an individual, a *Haecceity*, that enters into composition with other degrees, other intensities, to form another individual. [...] In short, between substantial forms and determined subjects, *between the two*, there is not only a whole operation of demonic local transports but a natural play of haecceities, degrees, intensities, events, and accidents that compose individuations totally different from those of the well-formed subjects [...] However, depending on their degree of speed or the relation movement and rest into which

> they enter, they belong to a given Individual, which may itself be part of another Individual governed by another, more complex, relation, and so to an infinity. There are thus smaller and larger infinities, not by virtue of their number, but by virtue of composition of the relation into which their parts enter. Thus each individual is an infinite multiplicity, and the whole of Nature is a multiplicity of perfectly individuated multiplicities.[2]

This idea of identity as haecceity is interesting. The individual is thus not seen as a closed off subject but rather as a degree of intensity that is constantly in composition with other intensities. It is this in-betweenness once again that is interesting to deploy here in the Schulz case. Approaching Schulz, or identity in general, as infinite multiplicities connected to nature and the "outside" is precisely the tool need here.

The first issue in the Schulz case that thus must be analysed is exactly that, namely the composition of the identity of the creator, and its infinite multiplicity, connected to the concept of haecceity. The mural was initially made to adorn the walls of a nursery. It is also a work of art that had been created with the intent to wordlessly illuminate the story of the Drohobych Jewish community at a time during which it was painted, detailing the struggle of the Jewish people. This was expressed utilising religious symbols and allegories. Schulz had for instance painted un-Aryan features on the queen in the painting, something that would have been unheard of, even forbidden, during the time when the mural was painted. On one part of the mural a dwarf's face appears to bear the artist's own self-portrait. This dwarf can be seen at the reins of a carriage. This is also very important to note, because at the time Nazi laws prohibited Jews from both riding in and driving carriages. Schulz's mural is thus at once a timeless and unusual act of disobedience and social criticism, a historical document, as well as a disputed object of cultural heritage, *and* when it was found it was still under the scope of copyright and as such formed an intellectual property asset.

Even though Bruno Schulz was highly influenced by Judaism, as has already been alluded, he was still a secular man and there are many testimonies that confirm that he considered himself to be, first and foremost, a Pole. He probably never saw the Polish people as his oppressors and his Polish-ness undoubtedly also influenced his work greatly, defined him as an artist and as a person, and ultimately played a great role in his life. The problem concerns the fact that if the work is deemed Jewish in some way (e.g. Jewish cultural heritage) and in giving prominence to the one side, Jewishness, it has to be asked whether the other aspects of "identity", Polish-ness, European-ness, are simultaneously being negated, and if so whether it is at all possible for Bruno Schulz's mural to belong to

2 Deleuze and Guattari, 2011: 279–280.

the Jewish and the Polish communities at once while at the same time remaining in Israel, and still being European? Or can it even be said to belong to the "entire human kind" in the words of the UNESCO conventions, because of its significance as a testament to the events that took place during WWII? The conflict has been settled between Yad Vashem and the Ukraine on a diplomatic level, as I will discuss below and in detail in Chapter 7, and the pieces of the mural have been given to Yad Vashem on a "long term loan" but where Yad Vashem states that the works are part of the cultural heritage of the Ukraine.

Regardless of this settlement agreement, the issue here, however, centres not only around the people or the community the work might or might not be attributed to, but also where it should be kept and who should be able to protect, control and in the extension also access it. Is it truly Yad Vashem and people who visit Yad Vashem? This is not a rhetorical question.

To deal with that aspect, one is put in the rather uncomfortable situation of having to *define* what Schulz was, and was *not*. Who was Bruno Schulz – a Polish Jew, or a Jewish Pole, or simply a European artist, a human being, who was a victim of Nazism? The question concerning not only the artist's identity but also his *Heimat* thus becomes inescapable. In these cases it is evident that the law appears to be presupposing certain notions of monocultural societies and definable and stable nationalities, identities and communities. When it comes to the lack of identity, or perhaps more accurately multi-identity, it becomes more difficult to handle these cases legally. In the wake of on-going current globalization with artists creating in a multicultural, interconnected world, this is not directly a dying issue. With migration that is constantly taking place, and where national identities are blurred and many territorial borders still remain problematic, undefined or under negotiation, these kinds of questions are not likely to disappear over time. On the contrary. So the concept of haecceity connected to the hyperobjects lends itself nicely for the analysis here, and becomes potentially a much more appropriate tool, that allows for a transdimensional reading of what is commonly referred to as "identity". I will argue that the reason we (we the lawyers, we the legal philosophers, we the scholars, *we the people…*) perceive Schulz's mural as an insurmountable problem is because there appears to be an incongruity between the notions of what art is (supposed to be), who the artist is (supposed to be) and in which constellations or spaces they *de facto* exist. In other words we often find founding assumptions in law that cultural works are created under uniform and clear conditions and that concepts such as: a) a work of art, b) an artist c) an identity d) a community exist and can be articulated, defined and closed in legally. These assumptions, that all of those concepts inherently correspond to some outside "reality" are obviously problematic when it comes to the absence of such connections or in the presence of pluralism, multi-centricity or indeed hyperobjectivity in terms of the works of art. As Benjamin Paloff so succinctly puts it with regards to Schulz:

> Born a subject of the Austro-Hungarian empire and later a citizen of independent Poland, Schulz found himself living briefly under Soviet occupation at the beginning of the war and was murdered because he was a Jew in the Third Reich [...] Remarkably, this is the story of a man who spent most of his life in one place.[3]

Eerily echoing Paloff, but written many years before his article, Deleuze and Guattari write about *the nomad* in the following manner: "the nomad is on the contrary *he who does not move.*"[4]

Ever since Roman law, there exists a division in law between property that is deemed to be fixed land, realty, and property deemed to be chattel, personalty, movable objects, not fixed to land. Furthermore, in Roman law objects, as well as living beings that were not citizens, *strangers*, were deemed to be chattel as they could not own land and in order to gain some kind of subjectivity they had to be subject to a landowner's protection. As a consequence animals, women, slaves as well as Jews during the Middle Ages[5] have legally been treated as chattel as they were, quite simply, not attached to land. The issue at hand is very similar. Created on Polish territory under German occupation, that later became the Ukraine, Schulz's mural no longer has a land, if ever it did. So we are forced to assume that the work, *as well as the artist*, legally can merely be understood as chattel, dead matter, and as such belonging to the landowner. Such reasoning naturally fails to see the full nature of the hyperobject, the fact that it is viscous, nonlocal, subject to temporal undulation and phasing, and that it ultimately is interobjective, where both the dichotomy between so called "living" beings, humans, and "dead" matter, objects, is inherently challenged as here, what we are dealing with is dead humans, some six million of them. It means that the founding dichotomy between space/land (dead matter) and human/property (living matter) collapses.

In Roman law, as we will see further in Chapter 7, we find the concept of *res communae* — objects that cannot be owned by anyone and are open to everybody by their nature. This concept can and will be connected to the notion of hyperobject, here specifically artworks that belong to a heterogeneous group collectively, works that depict the history and culture of the many communities they stem from, something that is worth protecting both in the short and the long term, as we will see when I discuss intergenerational aspects of the commons in Chapter 5. What is apparent is that

3 Paloff, 2005.

4 (Emphasis in original), Deleuze and Guattari, 2011: 420.

5 See e.g. Menahem Shohet, 1931.

Schulz created an artwork in order to beg silently for change and, if he had asked for change more vociferously, it would inevitably have meant an instant end to his life. Still he died *because* he was seen to belong to a community. How can such issues be captured legally as they are, at the core, issues concerning human suffering and (in)justice? How can the ownership, or belonging, of an artwork influenced by Judaism as well as the Polish culture, created under Nazi occupation, on occupied territory, be reconciled in law?

4.1.2 Fragments: nonlocality

Studying the mural adds layers of complication: the work has been destroyed, fragmented and it cannot be viewed in (any) one place in its entirety, as some parts are in Israel and some remain in the Ukraine. It is thus constantly exhibited elsewhere, always away from its "original" context, away from itself. What happens to such works of art when they are taken out of their original context, fragmented, broken, taken elsewhere? Does the artwork lose its value, or potential, does it become reified, misplace its hyperobjective qualities when it has been taken out of context, broken up, shattered? Or, is it the other way around?

These questions are particularly pertinent in relation to the issue of whether the five pieces, by being taken to Yad Vashem, were rendered "soulless" and "inauthentic" in Adorno and Horkheimer's[6] terminology, whether they became reified, or, on the contrary, whether in a Benjaminian sense[7] the act itself shattered the aura of the work and freed it from the burdens of its past, its original location, and unleashed its true potential emancipating it from its given and perhaps vastly constraining context. It can be argued that by taking the mural to Yad Vashem it attained another or maybe its ultimate, potential in that it can be studied independently from its original context, as it is placed in a new setting, among works from a similar context, in a new (Old) land. It can be viewed by larger numbers of people, be adequately preserved and can also be understood as relevant from additional aspects that may not be apparent had it been left in its original setting. Of course, Yad Vashem is not the sole claimant on the mural, there were, and still are many other claims.[8] To illustrate further this very nonlocal aspect in the Schulz case let us also look at another very similar case. It concerns the manuscripts left behind by Franz Kafka when he died.

6 Adorno and Horkheimer, 2007.

7 Benjamin, 2007.

8 Not just the Ukraine and Poland, but also Schulz's heirs, that I will not go into here. The last living heir to Schulz, Mr. Marek W. Podstolski is still fighting for the return of various Schulz works that were taken from the family during WWII.

The dispute concerning Schulz's mural has (so far) not ended up in court because of the settlement agreement between Yad Vashem and the Ukraine. The case of Franz Kafka's manuscripts however, unlike Schulz's mural, resulted in court action. The dispute concerning Kafka manuscripts differs on other key points as well, but can still be very relevant to the discussion here. In October 2012, a judge ruled that the collection of documents that Franz Kafka had left behind just before his death and given to his friend and publisher Max Brod, should be handed over to Israel's National Library from the private hands of the family of Esther Hoffe. Hoffe, now deceased, had been a friend and secretary of Brod's. Brod in his turn had left Kafka's documents to her. Her estate, controlled now by her two daughters, was in the possession of the documents.

In the ruling of the Kafka case, that itself perhaps was a little Kafkaesque in nature, the Israeli Judge Talia Pardo-Kupelman wrote:

> This case complicated by passions, was argued in court for quite a long time *across seas, lands, and times.* Not every day, and most definitely not as a matter of routine, does the opportunity befall a judge to delve into the depth of history as it unfolds before him in piecemeal fashion [...][9]

Judge Pardo-Kupelman continued to assert that this trial had opened "a window into the lives, desires, frustrations and the souls of two of the greatest thinkers of the 20th century [Kafka and Brod]."[10] The language that she chose in her ruling is clearly not *traditional* legal language, *dogmatically* used in adjudication. But how could she have used dogmatic language? When encountering a case of this type, passions, time, desire, frustration, concepts that are usually considered to fall *outside* the scope of the law, that are excluded and considered to be extra-legal, were at the heart of the case in front of Judge Pardo-Kupelman. These are hyperobjective qualities. There was no way of circumventing or excluding them. But there was also a genuine legal question that was presented before the judge, namely who was to be deemed to be the rightful owner of the manuscripts that Kafka had left behind. This was a question of property and inheritance law.

The issue was not easy. In order to deal with it, the judge transformed it from being a material legal question (who is the rightful owner?) into a question of burden of proof (have the heirs managed to show, as the burden of proof was theirs, that the manuscripts had been issued as a gift in their mother's lifetime?):

9 (My emphasis). This translation of the decision is Haaretz' translation and was taken from Aderet, 2012.

10 Aderet, 2012.

> Due to the strict *requirements of proof* required, I do not believe that the plaintiffs have met the requirements... the gift was never carried out to completion... One can determine that the Kafka manuscripts, like the Brod estate, were not given to the plaintiffs as gifts.[11]

Evading the legal question and after having analysed the arguments and the evidence presented in the case, the judge in the end conceded to the position of the executor of the Max Brod estate, Advocate Ehud Sol. Her ruling states:

> Indeed, letters providing for a gift were written. However, when examining the conduct of Brod and the late [Esher Hoffe], a doubt arises as to whether this is a *gift for delivery of the object or a gift of certain rights* ... both Brod and the deceased [Esher Hoffe] wrote letters as to giving gifts but they reserved the rights of ownership to themselves... on one fact I have no doubt, that Brod viewed these writings *as his property* and treated them as an owner, also after he wrote the letters of gift.[12]

It is no doubt interesting to see how the delivery of the object, i.e. the physical manuscripts, was separated from the immaterial aspects of the documents, e.g. the intellectual property rights in the writings. However, in her ruling, the judge disregards the delivery of the object as a gift, the documents were clearly in the possession of the Hoffe family, and had obviously been handed over from Brod to Hoffe. There was a gift-letter, but the interpretation of it was contested. Therefore, the judge focused on the rights aspect in the contents, concluding that a gift of the rights had not been given:

> [T]he Kafka manuscripts, like the Brod estate, were not given to the plaintiffs as gifts [and] should be handed to the archive, [of, as Brod's 1948 will stipulated] the library of the Hebrew University in Jerusalem or the Tel Aviv municipal library, or (that of) any other public institution in Israel or abroad.[13]

Finally Judge Pardo-Kupelman concluded the case, expressing her own *sentiment* and *hope*, writing "I *hope* that the inheritance of the late Brod will finally find its place according to the wishes of the deceased."[14]

11 (My emphasis), Aderet, 2012.

12 [sic] My emphases throughout. www.theworldlawgroup.com/index.cfm?cm=Doc&ce=details&primaryKey=53792 (this link has since been taken down by the law firm. It was last accessed on 31 May 2014).

13 Flood, 2012.

14 (My emphasis), Aderet, 2012.

Deleuze and Guattari have also written about Kafka's belonging. They argue that Kafka's entire body of work can be considered as a rhizome because it has "no privileged point of entry, no direct *chef d'oeuvre*, no extra-literary texts and no intrinsic hierarchy of fragments and completed works".[15] They argue that as such, as a rhizome, all Kafka's diaries, letters, short stories, novels, etc. play an equally pivotal role for his writing machine. I shall not engage in Deleuze and Guattari's readings of Kafka's works here more than to connect them with the claim of nonlocality and artists that create in a *trans*-language, have an *infinite-multi*-identity, a haecceity. Kafka's writings were dubbed "minor literature" by Deleuze/Guattari, a term that they coined to denote a literature that deterritorialises a language, that is political and that has a collective value. Deleuze and Guattari claim that minor literature engages in a linguistic dispossession. Kafka was writing in German at the same time as he was challenging German language, deterritorialising it, inventing it, enriching it "artificially, to inflate it with all the resources of symbolism, oneirism, esoteric meaning, hidden signifiers".[16] Yiddish was never absent from his writing either, even though it is a language that is only spoken, a language in continuous flux, according to Deleuze and Guattari.[17]

Now, let me connect the Kafka case to the Schulz case. The Schulz and the Kafka cases provide us with quite literal issues connected to nonlocality in terms of belonging. The artist must be given some type of belonging in order for the posterity to be able to designate the rightful owner of the work, as well as the rightful group of people it may be attributed to as heritage or as property. This in turn must be tied to a community and/or a territory. Belonging is then defined in an exclusory manner i.e. Jewish, Zionist, Polish or Ukrainian, and the group of people becomes stinted: a remembrance authority, a library, the people who are in Israel or have the possibility to be in Israel. All others are by extension excluded legally. This is of course not unproblematic either in the Schulz or the Kafka case. As Judith Butler notes regarding the Kafka case:

> It matters that Israel comes to own the work, but also that the work is housed within the established territory of the state, so that anyone who seeks to see and study that work must cross Israel's border and engage with its cultural institutions. And this is also problematic, not only because citizens from several countries and non-citizens within the Occupied Territories are not allowed to cross that border, but also because many artists, performers and intellectuals are currently honouring the cultural and academic boycott, refusing to appear in

15 (Emphasis in original), Bogue, 1989: 107.
16 Deleuze and Guattari, 1986: 34.
17 Bogue, 1989: 118–119.

> Israel unless their host institutions voice a strong and sustained opposition to the occupation. The Kafka trial not only takes place against this political backdrop, but actively intervenes in its reconfiguration: if the National Library in Jerusalem wins its case [which they did],[18] to have access to the unpublished and unseen materials of Franz Kafka one will have to defy the boycott and will have implicitly to acknowledge the Israeli state's right to appropriate cultural goods whose high value is assumed to convert contagiously into the high value of Israel itself. Can poor Kafka [and Schulz][19] shoulder such a burden? Can he really help the Israeli state overcome the bad press of the occupation?[20]

I will connect the issues of belonging and space more concretely in Chapter 5 below where I will refer to the notion of "subversive property" as developed by Sarah Keenan where she claims that property is constituted by entanglement between persons and space. Keenan thus shows how property is a spatially contingent relation of belonging, and as such it opens up for the idea of the commons.

4.1.3 Collective moral rights: temporal undulation and phasing

To address these questions of belonging within positive law itself and by solely utilising traditional legal methods is clearly difficult. As we saw in the Kafka ruling above, the court is forced to go outside traditional legal reasoning, or with the Schulz case itself outside law through a diplomatic agreement. Let me just look at the difficulty of this in the Schulz case.

The Schulz mural was created in the course of employment or under commission. The first problem that confronts us is which jurisdiction and which legislation to address. Polish law from the 1940s? Current Ukrainian law? International public or private law? In modern Ukrainian law these issues are generally settled upon on a national level. Much like most other European legislations, Ukrainian Law on Copyrights and Related Rights stipulates in Article 16.2 that works of art created during employment or by commission are to be vested in the employer. Interestingly though, Ukrainian law, unlike most other European countries, goes further in its protection of the employed creator and protects moral rights of the author also in the course of employment.

In a press statement, Yad Vashem stated the following after the removal of the five pieces from the Ukraine to Israel:

18 My note.
19 My note.
20 Butler, 2011.

> Unfortunately it is a fact that from the around 3.5 million Jews who lived in Poland before the Shoah, today there are only a few thousand Jewish inhabitants. Despite the fact that today most of the Holocaust survivors live in Israel, the remnants of the vibrant Jewish life and the suffering both of the victims and the survivors are scattered all over Europe. Therefore Yad Vashem has the *moral right* to the remnants of those fragments sketched by Bruno Schulz.[21]

The term "moral right" evidently catches attention particularly in the way it was used in the press statement by Yad Vashem. From a copyright law perspective this is an interesting choice of words, as the legal concept of "moral right" is not (directly) applicable here. Moral rights in copyright law are considered to be non-commercial, serving to protect certain softer aspects of the artistic creation such as the right of attribution (being named as the author) and the right of integrity. Moral rights are intended to be closely linked to the author's person. In contrast to the proprietary copyright, moral rights are there in order to protect the personality and reputation of the creators themselves. They are in most jurisdictions non-assignable and it is said that they also generally *die with the author*; to be exact, they cannot be inherited post mortem auctoris (after the death of the author). Simply put, moral rights are meant to protect the sides of the artwork that are part of the the author's "soul", and are as such meant to be inalienable from the author. When the author dies, so do the moral rights.

Attempting to determine the belonging of this work of art after the death of the author, and the employer, when the artist's nationality and belonging are additionally being disputed, as well as the fact that the work had been created under undue circumstances, is almost impossible to do under positive law. The strongly protected non-proprietary, inalienable moral right in the Ukrainian legislation, however, brings forth an interesting argument that is not only relevant in this case, but that also serves to illustrate a variety of other challenges to e.g. copyright law. In the Schulz case, for example, moral rights are precisely claimed post mortem auctoris, but not by the author himself, obviously, but rather by an *institution* decades after his death when both the copyright and moral rights had expired. The grounds for claiming moral rights appear as non-legal, at least dogmatically speaking, but were they really irrelevant? This claim raises the issue of intergenerational justice, particularly when it comes to works of cultural heritage. That the Schulz mural can be and is deemed to be cultural heritage is undisputed, but as we clearly see the dispute lies in whose heritage it is. So far I have listed various communities that are claiming it such as the

21 (My emphasis), Yad Vashem's press statement from 2001. Available at: www.ji-magazine.lviv.ua/inform/info-eng/yv-en.htm

Jewish, the Polish, the Ukrainian, but it could also be deemed to be a type of "dark" European heritage, reminding us of the atrocities committed during WWII. And here we have Yad Vasham claiming moral rights in this item of heritage.

Interestingly enough, had Bruno Schulz been alive today he himself would have been able to bring an action for breach of moral rights due to the mutilation, fragmentation and destruction of his work as a breach of the moral right of integrity. Yad Vashem as an institution was created in order to honour the people who lost their lives in WWII and to preserve the memory of the victims, so that the Holocaust would never be forgotten. Could it be argued then by extension, and that by virtue of being able to protect and preserve the works of the victims of the Shoah, certain rights ought to be directly extended to, for example, Yad Vashem or similar institutions, where there were grave circumstances present at the time of the creation, such as exploitation, incarceration, coercion or worse still – genocide? It would mean extending the idea of the "human" life, making it more-than-human, posthumous or posthuman, through the institution meant to safeguard exactly human life. What would such a solution mean for e.g. the public interest in works such as Schulz's mural? Copyright law, and the concept of moral rights, do not lend themselves to these types of solutions. However, in circumstances like these, questions of the duration of life cannot be escaped – particularly in light of the war crimes connected to the destruction of cultural heritage.

Copyright law regulates the sphere of the private domain primarily, but also it accommodates for the public interest. Therefore, it has to be asked, in view of all of the above, whether it should be at all possible to "own" works of art such as Schulz's mural after the death of the author, i.e. in the traditional sense of private, individual ownership. Ought, for example, a notion such as *force majeure* be made visible legally when it comes to ownership, control and access to works of art that have been created under these types of circumstances such as wars, and that, through disputing the ownership, the work itself runs the risk of destruction or peril, something that undoubtedly is a collective loss, or worst yet, a war crime? Moral rights, extended or otherwise, are probably not the appropriate tool to make provisions for this but they do reveal and draw attention to the temporal aspects of the hyperobjects. The question of ownership might therefore not be interesting at all, as determining who can have access to the work intergenerationally, might be far more acute.

4.1.4 Geissler's installation and interobjectivity

The case of Bruno Schulz's mural does not even end there and it keeps challenging many of the most fundamental legal principles we take for granted, some of which date all the way back to Roman law. On top of everything that we have seen so far, we can now also place the case in the context of Benjamin Geissler's mobile installation called *The Picture Chamber of Bruno Schulz – The final work of a genius*. Thus, additional issues emerge. In that exhibition, Geissler recreated the mural virtually in an installation that takes the work into the twenty-first century. The installation can be described as follows:[22]

The viewer enters into a constructed chamber created as a true-to-scale reconstruction of the Landau nursery in which the mural was originally painted. There are images being projected on the four walls, and the images change continuously, they show the mural reconstructed but also other images. All the phases – from the moment of discovery to the various moments of destruction of the wall, to the moment of reconstruction with all the known fragments – drift past, slowly fading in and out, accompanied by music composed exclusively for the installation. Ten visual presentation boards in A1 clip-on picture frames for multi-lingual texts allow the viewer to learn more about Bruno Schulz, Drohobych, the origin of the mural, the virtual reconstruction, the meaning of the fragments and the significant influence of Schulz as a source of inspiration to artists all over the world. Outside the installation there are films being shown that were inspired by Schulz's work, lectures on Schulz etc.

That Schulz's work challenges territoriality[23] is obvious and this is wonderfully captured in Geissler's installation. As a nomadic, travelling, movable, digitised space, (a lawscape?) that reconstructs the mural and places the original into a present-day context, the installation is a subversive act of defiance in its own right. It *deterritorialises* the mural once again and functions as a genuine alternative that challenges the dichotomies of the inside/outside, here/there, movable/immovable, material/immaterial. The installation constitutes an itinerant space where the mural can be experienced in a simulated, yet true-to-scale environment. It enables access to the work, even though it is fragmented. The work is simulated, projected onto walls of the mobile chamber inside the travelling installation that can take the work around the world while at the same time remaining physically *elsewhere*. The installation reconstructs the room where the mural was originally painted and as it does so it also re-imagines it, moves it, and opens up a portal through time for the audience to enter it.

From the physical work as it once was, to the broken, dispersed and fragmentised work as it is now, the digital technology allows us to have the work recreated and simulated, in a mobile environment. It is like picking up the broken pieces of the work and reassembling them when entering

22 The presentation of the installation here is mainly taken from the exhibition catalogue for the exhibition *The Picture Chamber of Bruno Schulz – The final work of a genius*, Geissler, 2012.

23 For a more detailed study of the Bruno Schulz case with a full legal analysis see: Bruncevic, 2011.

Geissler's installation. It is as if freeing the mural from all burdens of its past, present, and territories. Legally this is a very interesting discussion with the added complexity of a digitised derivative work. How to provide adequate legal protection while still encouraging creations of this kind and similar spaces where artworks can be accessed virtually, by reproduction, and where also a creative communication and sharing of art can take place. Incontestably, here traditional legal reasoning and the binary logic is challenged: the work clearly does not have to only be seen as either a private asset or a public heritage, not have to be deemed as either fixed (onto land, or a building) or movable chattel (as a painting), or something that either belongs to one people or another, something that has to be either here or there. In this instance it appears to be freed. A space like Geissler's mobile installation is a room but not realty; it is movable but not chattel. It could be argued that it is a hyperobject, but so is Schulz's mural itself, so is Schulz, so is Geissler, so are we.

4.2 Wikimedia Commons and art in public spaces

On 4 April 2016 the Swedish Supreme Court (*Högsta Domstolen*)[24] delivered a verdict whose potential ramifications were heard internationally. As a precedent, it was not just a ruling on a copyright matter, it was also an application of one of the exceptions in Infosoc, as well as a principle stand regarding access to art in public spaces vis-à-vis digital spheres. The facts of the case were as follows.

The parties involved in the matter were the claimant, the Swedish collecting society for visual artists *Bildupphovsrätt i Sverige,* (BUS) and the respondent, *Wikimedia Sweden.* The respondent is a sub organisation to the global Wikimedia, and part of the overall non-profit foundation that oversees Wikipedia. In Sweden, the organisation also hosted and ran a database that was free and open to the public called *Public Art* (*Offentlig Konst*).[25] One of the organisation's main aims was to provide access to public art to the general public, without profit. The database provided maps, descriptions and images of artworks in public spaces such as e.g. landmarks, sculptures and monuments. The database focused on larger-scale works. The public were encouraged to also take pictures of any artwork that they found in a public space, upload it on the Offentlig Konst site, and indicate on the map the work's whereabouts. Or, if a work was already listed but not photographed, the public were encouraged to provide images. It was also possible through a search function to look for

24 The Wikimedia Commons Case, Högsta Domstolen, NJA 2016 s. 212 (NJA 2016:20). Delivered on 4 April 2016. The case was also decided in the first instance court (Stockholms Tingsrätt, Patent- och marknandsdomstolen) in Stockholm. Case number: PMT 8448-14. Delivered on 6 July 2017.

25 www.offentligkonst.se

works by a specific artist and then all available works by the said artist that are in a public space would appear in the database.

The publication of three specific artworks on offentligkonst.se was disputed by BUS. The artworks in question were:

- *Duo* by the artist Thomas Qvarsebo from 1988 that is placed in the one of the more popular areas in Stockholm called Södermalm. The statute can be found by Pustegränd and Brännkyrkagatan;
- *Moby Dick* by the artist Johan Paalzow from 2004 placed in the area called Konradsberg, in Stockholm; and
- *Binär* by the artist Eva Hild from 2012 that is placed on Jakobsgatan by the entrance to the building that houses the Swedish government and the Finance Department in central Stockholm.

The creation of all three artworks had been financed by public funds and they were made specifically for the purpose of being displayed in a public space.

The database offentligkonst.se was launched in October 2013. It was funded by Vinnova, a Swedish governmental agency working under the Ministry of Enterprise and Innovation that acts as the national contact agency for the EU Framework Programme for R&D.[26] Vinnova is an agency with the mission to fund and "promote sustainable growth by improving the conditions for innovation, as well as [...] needs-driven research."[27]

BUS sent the first cease and desist letter to offentligkonst.se in December 2013, three months after it was launched. In the letter, BUS claimed that the activities conducted by offentligkonst.se, i.e. photographing, cataloguing and uploading the three works in question, constituted copyright infringement of the rights held by the three artists which are their members, and that activities like these require copyright holder's permission and clearance. BUS could show that earlier, prior to the launch of offentligkonst.se, whenever images of the three disputed works were posted online, that this had been done with their or the rights owner's permission. BUS claimed a preliminary injunction against the publication and distribution of images of the artworks on offentligkonst.se, and sought damages for breach of copyright. The claim was supported by the fact that a substantial part of their regular business activity is licensing out non-exclusive rights for online publishing of works made by their members.

Wikimedia on the other hand responded that their publication and distribution of the images of *Duo, Moby Dick* and *Binär* on the site offentlig-konst.se was to be understood as permitted use under the exception stipulated in art. 24 section 1 Swedish Copyright Act, that states the following:

26 www.vinnova.se/en/About-Vinnova/
27 Ibid.

1 Works of fine art may be reproduced in pictorial form [...] if they are permanently located outdoors on, or at, a public place [...]

They claimed further that their database did not incur any damage to the rights holders and that the use of the images was in accordance with the exceptions provided by Swedish copyright law. When the case was initiated in the court of first instance (*Tingsrätten*) in Stockholm two specific questions were referred to the Swedish Supreme Court for clarification. These were:

1 The term "reproduction" in art. 24 section 1 – should it be understood to also include reproduction and distribution of images online, where there is no permission from the rights holder?

2 Does the answer to question 1 differ if an activity is commercial in nature or if such online distribution is part of a non-profit, for public interest, activity?

To the first question the Supreme Court replied that since the inception of the current Copyright Act there have been a number of amendments made to it. This has meant that the concepts in Swedish copyright law are generally to be seen as fragmented and ought to be interpreted in the light of the times when they were incorporated in law. The issue at hand, the Supreme Court argued, precisely points out one such matter where the terminology in art. 24 does not correspond with the main, older, copyright terminology as expressed in art. 1 and 2 of the Swedish Copyright Act (the two sections outline the scope of copyright in Swedish copyright law). This means, the Supreme Court argued further, that a systemic interpretation of terminology regarding the scope of copyright in art. 1 and 2 read together with the exception 1 in art. 24 cannot be conducted as they differ in nature, and as they were incorporated in the Act at two different stages in time. The scope came with the inception of the Act, the exception in art. 24 with the implementation of Infosoc in Swedish law. Furthermore, the Supreme Court claimed, each individual exception comes with its own rationality justified by a particular aspect of the public interest it is meant to govern. The exceptions need therefore to be interpreted in view of this fact and in order to understand art. 24, a holistic interpretation of its context needs to be conducted.

The founding rationality behind the exception in art. 24 is that it enables reproduction of works in public spaces in "pictorial form" (two dimensionally), the Supreme Court continued. They argued that this is a socio-political public interest concerning the interest of keeping certain things outside the scope of the exclusive sphere of copyright, here the right to pictorially reproduce artworks that are placed in a public space. They also pointed out that the interpretation of this exception must be done in light of and in accordance with Infosoc. The relevant section in that directive that needs to be taken into account is art. 5.3.h, which lists the exceptions stipulated in the directive. The list of exceptions in Infosoc is a so called open list, meaning that the exceptions that are listed there are examples of exceptions Member States could have and that the list is not exhaustive. However, if a Member State chooses to incorporate any of the exceptions listed in Infosoc, the national legislation may not have a more limited scope than the one provided for in the directive. It is thus stated in Infosoc:

> Member States may provide for exceptions or limitations to the rights provided for in Articles 2 and 3 [scope] in the following cases: [...]
>
> (h) use of works, such as works of architecture or sculpture, made to be located permanently in public places.[28]

Furthermore, the Swedish Supreme Court pointed out, all exceptions to copyright need to be interpreted in accordance with the times, and as societal and technological conditions change, so should the interpretations. In the case at hand it was argued that there is a clash of two interests: the economical interest of the rights owner, and the public interest of unrestricted access to the works financed by public funds and placed in a public place. An exception to copyright here should, however, not be too onerous on the economical rights, even where the use of the work happens in accordance with the exception for non-profit reasons. Therefore, the Supreme Court concluded, the exception in art. 24 section 1 did not include the activity conducted by offentligkonst.se, as it was seen as potentially too onerous on the economic right. As such, it did not matter that offentligkonst.se was non-profit.[29]

4.2.1 Conflict of interest: possession – access

In its reasoning the Swedish Supreme Court identified two opposing interests in the case at hand, private ownership and public access. Elsewhere[30] I have analysed a decision by a Dutch first instance court where an artist had used a trademark in a derivate work in order to express a political opinion. There, in a similar manner as the Swedish Supreme Court, the

28 Infosoc, art 5.3 h.

29 The Supreme Court decision only concerned the two questions posed by the first instance court. The first instance court delivered their verdict a year later (6 July 2017) where they reiterated that copyright had been infringed. An injunction was imposed and it was stated that Wikimedia not only has to take down the images, but also pay damages for copyright infringement as well as the litigation costs incurred by BUS (around 60 000 Euros plus damages for infringement which were not specified in the decision).

30 Bruncevic, 2014: 182 aa.

Dutch court identified two opposing interests (freedom of expression and right to possession), writing:

> Since the case concerns fundamental rights that are *on an equal footing but conflicting*, according to established case law of the European Court of Human Rights, a fair balance should be sought between the general interest and the interests of the parties involved.[31]

While the courts in both of these cases are clearly putting two different interests on equal footing they add in their reasoning that the two can be, and often are, conflicting. It is of course undesirable at least from a dogmatic legal point of view that some parts of the law should conflict with others, because that arguably creates incoherence, which in turn is also undesirable. Thus, the only way to deal with these conflicts of interest is to pit the two against one another so that they in the end have to form an oppositional pairing. This can be understood as the "oppositional identity" of law, as Philippopoulos-Mihalopoulos refers to it, that allows law as a system to maintain its internal boundaries.[32] Such oppositional identity constantly requires compromises and balancing acts like the one in the Dutch case between e.g. the notion of property as opposed to the notion of freedom of expression. It also constantly requires compromises and balancing acts like the ones in the Swedish, as well as in the Dutch, case namely those between e.g. the notion of possession of property through intellectual property laws as opposed to the notions of the public interest in access through e.g. the exceptions in the same laws or fair use.

Possession as a concept is seen as something that is enclosable, exclusive, private, and *access* as its opposite, namely open, non-exclusive, public. I will discuss this closer in Chapter 7, p. 178 aa where I will introduce the notions of static and nomadic possessions, the Deleuzeoguattarian forms of possession. For now, I want to show that this reasoning, where possession is merely understood as "static" or as enclosable and exclusive, also assumes that the two interests, public and private, will always be: a) comparable and commensurable, and b) in conflict with one another. I shall also return to a closer study of intellectual property as a construct in Chapter 6 and the notion of possession as put forward within the context of intellectual property law, but already here the following question may be warranted, are the notions of possession and access really commensurable? Do they weigh the same? Always? Can we ever really measure what is possessed against the enabling of access? Because that is exactly what is being done

31 (My emphasis). The unofficial translation of the so called Darfurnica ruling, referenced in Guilbault. See p. 16 of the translation of judgement, and p. 254 of the Guilbault article, 2011.

32 Philippopoulos-Mihalopoulos, 2013.

here, comparisons that might be impossible as we soon shall see, but the courts of law are making them nonetheless.

4.2.2 Right to roam – access to the city

An issue that may not be apparent from the Swedish Wikimedia case is that the line of reasoning followed by the Supreme Court in this decision directly affects the possibility of interaction with public spaces and as such impacts on the various rights of access to the city and the urban spheres. Obviously, this can be connected to the writings of Henri Lefebvre regarding the right to the city.[33] But, as Iljadica very well points out, this right, "right to the city" – is of course not a "legal" right but it encompasses a bundle of various different rights such as the right to information, various rights connected to freedom of movement, to citizenship, etc.[34] The movement connected to access to the city as an urban commons will be discussed in greater detail in Chapter 5. Allow me only to begin that discussion here by stressing this particular issue, in conjunction with the case of offentiligkonst.se and Wikimedia Commons in Sweden. It is important for two different reasons. The first one is to begin to expressly connect the copyright legislation to physical spaces and show how it is not just a matter of accessing works online but how it quite literally also can interfere with how and where we are allowed to move and what we can do (in the public sphere). This is what will furthermore, secondly, allow me to make a theoretical point about the materiality of the lawscape.

In their ruling against Wikimedia Commons the Swedish Supreme Court argued that the issue at hand was not one that fits within the exception in art. 24 p.1 (two dimensional reproduction) but rather a case concerning the creation of a database containing digital reproductions of artworks, and making such a database open to the public. Making an artwork available through a database, the court argued, must be seen as an activity that typically has a "not insignificant commercial value"[35] either as a database in its own right or as various services that can be connected to such a database, and as such these commercial rights must be reserved to the copyright holder. Whether the database itself is commercial or not is irrelevant, the court concluded. What the court of course failed to do is to connect the database to the right to the city as the underlying assumption is that a work exists either in the physical sphere (as part of the physical commons, governed by such rights as e.g. land law, right of movement, right to roam, "right to the city" etc.) and its image exists in the virtual sphere (as part of the intellectual commons, governed by such rights as

33 Lefebvre, H. 1991.

34 Iljadica, 2017.

35 Swedish expression: "ett icke obetydligt kommersiellt värde".

intellectual property law, right to information, freedom of speech, freedom of expression). As might become obvious, if it is not already, is that this dichotomy is if not highly flawed, at least problematic to uphold.

In subsequent statements, BUS has argued that this ruling does not, nor will it, affect private users nor prevent individuals from taking photos of public art and uploading them on e.g. their social media profiles. Focusing precisely on the issue of "database" it has been claimed that this ruling does not affect how the general public is allowed to interact with the artworks placed in public. However, there seems to be a silent addition to that statement that is not being addressed: the ruling does not affect how the general public is allowed to interact with the artworks in public, *in principle*. I will return to that in a moment.

Let me linger here and discuss how still the implications of the decision and its connection to the access to the city must be clarified and made visible. There have been numerous projects lately that have been rethinking the city and connecting it particularly to the so called urban commons.[36] Particularly, what those studies do, both the founding primary studies[37] as well as the secondary studies,[38] is to show that there is an interaction between the cityscape and people's perception of it. This interaction can simply be explained in the following manner, when we walk in the city we become entangled with it. As we perceive the spaces of the cityscape we take them in, they become our memories, knowledge, our senses, part of us. So when we for instance take a photograph of the city we are in fact not only reproducing[39] what we see (because that assumes that we are divided from the city and our surroundings, which goes contrary to the idea of the hyperobjects as I have established it so far), but we also become connected to the city, *it sticks to us*, and the connection between us and the city becomes interobjective. And this interobjecitivity continues when we for instance then share our images on social media, or conversely, when we access images online uploaded there by others.

By understanding this phenomenon as an interobjective connection we can begin to reveal how the physical commons (the cityscape) enters into the intellectual commons (our expressions, our creative output, our memory, our knowledge, our *body*): they become entangled, they stick to each other, to us. What the Swedish Supreme Court is arguing in this case is of course the opposite. They take the distinctive view that the physical (the works in the public space) is separated from the intellectual (the intellectual property and interaction with those works). The Supreme Court also assumes, wrongly so, that the two can be separated. In arguing

36 I will engage with these studies in a more detailed manner in Chapter 5.

37 As e.g. Harvey, 2001; Harvey, 2004; Sloterdijk, 1998; Sloterdijk, 1999; Sloterdijk 2004.

38 Ostrom & Hess, 2007.

39 Iljadica, 2017.

that a database is a commercial right that belongs to the individual copyright owners only (as part of their intellectual property) denies precisely the fact that the images of the city are equally entangled with and constitutive of the individuals that roam the city (on the surface as part of their urban commons, but more precisely, as part of themselves, as they have become entangled with the hyperobject that is the cityscape and the artworks exhibited therein).

The legal question, that might not be particularly interesting from a philosophical point of view, but that is pertinent nonetheless, is whether the copyright exception could be read in this manner, to more broadly also incorporate the wider sharing and access that happens when it can be shown that the physical commons extends itself to encompass the intellectual commons too. The answer to that question, I fear, is no, because intellectual property law is fully embedded in this founding division between the physical and the intellectual, the material and the immaterial, private and public. The Fair use, exception rules in Infosoc and in the national legislations do not include the virtual extension of the public space as such, nor do they appease these dichotomies, they merely reinforce them, which is clear from the Swedish decision. In a balance of interests between the private (property) and the public (space/access/etc.), the private generally tends to weigh more. We all know why that is, but if it needs to be stated expressly, it is because of the preferences of the capitalist system that requires such an imbalance. However, that fails take into account that the entanglement that happens between the so called private and public here is equally "private" for the person that interacts with the cityscape as it is for the person that holds the intellectual property in the public art. Furthermore, the cityscape extends itself in the virtual sphere too.

This is of course of utmost importance to the discussion that I will carry on in Volume II in terms of the entanglement that happens between humans and their so called "surroundings", "environments", and ultimately the commons. The point that needs to be made here, which takes us back to the introduction of this book, the walk in London, the *allemansrätten* connections – is while there is such a thing as a right to roam in the physical commons, how can we imagine a right to roam, in all senses of the word "roam", that encompasses the movement of the hyperobjects that are always interobjectively relational and connected to other hyperobjects?

4.2.3 Right to roam 2.0 – UGC and property rights

The second point that emerges from this is the fact that a database that is highly dependent on user generated content (UGC) is seen as something that is a) a solely commercial right and b) mainly part of the (intellectual) *property* rights held by the original copyright owners. Within the context of this case study let me just discuss the implication of UGC here. I have already introduced the notion of the prosumer in Chapter 3 and his or her connection to the hyperobjects. Here it can be developed a little further in connection to this particular case.

Above, the point was made that there is a space or a spacetime that hyperobjects produce relationally – i.e. they function co-constitutively. When that is shown the founding idea of a "unique" artwork and the dichotomy between human and non-human becomes highly problematic. Equally then, the notion of "author/creator" becomes questioned particularly within the context of UGC, as content is constantly created by others, uploaded digitally, through a database or a digital platform, where the creators are users, consumers, machines, all at once. This moves us beyond the subject–object rationality into firstly "automatic subjectivity", where actors that are traditionally seen as non-human may gain agency and subjectivity (such as e.g. the cityscape, nature,[40] the database[41]) by showing their hyperobjectivity. These hyperobjects then are all at once human but also automatic, a-human, more-than-human, mechanical.

What implication does this insight have in terms of allocation of property rights and the right to the city? There is a clear increased fluidity between notions such as original–copy, consumer–creator, person–property, etc. This very fluidity is noticeable through the viscous nature of the hyperobject. Particularly the distinction between personhood and property will be further challenged and discussed in the next case study and then in Volume II. For what happens, as e.g. Käll asks, when subjects and objects become entangled through practices of digital property into what she refers to as "object-space", that I am here referring to, as already established, hyperobject.[42]

The convergence of personhood, property, space, and digital platforms is something that needs further attention before we arrive at the discussion of the commons. Because suddenly the right to roam the city means something else when everything, quite literally, becomes a territory that can be traversed.

4.2.4 Convergence: transmedia as hyperobject

Which leads us back to the statement above claiming that this ruling by the Swedish Supreme Court does not or will not affect how the general public is allowed to interact with the artworks in public. Drawing on the above, quite on the contrary, in fact, we can with full certainty claim that the decision will affect the public *in every way*. So let me conclude this case study by looking into the future through showcasing an interesting development connected to this decision.

40 Safi, 2017.
41 E.g. artificial intelligence.
42 Käll, 2017.

The Swedish Supreme Court delivered their ruling in April 2016, a couple of months before the vastly popular Pokémon Go game was rolled out globally. For the uninitiated person, who has not spent the summer of 2016 catching Pokémons in the most unlikely of places,[43] this is a so called "free-to-play, location-based augmented reality game developed by Niantic for iOS, Android, and Apple Watch devices".[44] Simply put, it is a game where players connected through the GPS systems in their phones can enter into an "augmented reality" based on their geographical locations. Players move through the "real world" while their avatars in the game move in the augmented reality within a map that is provided by the game. The game then takes players who have to walk (and not travel or be in a vehicle) around in their local surroundings, visiting real local landmarks and monuments in order to both catch and train their Pokémons in the game.

The interesting aspect that came up was of course that the landmarks and images thereof were not provided for the game by Pokémon/Nintendo but were rather user generated through the so called Ingress-community. No permissions or rights clearances had been done before the images were taken by Ingress and sold to Nintendo. Ingress is also a similar game to Pokémon Go, and it could be said that it was its forerunner. Wikipedia explains for instance that the Ingress game "consists of capturing 'portals' at places of cultural significance, such as public art, landmarks, monuments, etc., and linking them to create virtual triangular 'control fields' over geographical areas."[45] The Ingress game was made in 2014 and launched in 2015.

This type of so called "transmedia storytelling" or "transmedia narrative" entails telling a story, while at the same time experiencing a story, though various multimedia and digital platforms using for instance mobile or GPS technology. The augmented reality is, so to speak, just plain reality. No prefix.

BUS has so far chosen not to challenge Pokémon Go (or any other digital platforms that can be understood as a databases in this sense and that contain UGC of artworks in public places as e.g. Instagram, Facebook or Twitter) for infringement of copyright even though they now have the precedent in the Wikimedia case. We can only speculate why this is the case. That Pokémon Go as transmedia storytelling has a commercial nature is undisputed, and is much more so a (once again commercial) database than the offentligkonst.se site ever was. So two arguments can conclude this case study, firstly these types of engagements with the cityscape mean that the urban commons becomes entangled with the human in a more constitutive sense than previous interactions between the digital and the analogue, because in a transmedia setting the real world and the "virtual"

43 Throughout global cityscapes and landscapes but also in very unlikely, and arguably inappropriate places, such as hospitals, Auschwitz etc.

44 https://en.wikipedia.org/wiki/Pok%C3%A9mon_Go

45 https://en.wikipedia.org/wiki/Ingress_%28video_game%29

world converge. How, or whether, to divide the one from the other, how to divide intellectual property from the urban commons, the environment from the human, becomes increasingly difficult. Secondly and on a final note, by reasoning as the Swedish Supreme Court has done, and by giving prominence to the intellectual property over the right to access or the right to the city violently restricts not only access to art, but also quite literally our movement and freedoms within the urban commons and the city scape.

4.3 Richard Prince and art on Instagram

New Portraits, a series by the artist Richard Prince, has in the last two years become one of the most discussed artistic creations. Using the images posted by people that he follows on Instagram, and only making some minor edits to the captions, Prince blew up the images and printed them on canvas. One of the canvas images was sold for USD 90 000. Prince is known for his "re-photographing", repurposing and appropriation techniques. He is also quite used to finding himself in litigation, subject to claims for among other things infringement of copyright laws, for instance in the now famous case *Cariou v. Prince*[46] where a French photographer Patrick Cariou brought a copyright infringement claim against Prince's appropriation of images. Cariou had taken images of members of a Rastafarian tribe that were subsequently altered and repurposed by Prince. Prince won the case for 23 out of the 25 images on a fair use defence, and the two artists settled regarding the last two images. *New Portraits* has now also been legally challenged by among others the LA-based photographer Donald Graham whose Instagram post was one of the images used in *New Portraits.* The case raised by e.g. Graham shines a light on a number of issues connected to *New Portraits* in terms of the notion of the artistic subject, the legal subjectivity and privacy-based rights that emerge within the virtual sphere, or the *infosphere.*

4.3.1 The Death of the Author

In the essay "Death of the Author"[47] Roland Barthes, very poignantly so, claims that the "author is a modern figure, produced no doubt by our society [...], at the end of the middle ages, with English empiricism, French rationalism and the personal faith of the Reformation, [that] discovered the prestige of the individual, or, [...] more nobly, of the 'human person'". Beginning with this Barthian quote, we can start to explore *New Portraits,* in order to discuss the idea of legal subjectivity formed in copyright law specifically. From there on this will be connected to certain aspects of for instance rights to information and privacy rights.

But first, some more words about the exhibition:

46 Cariou v. Prince, 714 F. 3d 694 (2d Cir. 2013) [USA].

47 Barthes, 1967.

New Portraits became a notorious global exhibition in 2015. Audiences around the world flocked to see Prince's images in the Gagosian galleries where they were exhibited. Many of the patrons also took their own photos in front of the images exhibited, uploading them on their own Instagram accounts. As such, the exhibition existed both in the "real world" and in the virtual sphere, simultaneously. It became continuous, open for everybody to engage with and make additions to. The overwhelming sensation of simultaneously being exposed to both the presence and the absence of the author was clear.

It can be claimed that the exhibition is marked by *the presence of an omniscient author* in an almost traditional, romantic, sense. The art being exhibited is made by one of our time's most prominent contemporary artists. Prince is well known both in the connoisseur art world as well as to the broader public. He has been a practicing artist since the 1970s and his oeuvre is already well established. To people who are familiar with his works he is associated with appropriation of popular culture, exploration and critique of morality, exposure of the body as well as works that are based on collage. *New Portraits* is in no way an exception from this style. Prince's established artistic persona is very much present in this series.

This exhibition was curated and exhibited in a very classical manner where the author is put at the forefront: a solo exhibition that comprises of printed physical works exhibited in a traditional gallery space. The works were shown and sold through one of the most prominent and influential galleries in the world, namely the Gagosian Gallery. There was a catalogue, a press-release, a commercial framing of the exhibition where the author no doubt was placed centre stage. Artistically, the omnipresence of the author was thus unmistakable. The images appear to be very much auteur-based expressions. The gaze of the artist (some might say a very much white, male, middle-aged, Western, gaze, but a gaze nonetheless) is unquestionably present in every image. There is a clear narrative being recounted by the author, and the images are equally confrontational as they are provocative, thus making the author's presence unquestionable

At the same time, there is an almost uncanny *absence of the author*. The images being exhibited are neither paintings nor photography in a traditional sense. In fact, the exhibition comprises of images posted by people that Prince follows on Instagram. After posting a comment on the images on the Instagram platform, Prince then took a so called "screen grab" of the interaction, blew up the image with his comments visible, and printed it onto physical canvases. None of the images were thus actually taken by him. All of the images were in some shape either self-portraits ("selfies") taken by the people themselves, or regular portraits that people around the world posted on their Instagram feeds taken by someone else, but not Prince. For the purpose of his prints on canvas Prince has chosen to keep everything as it appeared on his screen, to e.g. keep the Instagram interface and not edit the images. He also kept the Instagram letter font, he did not alter the images in any way, he kept the real user handle (username) of the people whose images he screen grabbed. The only thing that he altered were some of the captions (comments). The comment alteration was done by an act of "hacking", as he calls it. He explains his so called hack in the press material that accompanied the exhibition:

> But somehow I figured out how to hack into Jessica's feed and swipe away all her comments and add my own so that it would appear under her post. The hack is pretty simple and anyone can do it. You hit the gray comment bar and pick a comment you don't want and swipe with your finger to the left, and a red exclamation mark appears. You press on the exclamation mark and four things come onto the bottom of your screen.
>
> 1 Why are you reporting this comment?
> 2 Spam or Scam
> 3 Abusive Content
> 4 Cancel
>
> To get rid of the comment, you click on Spam or Scam. It's gone. Just like that I could control other people's comments and Jessica's own comments. And the comment that I added could now be near enough to Jessica's photo that when I screen saved it, my comment would "show up." Make sense? It's about as good as I can do. What can I say? Einstein and cuckoo
>
> [...]
>
> So now...
> So now I was in.
> Waiting to follow.
> Richardprince4 would appear at the bottom of Jessica's final portrait.
> My comment, whatever it would be, would always be the last comment.
> The last say so. Say so.[48]

This manipulation of comments is the only visual presence of Prince in the images. Otherwise it can be claimed that as an author he is absent in the sense that if we did not know better this exhibition would appear to be a collection of works by a number of unnamed (no real names, only handles), people. So who is the author of these works? The one who creates the content or the one that edits and curates the content?

48 Prince, press release for New Portraits.

This is not, by far, the first time the question of who is the author in contemporary art has been posed. Nor, by extension, is it the first time that the adjacent question of "what is an author" has subsequently been raised. And it certainly is not the first time these questions have been juxtaposed with the legal questions of authorship and the creation of artistic works in for instance intellectual property law. And finally, this is not the first time, that the infosphere and spaces of artistic creation have been explored for their potential in the creation of subjectivity. So what does this case study have to add to all of this? It puts them all together, exploring their role in terms of questions connected to the notion of the author (dead or alive?), production of space through artworks as hyperobjects, production of legal space through application of *lawscape*, all of this will later on be necessary in advancing the discussion concerning the commons.

4.3.2 Private and individual author-genius as the legal subject

In copyright law the author is given a (limited) monopoly or an exclusive right to copy, distribute, sell the works that they have created. Based on a Western, Enlightenment idea – copyright relies on the Lockean justification of property – that when someone takes something from the commons – and adds their own work and labour to it – they are then rewarded with a property right in the thing – be it material or intellectual. Copyright, as opposed to "general" property rights in Western legal systems vested in tangible property, is limited in time. It is limited in other ways too e.g. in order for copyright to subsist in a work an expression of an idea is required and not an idea itself. There are also exceptions to copyright through various fair use/fair dealing principles. Ideas, information and "facts" are seen to be in the public domain or in the commons, which the author takes from – adds work and labour, skill and genius onto, and thus makes what was taken their own.

As we already began to explore in Chapter 3, intellectual property law is founded on this very idea of the "God"-like creator who is seen as the "inventor" of a work, the work is always assumed to have been created as a result of the author's genius, hands, skill and labour. The God-like/genius creator is always assumed to be a human being (copyright cannot be vested in animals or nature). The human being who is the author is also the first holder of the copyright.

Let me connect the notion of the author, the first holder of copyright, as the legal subject in intellectual property law, to the notion of the broader legal subject in general. Normally, the legal subject is constructed around the idea of a human being, of a definable, singular individual. Furthermore, it relies on a distinction between the public and the private sphere. That means that an individual is assumed to have a private sphere which is connected to the self: both the corporeal and the extended self that includes property, body, the intellectual traits of an individual such as his/her sense of identity, integrity, thoughts and so on. This private sphere is protected by assigning it certain rights – e.g. human rights or intellectual property rights. As a legal construct the legal subject is therefore enclosed – that is, it is constructed around the idea of one single, private individual/ human being whose private sphere is protected by rights.

The concept of the author in copyright law is enabled by this very construction of the legal subject. The legal subject is of course a core concept in law (at least in liberal Western jurisprudence). It is a formal construct – that is it connected to the legal state – the *Rechtsstaat*.[49] The state thus constructs the legal subjects onto which rights and obligations are attached in order for them to be protected. The first question here is whether the individual as imagined by the construct of the legal subject encompasses the human being in its full extent, i.e. whether everything that is "human" in a human being is covered by the notion of the legal subject? And does being human mean creating a clear dichotomy between that which is seen to be human and conversely non-human? And the subsequent question of course being, to what extent are the non-human qualities part of that which is considered to be the human body, such as their property, intellectual property, social media profiles, their portraits, the digital content that they create online, etc.?

Obviously, the notion of an "autonomous individual" that is a "human" has natural connotations to a liberal, occidental, tradition in jurisprudence. Attached to the autonomous individual are the ideas not only of a definable and unified human being, delimited by the human body, but also the construction itself relies on the idea of privacy, the enclosure of the private sphere and the rights connected to each human being individually. And then there is of course another poignant assumption, and that is that the legal subject must correspond to a definable physical individual – the human being – whose boundary is the human body, as famously expressed by Savigny in *System des heutigen römischen rechts*,[50] which in turn is connected to the Kantian tradition that rests upon the idea of the moral autonomous subject, onto which private rights such as ownership are bestowed.

What happens then when we try to apply this philosophical tradition, onto which the notion of the legal subject rests, on the idea of the author in copyright law, and how is it connected to the Prince case? Can the notion of the liberal legal subject be separated from the social subject? What are the boundaries of the subject? Merely the physical body or can the human (or *post*human) body be seen to incorporate not only the physical body but also the representation of the body too, e.g. in the form of a portrait? And

49 Bruncevic, 2017.
50 Savigny, 1840.

can an Instagram portrait be equally material as any other part of the human body, say for instance, a limb or an organ?

4.3.3 Dichotomies of creation and inforgs

Let me now take a short diversion from the idea of the author in copyright law to the notion of an information carrying organism or *inforg* as referred to by Floridi, namely a posthuman conception of subjectivity. To do that in connection still to copyright law and creation of art and the Prince case in particular we have to first take a closer look at a couple of founding dichotomies that underpin copyright law.

Dichotomy 1: ars-poïesis

First of all: what is it that is being created? These portraits that Prince has created, or appropriated, can they be considered as intellectual creations, and in turn, art? Etymologically the word "art" has a meaning referring to "skill as a result of learning or practice". It stems from the Old French word *art* (10c.), which in its turn stems from the Latin word *artem* meaning "work of art; practical skill; a business, craft". Understanding art in this sense means connecting the concept to physical production that happens through skill and workmanship in order to create an object. It can be questioned whether Prince's New Portrait series can be defined as art in this sense and whether he de facto created anything. Screen grabbing some Instagram images, and choosing a number of them to print on canvas (the printing was not done by himself either), could that be understood to be creation of art in its etymological sense?

This is not merely a rhetorical question nor does it mean that Prince's work must be dismissed as non-art, non-creation or non-artwork *toute suite* either. Another etymological meaning of art can be found in the Middle English usually used in the sense of "scholarship and learning" (c. 1300), especially found today in the concept of seven sciences, or "liberal arts". This sense of the word "art" remains in e.g. the term Bachelor of Arts. This meaning is not tied to the skill and craft per se but to the intellectual or human workmanship (that is, creating something out of the intellect as opposed to working on something that emanates from the physical nature as e.g. painting on some kind of a surface). So if *New Portraits* can be seen not as a creation of tangible objects as paintings, but rather primarily as production of content, science, knowledge, and discussion, then this act of creation can instead be branded as *poïesis*. *Poïesis* (Ancient Greek: ποίησις) means "to make". The word, the root of our modern term "poetry", was initially a verb, meaning *an action that transforms and continues the world*. It refers to neither technical production nor creation in the romantic sense. *Poïetics* rather reconciles the person with the surrounding world.

It can be claimed that the broad and strong copyright law that we have today regulates creation of art in both meanings of the term, namely both as a labour/skill production as well as poïeis. However, the question is then whether copyright law was always meant, or whether it ought to, contain under its scope the act of poïesis – that is those intellectual acts that have to do with engaging with the world, with political acts, that make up creation of content, information and other comments that further society?

Dichotomy 2: creating–curating

To repeat, in copyright law there is an assumption that the author genius invents a work by inspiration and creates it by hand by taking ideas and resources available in the public domain/commons and making them into (art)works. Here on the other hand we have an instance of artistic creation that seems to be more connected to editing and curating, rather than that of traditional hand craft or skills-based creating. Such a curating action can in principle involve information gathering.

If we accept that *New Portraits* constitutes a creation of art in the second etymological sense, namely poïesis, and if we take the term to "create" to denote, not creation of an object *ex-nihilo,* but rather an action that transforms and continues the world by engaging in discussion and dialogue – then certainly Prince can be said to be the author of these artworks – because clearly *New Portraits* is a comment on and continuation of our current society. So how do we administrate legally the act of poïesis, creation of knowledge, public opinion and political engagement if it is *ab initio* captured by the private copyright law? And how does that affect public laws connected to e.g. the rights of information or freedom of speech for instance? If we accept that the act of poïesis carries within itself an action that transforms and continues the world, then it must be asked whether this at all ought to fall under the scope of a private (copy)right.

It is worth noting, and perhaps ironically one might say, that the entire *New Portraits* exhibition and all printed and promotional material connected to it is marked with the following copyright notice: "All images are subject to copyright. Gallery approval must be granted prior to reproduction". One cannot help but then ask, at least rhetorically, *whose copyright are the images subject to?*

Dichotomy 3: author–curator

In "What is an Author"[51] Foucault cites Beckett who in turn asks "what does

51 Foucault, 1998.

it matter who is speaking?".[52] Foucault then answers that the author's name cannot be simply disregarded, it *does* matter who is speaking. Foucault writes:

> [A]n author's name is not simply an element in a discourse [...]; it performs a certain role with regard to narrative discourse, assuring a classificatory function. Such a name permits one to group together a certain number of texts, define them, differentiate them from and contrast them to others. In addition, it establishes a relationship among the texts.[53]

Therefore, the name Richard Prince here is not insignificant – it is the organising devise which groups together a number of discourses: the artistic expression through appropriation, the societal comments, the critique of the self, the notion of privacy, etc. His name acts as a hub or as a focal point, a *space*, giving the collected portraits taken from Instagram a (new? additional?) meaning. Intellectual property law and the copyright system allow us to frame this entire "event" that Prince has created into an intellectual resource, something that can be formulated within the scope of copyright, which can be bought and sold through the mechanisms of the copyright monopoly and other property laws. This is indicated by among other things the copyright notice that accompanies the exhibition. Prince, of course, is claiming to be the author and as such that the works are his own.

We have seen here how the value of the images, both artistic and proprietary value, that is being created, is directly connected to the fact that the images have been appropriated by and claimed within the scope of Prince's artistic work, his copyright, his oeuvre, his persona. The images have been claimed by him as creations on the basis of how they were *curated* and not necessarily how they were *created*, or by whom they were initially created. Prince never claimed that he took any of the photographs. If we assume that someone (else) holds the initial copyright in these photographs, is it then really Prince that ought to be assumed as the holder of copyright in the *New Portraits* series? And if so, how does that affect the rights of the people in the images, the original photographers, *Instagram*? And furthermore, is Prince really at liberty to sell these works, even if they are considered to be derivative, or within some kind of fair dealing/fair use permitted use, by exercising the monopoly granted to him by the construction of the legal subject and in extension the author in copyright law?

52 Foucault, 1998.
53 Ibid.

Dichotomy 4: personhood–property

Before that question can be answered let me briefly concentrate on what it is that is being sold and the last dichotomy here namely that of personhood (connected to Prince as well as the people whose images he used) and property (connected to the portraits as works, the copyright monopoly and the ownership in the physical print).

Margaret J. Radin writes for instance in *Reinterpreting Property* the following:

> Most people possess certain objects they feel are almost part of themselves. These objects are closely bound up with personhood because they are part of the way we constitute ourselves as continuing personal entities in the world. They may be as different as people are different, but some common examples might be a wedding ring, *a portrait*, an heirloom, or a house.[54]

While Radin still upholds the liberal dichotomy between personhood and property as noted by e.g. Sarah Keenan,[55] her finding is not insignificant here. It shows that there is a sliding scale in types of property. This is part of Radin's larger argument that certain things become so entangled with the person that they become part of that person to such an extent that they cease to be property, at least *fungible* property, that is, replaceable property. There is something in a portrait that connects people to it, more than how people are connected to fungible property. The most obvious example of a fungible and therefore replaceable property is money. However, according to Radin, there is something in other types of property, e.g. a portrait, that makes up an excess, a space that is connected to the person represented in the portrait, that escapes the idea of (fungible) property as being entirely separated from personhood.

If we look at the portraits that Prince has included in the New Portraits series it is obvious that they are intimately connected to their subjects. Some of them are explicitly sexual, some of them allude to sexual behaviour, some of them are intimate in other ways, or confrontational – all of them somehow challenging the notions of race, sex, gender, moral norms etc. These images were of course voluntarily posted on people's personal Instagram feeds, but when they became part of Prince's expression, part of his curated view of the world – they acquired an additional meaning. They were filtered through his authorship. Obviously, they became famous but as such they also became (someone else's) property. And, while they theoretically already were available to everyone on Instagram, due to among others the sheer volume of the content on Instagram, in actuality they remained rather "private" – only

54 Radin, 2009: 36.
55 Keenan, 2014: 86.

shared between the people on the images and their immediate followers. That is, before Prince re-appropriated them and made them truly public and undeniably property by claiming them as part of his oeuvre, a part of *his intellectual property*.

Today most of us would with ease agree that our social media presence forms an extension of ourselves, of our lives, our personalities, of our private sphere, and properly speaking, also our bodies. Social media forms a natural and integral part of who we are and part of what constitutes our daily lives. Our online presence has become equally constitutive of us as our off line analogue presence. If we subscribe to such a line of reasoning, then we must admit that there is a special entanglement between for instance the Instagram handle "killthemfortheurl" whose image Prince used in *New Portraits* and the real person on the image – making her at the same time both a private person, and a property in the guise of her image.[56] And as Radin notes:

> Once we admit that a person can be bound up with an external "thing" in some constitutive sense, we can argue that by virtue of this connection the person should be accorded broad liberty with respect to control over that "thing".[57]

Does this mean that the person behind the handle killthemfortheurl ought to be given a broader respect and control of her portrait and of "her" data because by being part of her social media presence they simultaneously constitute her and her body? Again we are exploring this space that is created here between a person and a "thing" (here a portrait on a digital platform), in a constitutive sense, where the thing and the person have become entangled, forming an assemblage. This space includes the selfies, images, or personality of killthemfortheurl that have been created, curated and posted on her Instagram feed. But then in turn, these are all given a meaning only in the network, within the social media platform of Instagram, when they are shared with other people – and in extension when they became property strictly speaking by Prince's appropriation of it.

4.3.4 "Body" – a process of oscillations between material and immaterial

"It is not enough, however", writes Foucault

> to repeat the empty affirmation that the author has disappeared. For

56 She is also property as data that emanates from her Instagram account in the form of e.g. Big Data.

57 Radin, 2009: 37.

> the same reason, it is not enough to keep repeating that God and man have died a common death. Instead, we must locate the space left empty by the author's disappearance, follow the distribution of gaps and breaches, and watch for the openings this disappearance uncovers.[58]

Whether the author is an author-God in the sense of intellectual property law or a disappearing act in Foucault's sense can be discussed. When the disappearing author morphs into the curator of the infosphere, it further warrants the question what has become of the space left empty by the old author-God? Who is really speaking in the *New Portraits* series? In terms of artistic production and after Duchamp we are certainly no longer really expecting artists to be author-Gods: creators of objects *ex nihilo,* but rather, the author of contemporary art can very well be someone who takes a thing (a urinal, an Instagram image), from its original place (a toilet, a social media site) and places it elsewhere – e.g. in a gallery or a museum. Still, the very same notion of the presumably dead author-God seems somehow to be persistently lingering in copyright law. This is not a controversial claim, it has been repeated for many years now.

Yet, Prince is here, however contemporary his art might be, nonetheless invoking the notion of the author-God in order to claim copyright. He is claiming copyright for the act of curating and not the act of creating: copyright for poïesis. And in that case as a practical legal matter a number of conflicting claims on the copyright of these images could be made at the same time here: by the people whose images were used, by whoever was the original photographer, by Instagram, potentially even by the Gagosian Galleries, etc. The *New Portraits* series seems to have created a sphere, connected to the personhood of the self, and property of the other, a space that constitutes the self, that can function as both an escape from such a regime that can be propertied by copyright law and its legitimisation. Equally, this space can be connected to the human body, as an extension, excess, or simply be seen as the widened contours of a (human) body. In a posthuman understanding of the human, the inforg is as much human as it is information.

In the infosphere we have namely all become inforgs, information carrying organisms, claims Luciano Floridi in the book *The Fourth Revolution,* where the notion of the online and off line has been merged into one, into "onlife". Floridi writes:

> Our culture, so imbued with ICT ideas, finds sci-fi scenarios in which you swap your old body for a new one, or the suggestion that

58 Foucault, 1998.

> the self may be a cross-platform structure, like an app, perfectly conceivable.[59]

In the infosphere where the online and offline existence merge into onlife, there is a becoming (post)human that takes place and a space is created that seems to be contrary to the logic of copyright law that relies on the distinction between the author and the work. Nonetheless, something happens when images from onlife are severed and transposed into offlife, the analogue world, too: when they are moved back into the physical realm, made into physical objects, exhibited and sold in a gallery. So reading that together with Radin above – could it be claimed that making prints of other people's portraits could encroach on their bodily rights? That means perhaps that as much as no one is allowed to sell a part of my physical body, e.g. a limb or an organ, in the analogue sphere, Floridi's argument read together with Radin seems to be pointing towards that the same could be claimed for parts of our extended bodies that are included in the onlife, e.g. the information about us on our social media platforms.

This leads me to conclude that this extension of the body is directly connected to access to data and information. Privacy, property and public space merge in the *New Portraits* series – become entangled within the human body, forming a new assemblage. And to make this claim even broader. This case seems to be indicating that the traditional separation in occidental legal tradition between the private legal subject and public information seems to be problematic when subjects in themselves are becoming information carrying organisms. This shift requires a further discussion regarding the legal subject as a construction. Could it be that we are moving towards a more nomadic legal subject that forms a constellation between the private and the public and oscillates between the two?

4.3.5 The nomadic legal subject as an assemblage

What can be demonstrated here is that the notion of the author in copyright law is enabled by the construction of the legal subject. There is a difference between art and poeïsis – creation based on a technical skill or labour and creation as a process of commenting on the world, an act that continues the world. It can be argued that also the act of poïesis falls within the scope of copyright law. However such an interpretation of copyright law might be problematic as it takes information from the commons and encloses it into a private domain.

Creating and curating in terms of copyright law can be put together here. Certain content is directly connected to human beings or inforgs. This information exists openly online, and by incorporating it in private

59 Floridi, 2014: 69.

law regimes it may constitute an appropriation of personhood. In the infosphere they become entangled: online and offline existence becomes *onlife*, a space that is equally public and private. The Prince case is an example of this – portraits that exist online were transposed into printed works, made into physical objects exhibited and sold in a gallery. Does such an act encroach on bodily liberty – specifically if the inforg's body is seen as extended and as incorporating our social media online profiles and our digital information as well?

There is not one definable, individual, private legal subject at play here but rather various strata of authorship present in the case at hand (the original photographers, the subjects of the images, Instagram, Prince, curators, galleries, the public, etc.). Altogether they form part of an itinerant, network-based legal subject, or *creator-user*, which I have been referring to here, following Floridi, as an information carrying organism (or inforg).[60] This concept is, I argue, a hybrid between public and private law – where the artwork as hyperobject binds them together.

The nomadic legal subject thus forms an entanglement of property and personhood, of information and creation, of public and private rights, a borderland between shared information and privacy. This highlights a nomadic legal subject as a lawscape – a space where the inforgs exist and fight for coexistence. In this space they are not necessarily equal, autonomous nor do they all have the same rights.

In Volume II I will also discuss how this is connected to property rights (Chapter 5) and intellectual property rights in more detail (Chapter 6). It seems to me that the only property that appears to be standing strong, and the one that can still be upheld legally, is in the end the one connected to the so called "dead" author. However it is also a hoax because the author, while dead, still seems to be walking among us, feeding on our body parts: we have created *the author-zombie*. His disappearance act, as claimed by both Barthes and Foucault, appears to have been a rouse, an illusion, because it is still the undead author's name, his performative exclamation, his *fiat lux*, that has framed this entire exhibition, moving it away from the sphere of personhood into the sphere of property, into something that can be dismembered, and where each separate limb can be sold for around USD 100 000.

60 Floridi, 2014.

INTERMEZZO

Approaching the theory of the rhizome and in extension rhizomatic jurisprudence is not the simplest of all endeavours. As we have seen so far the Deleuzeoguattarian concept of the rhizome is presented in the introduction of *A Thousand Plateaus*. It is often stated that a text must be *seen* before it is *read*. So far I have approached the rhizome the other way around. I have read it, before looking at it, before studying it visually. Before we go on to Volume II then, let us linger here for a while, look at the text, and once again remind ourselves what a rhizomatic reading of jurisprudence can be. To do that, after we have *read* the rhizomatic theory in this first Volume, we now need to *look* at Deleuze and Guattari's introduction to the rhizome, before we move on to the second Volume. We take a break in the walk here. We experience the *intermezzo*.

A bizarre looking image of jumbled, creased, notes on a graphically represented musical score sheet opens up Deleuze and Guattari's introductory chapter, not words. Looking more closely at the image it can be discerned that this is the *XIV piano piece for David Tudor* written by the avant-garde composer Sylvano Bussotti. However, it does not look like a normal musical score, it rather looks as if someone has taken the notes written on a music sheet, stretched them all out, broken them, jumbled them and then haphazardly thrown the mess back on the paper. The image almost looks three-dimensional. Like that, it also appears to be a graphic representation of an instrument and not a carefully composed, meticulous musical score: it does not have anything in common with a neat musical score sheet one is used to seeing – it almost looks like an anti-composition. So can this image that opens *A Thousand Plateaus* divulge the secrets of the rhizome theory?

Plateau: on Sylvano Bussoti[1] and the avant-garde art

Bussotti is one of Italy's most well-known composers. He was born in a

1 Interestingly and as a curious matter of fact, Deleuze and Guattari misspelled his name, and the translator to the English version has stayed faithful to this and reproduced the misspelled name also in the English version. The correct spelling of the name is Sylvano Bussotti, with two "t"s.

cosmopolitan Florentine family in 1931. He is a classically trained violinist, and was a student and later also the lover of Heinz-Klaus Metzger who in turn was one of Theodor Adorno's most brilliant music students.

Plateau: David Tudor and John Cage

The music piece that we are looking at here has been composed by Bussotti for the pianist David Tudor. Tudor is otherwise mostly associated with the avant-garde composer John Cage, whom we have already met in Chapter 3, p. 68. He performed Cage's *4:33* piece when it premiered. From the opening image of *A Thousand Plateaus* and onwards, we are waiting for him to begin his performance of Bussotti's *XIV Piano Piece.*

Plateau: the connection with Frankfurt School

Bussotti was for a time the artistic director of *La Fenice*, the opera house in Venice. A post from which he officially resigned at the Venice Biennale in 1991 by bringing a prostitute and a pornographic star to deliver the keynote address, one that he himself was supposed to give. This was done as a protest against the corruption that he felt reigned within the art world. That Bussotti mixed "highbrow" and "lowbrow" art in his music and adopted it as part of his own public persona, and that he challenged the traditional cultural industry, as well as Adorno's definitions of it, is apparent.

Plateau: the connection to La Fenice

La Fenice, this ill-fated, Venetian opera house, has burned down to the ground twice, once in 1836 and then again in 1996.[2] Eerily, its own name, *la fenice,* the Italian word for the mythological bird *the phoenix* that famously burns down and rises out of its own ashes, echoes the faith the opera house itself was to have, twice. La Fenice represents classical as well as Italian *art*; it is a monumental *symbol* of Venice, but it also simultaneously represents tragedy, destruction, violence and perhaps even corruption in order for a rebirth to take place.

Plateau: the connection to Venice

A sinking city. One of the most mystical and mythical places in Europe and perhaps in the world. A city like no other, on water, connected by *canals* instead of streets, with secret alleys, hidden houses filled with artistic

2 For a brilliant account of the 1996 fire, La Fenice, and of the city of Venice and all its residents, see Berendt, 2005.

heritage and treasure. In Venice, nothing is what it appears to be on the (water) surface. On the contrary, there are subterranean undercurrents that carry the city on its shoulders. It is a city that is not built upwards but sideways, and not on soil but on water. Constantly deterritorialising itself. It is a city that is not situated on firm ground, but one that *flows*. A city confined to the rules and strengths of the sea and not of the land. Smooth not striated. A city dependent on the fickle mood shifts of tides as it alternates between ebbs and flows.

Plateau: "The average rise and fall of the tide is about three feet", wrote Ruskin in The Stones of Venice but "it is enough to cause continual movement in the waters"

A connected city – but a city dependent on fluent, moving, temperamental waters, a city that in turn is connected by slow (man-made) canals, not by hard roads or fast transportation. A city that is difficult, if not impossible, to fully represent on a *map*, as it is constantly moving and changing. What does the urban commons look like for the Venetians?

Plateau: beyond arborescent thinking – can we see the wood from the trees?

Venice is a city on water and it forms an image of what we should be thinking about here, water, canals, movement, beyond the idea of fixed origins, static cities with arborescent roots. Canals instead of trees. But we are used to thinking arborescently. We are used to imagining thought as a tree. Deleuze and Guattari say:

> The West has a special relation to the forest, and de-forestation; the fields carved from the forest are populated with seed plants produced by cultivation based on species lineages of the arborescent type; animal raising, carried out on fallow fields, selects lineages forming an entire animal arborescence. The East presents a different figure: a relation to the steppe and the garden (or in some cases desert and the oasis) rather than a forest or a field…[3]

So we must *refrain* from territorialising the forest. Which brings to mind something Agamben wrote in *The Open* about Baron Jacob von Uexküll:

> There does not exist a forest as an objectively fixed environment: there exists a forest-for-the-park-ranger, a forest-for-the-hunter, a forest-for-the-botanist, a forest-for-the-wayfarer, a forest-for-the-nature-lover, a

3 Deleuze and Guattari, 2011: 20.

forest-for-the-carpenter, and finally a fable forest in which Little Red Riding Hood loses her way.[4]

Plateau: we must refrain, refrain: the notion of territory?

The eleventh plateau in *A Thousand Plateaus* is called *On the refrain.* There, Deleuze and Guattari connect the repetitive nature of the musical refrain to a territorialising force. The refrain is what territorialises the song. The refrain is what territorialises our thinking. The refrain is the incantation of territory, the claiming of space, as famously explained by Deleuze in *Abécédaire*, a French film, an eight-hour long interview where he comments on his terminology from A (animal) to Z (zigzag):

> When do I do Tralala? When do I hum? I hum in three various occasions. I hum when I go around my territory…and that I clean up my furniture with a radiophonic background…meaning when I am at home. I also hum when I am not at home and that I am trying to reach back my home…when the night is falling, anxiety time…I look for my way and I give myself some courage by singing tralala. I go toward home. And, I hum when I say "Farewell, I am leaving and in my heart I will bring…". That's popular music "Farewell, I am leaving and in my heart I will bring…". That's when I leave my place to go somewhere else.
>
> In other words, the ritournelle (refrain), for me, is absolutely linked to the problem of territory, and of processes of entrance or exit of the territory, meaning to the problem of deterritorialization. I enter in my territory, I try, or I deterritorialise myself, meaning I leave my territory.[5]

Plateau: "Play it again, Sam!"

Deleuze and Guattari said that *A Thousand Plateaus* should be read like you listen to a record. Sometimes you can skip parts, other parts you will play on loop, sometimes you can listen to it chronologically, from beginning to end. Sometimes you just play your favourite song. Which means that the image in front of us that opens up *A Thousand Plateaus* forms the sound-track of this book, it paints the sound of the rhizome.

4 Deleuze, 1994.
5 Agamben, 2004: 41.

Hold on, I think I understand now. We must go back to Agamben and Uexküll in *The Open*:

> Where classic science saw a single world that comprised within it all living species hierarchically ordered from the most elementary forms up to the higher organisms, Uexküll instead supposes an infinite variety of perceptual worlds that, though they are uncommunicating and reciprocally exclusive, are all equally perfect and linked together as if in a gigantic musical score [...] like two notes on the "keyboard on which nature performs the supratemporal and extraspatial symphony of signification" though it is impossible to say how two such heterogeneous elements could ever have been so intimately connected.[6]

Well that answers the question. We not only have to see a text, we have to listen to it too. And when we *hear it* we then know what the rhizome theory is about – and Deleuze and Guattari say so themselves, already in the introduction to *A Thousand Plateaus*: it is about music.

> Music has always sent out lines of flight, like so many "transformational multiplicities", even overturning the very codes that structure or arborify it; that is why musical form, right down to its ruptures and proliferations, is comparable to a weed, a rhizome.[7]

Plateau: and what of jurisprudence?

Can we see law? Can we hear law? What does the theory of the rhizome give to jurisprudence?

The first volume of this book has read jurisprudence in this very manner, like music, moving from plateau to plateau, exploring the connectivity and possibility of various plateaus of law, art, and spaces where they linger. Rhythmically. The one-two-three of the waltz, forming a territory, a lawscape. I have refrained from reading jurisprudence or art as a tree, a structure, but rather approached them as a rhizomes made up of fluent, liquid, viscous plateaus. The legal machine, the positive law or dogmatic legal reasoning have served as a counter current – one that grounds and territorialises the rhizomatics of law.

Whenever legal concepts are territorialised or, attempted to be territorialised, sooner or later lines of flight will occur, lines of flight that flee the striated territory, force it to move.

6 Agamben, 2004: 41.
7 Deleuze and Guattari, 2011: 13.

So we move.

Difference and Repetition was Deleuze's doctoral thesis. It engages in a critique of representation. In its seven chapters Deleuze sets the stage for his future place in philosophy. There, he engages in a dialogue with philosophers before him and the history of philosophy. In the first part of the book he sets in motion a depersonalisation of philosophy (in Chapters 1 and 2) and a prolegomena of philosophy in Chapter 3. In the second part of the book he does philosophy "in his own name", creating an internal repetition in the book. That he provides a repetition of the introduction in the conclusion, and how his Chapters 1 and 4 and 2 and 5 mirror each other in *Difference and Repetition* have clearly inspired the structure of this book.

Commonly, difference impedes repetition, as that which differs from something previous cannot and is not repeated *per se*, it is something new. Deleuze, however, claims that difference inhabits repetition.[8] Central to the concept of repetition for Deleuze is that it is subject to time, it is also subject to the law of the identical and to a previous model of time, i.e. "to repeat a sentence means, traditionally, to say the same thing twice, at different moments. These different moments must be themselves equal and unbiased, as if time were a flat, featureless expanse".[9]

Thus, we move on to Volume II now, inspired by this, moved by this. Volume II mirrors (refrains, but composes a difference at the same time) Volume I, but then additional aspects are added on. Chapter 5 mirrors Chapter 2. It is also a theoretical chapter, but it does not study rhizomatic jurisprudence, it studies the commons. Chapter 6 mirrors Chapter 3. It too deals with the artwork, but the artwork is now placed inside a territorial, striated intellectual property law that attempts to ground it, territorialise it. The territorial intellectual property law is moved by the deterritorialising movements of the global advanced capitalism, that will also be followed in that chapter. Chapter 7 mirrors Chapter 4. It returns to and deals with the questions of possession, but there possession does not serve as conflict, instead, we study how various models of possession have been and are used in order to create solutions but also in order to reterritorialise the movements of law, art and commons. These (re)territorialising forces may striate and ground the legal concept of the commons, but they also make it visible and conceivable.

This approach mirrors the Deleuzian and Deleuzeoguattarian approaches. It moves between plateaus rhythmically, evolving from the rhizomatic jurisprudence to de/re/territorialising law, towards the lawscape and finally arriving at the legal concept of the cultural commons...

8 Deleuze, 2010: 76.

9 Anon. Internet Encyclopedia of Philosophy.

Volume II

(Re)Constructions

Part 3

Commons

Chapter 5

Commons

Being(s)-in-common

5.1 Property

In the book *Common as Air,* Lewis Hyde writes that "[h]ow we imagine property is how we imagine ourselves."[1] Let us now go over to the discussion concerning the commons through precisely that statement i.e. in the imagination of property and how such a conception in turn affects how we imagine ourselves. What ties property to personhood, to us, if people and property ever were two separate entities, is the very idea of the commons. So the first commitment to the idea of the commons, if we must have one is: commons is the space, the in-between, the very excess, created through the entanglement of personhood and property.

This entanglement is not always visible, even denied legally, and there exists a powerful division in law, a seemingly insurmountable jurisprudential divide between persons and property. In Roman law for instance, only free men were able to own land, deemed to be immovable property. A division was thus created between the person ("free man') and the property ("land"). According to Roman law principles not even all human beings were all considered to be persons. Those who were not free (male) citizens were, much like property, deemed to be chattel because they were not able to own land, and legally seen as attached to the land and thereby to the landowner. Non owners of land had to be subject to a landowner's protection in order to be granted the status of a legal subject, and thus personhood.

The discussion about the commons must then begin there, in the connection between the person and ownership in a) the land(scape), b) the commodity and finally c) the content. All these three types of ownership exist in law, but all three are also divided from the person on a principle level. The discussion will then carry on to the notions of space and their connection to the person. Finally, I will discuss various conceptions of the commons (as a resource, as a network) before arriving at my

1 Hyde, 2012: 26.

own definition of the commons namely as an ecology, as the in-between or the entanglement of personhood-property-space.

5.1.1 Landscape: immovable property

Immovable property is a static form of property, which is based on (occidental, if we are to briefly interject with Deleuze and Guattari) notions of cultivation and exploitation of land and the wealth that stems from it. The production of wealth is thus organised by relying on income structures stemming from the exploitation of land, by tending the land with manual labour. Manual labour, at least in Roman times, was provided by slaves, who were, once again, deemed to be chattel, attached to land as any other tool or machine. This is explained by the so-called "occupational theory"[2] something which was initially developed in legal doctrine by Samuel Pufendorf[3] and then by Hugo Grotius.[4] It presupposes a quasi-religious notion of land as something initially held in common and then given to Man "on loan" by the will of God. Blackstone's comments on this are now famous:

> [t]he earth... and all things therein, are the general property of mankind, exclusive of other beings, from the immediate gift of the Creator... all was in common among them, and that every one took from the public stock to his own use such things as his immediate necessities required.[5]

Thus, as per the occupational theory, the individual who is the first to occupy a part of the common (land), or who occupies the territory and the people (enslaves others, making them his chattel) on that land, will be seen as the rightful owner of that which has been passed on from God to man.[6] By the act of enclosure man creates ownership of land and the chattel attached to it. The focus, when it comes to immovable property in property law lies on exclusivity of land, and extracting the value from *land* and its

2 Although the occupational theory could be developed here and is very interesting particularly in terms of indigenous people's rights to land, it will not be further discussed, so as not to create undue diversions from the discussion at hand. But see e.g. Mabo v. Queensland (No.2) (1992) 66 Australian Law Journal Review 408 in which the High Court of Australia recognised the communal native title of the Meriam people to land on Murray Island.

3 Pufendorf, 1703.

4 Grotius, 1925.

5 Sir Blackstone, 1979.

6 This is of course classical property theory, that we can see also in e.g. Locke, 1690, Book II. In common law see the principal case Pierson v. Post 3 Caines. R.175 (N.Y. Sup. Ct. 1805) that appears to distinguish two principles of occupation, the act of enclosure and invested labour.

resources that are there, by nature. This logic is based on so called primitive accumulation as value creation, namely occupation by enclosure of land and the labour on the land.

The dominant legal field that regulated, and still regulates, this occupational form of ownership and that closer attention ought to be paid to is *land law*.[7] Some existing legal principles that are very interesting to study in terms of the legal framing of the commons are particularly principles connected to ownership of land such as the rights of passage, way leaves,[8] as well as *allemansrätten* that we began with, and conversely their opposites such as *trespassing*.[9] Other interesting legal principles to comment upon from an immovable property and land law point of view could be tenancy, easements, servitudes and the like, all of which could be beneficial to bear in mind when discussing the commons. I will also consider the different forms of exclusions and enclosures of certain spaces by e.g. fencing, whereby parts of the land that were initially held in common become property by the act of occupation and can thus only be privately accessible (or by a right of way). That it is possible to find indispensable knowledge in land law and its general principles in terms of commons will, if it is not already so, become obvious.

I want to keep making these connections using Deleuze and Guattari's rhizomatic theory and nomadic method. Establishing all these connections will carry the discussion forward, onto other plateaus, and show that what we are really discussing when we are studying the commons, might not be as foreign for the legal sphere as it might initially seem, particularly if we are making connections across traditionally divided legal fields. The underlying claim I am advancing is of course that the idea of the commons is in fact not particularly new or unexplored as a legal phenomenon, as it may have been assumed. Even if it can be argued that the idea of the commons is, primarily, a medieval principal, the discussion really ought to begin in Roman land law, in order to arrive at the present day and the digital knowledge society, bio power, global capitalism and ultimately the legal concept of the (cultural) commons.

Particularly the principles of way rights and easements ought to be stressed where access to the commons is enabled without, for that sake, (seriously) denting the underlying ownership of land. This is significant as these principles allow us to demonstrate how there already are existing legal tools that could be put into play in constructing a legal concept of the commons. It has for instance never been all that controversial to limit

7 Iljadica, 2017.

8 Cf. the concept of *allemansrätten* in Swedish law, see also the Swedish Supreme Court decision NJA 1996 s. 495 and Swedish statutory law 2 kap. 18 § 3 st Regeringsformen, as well as the Swedish Environmental Code, 7 kap. 1 § Miljöbalken.

9 Hemmungs-Wirtén, 2004; Hemmungs-Wirtén, 2008.

property rights in land when it comes to e.g. rights of passage or rights of way. Quite the contrary, it has been argued, historically through to our day, that it is a sensible inconvenience for the benefit of public good. If we are all to enjoy the good life we must have access to the commons. In order to be able to build roads, infrastructure, enjoy nature, fresh air, and so forth, interests that have always been premiered in law, while still simultaneously managing to uphold (individual) ownership of land, we have to accommodate for the commons. Professor Eric T. Freyfogle even phrased it as such that the public access to the commons must be seen as the primary right, or as the *de facto* state of nature, while the private ownership of land must be seen as secondary or as a legally constructed exception or encroachment on such a primary state.[10] Through such reasoning the private right is thus understood as a social construction put in place in order to regulate the already excising "natural" commons with an inherent public access and to delimit the, again, already existing state of nature that is, a commons open to all; and not the other way around.

Some argue that e.g. *allemansrätten*, wayrights or easements are so called "soft values", principles that have been incorporated in law so as to balance the "hard" property right, that these are values that mainly promote public interest such as health and recreation.[11] While this may seem to be true to a certain extent, these statements are based in a dogmatic understanding of law, where there is a difference between hard property rights ("inside" of law) and soft values (policies, "outside" of law). The analysis here does not necessarily, or at all, follow such a line of reasoning, as it is not a question of creating a balancing act between hard and soft values. Instead it is argued that by presenting the issue in the manner of occupational theory, presenting exclusions, enclosures, stints and privileges that come with exclusivity rights as the only way to regulate this sphere, that such statements in actual fact constitute violent acts, an exercise of power over the public right and in extension the commons.

5.1.2 Commodity: movable property

But if we are to move a little bit further in history from Roman law, and look more closely at also movable property we find other legitimising aspects to the commons. Industrial production strengthened the economical as well as legal significance of chattel, so that it could be exploited in new ways. Naturally, it also meant that the feudal structures slowly merged into bourgeois structures and the monetary institutions obtained a strengthened symbolical significance. With the new organisation of industrial labour everything could be calculated in monetary terms, even

10 Freyfogle, 2013.
11 See e.g. Åslund, 2008: 22.

time. While immovable property had been permeated with notions of parochialism and stasis[12] (a "sedentary form of possession" in Deleuzeoguattarian terms[13]), ownership of movable property constituted a new movement, one that also generated a new type of wealth, based on commerce ("nomadic form of possession" in Deleuzeoguattarian terms[14]). The value creation here is no longer necessarily tied to extracting as much value as possible from the immovable land, but rather extracting wealth from *labour* and investing it into movable commodities. Though we saw above that occupational theory can be used to explain the ownership of land, when we move into the industrial paradigm and the commodity paradigm, the theory of labour becomes more pertinent.

Locke and the ideas that had coloured the revolutions before industrialism sought to argue that there was a natural connection between commodities (objects), the labour (people) invested in them, and ownership. Here, ownership thus expressly becomes linked to labour not through occupational theory as in land law but through an idea that a right to private property is a result of the labour invested in an object. The dichotomy human–object, person–property is thus created and perpetuated. However, the only distinction between owning land and owning commodities was that when it comes to the second, appropriation does not necessarily happen by the act of occupation but instead by investing (human) labour into resources initially held in common. Following the Lockean understanding that if labour is the only way through which humans can appropriate things that are not fixed to land, it becomes clear that man cannot appropriate objects endlessly, since there are limitations due to scarcities in nature. That which exists on Earth constitutes the limits of what can be appropriated and owned. The notions of scarcity and with that also exclusivity of things are two guiding principles here. However, with the introduction of money of course, no similar principles of exclusivity and scarcity are necessary, as there had been for natural goods. Money could, at least in theory, be produced endlessly. As we saw in Chapter 4, p. 106 following Radin, it is a fungible type of property, replaceable.

As large-scale industry eventually replaced agriculture as the hegemonic form of economic production, Hardt explains,[15] it once and for all prevailed over the rural economy as the dominant form of production. It meant that the new form now *over-spilled* and *coloured* the former. Agriculture had to become more like industry in order to still generate wealth, it had to become industrialised in order to derive profit and it also

12 Hardt, 2010: 347.
13 See Chapter 7.
14 See Chapter 7.
15 Hardt, 2010: 348.

had to adhere to and adopt to the "regimes of mechanisation" that marked the industrial paradigm such as discipline, work rhythms, working days/hours, other industrial temporalities such as leisure/holiday times, and so forth.[16]

The tendency that is interesting is this very *colouring* that occurs when one form of production overtakes another, forcing the old to adopt certain traits previously unnatural to it. However, what is equally fascinating is that the opposite might also be intriguing to expose. At least during a transitional period, as a new form of production and a new dominant form of property is emerging, the new form seems to initially be organising itself in a similar manner as the old, by pretending, or assuming to be, more like the previous production form than it is in actuality. For instance, early industry made itself dependent on natural resources such as mining and forests that until then had been subject to the agricultural economy. As one dominant form of production gradually morphs into another, lines become blurred and it becomes impossible to tell where the one production form ends and the other begins. It can be observed that such shifts also produce hybrid forms of production, that are somewhere *in-between*, it can either be that the new form colours the old, or that some traits of the old linger and remain embedded in the new. A deterritorialising act (here e.g. the industrial revolution) takes flight into the new, unregulated, *smooth space* (previously unknown economic form of production), but through acts of reterritorialisation (the industrialisation of agriculture and the agricultural dependence of the industry) the line of flight is then moved back into the striated space and once again territorialised, at least temporarily.

Thus we can see how property law evolved away from focusing mainly on land ownership and placed larger importance on personalty (in common law) or movables/movable property (in civil law), that is chattel. The industry was creating commodities and it was no longer just about the question of who owns the land, or who owns the industrial production but indeed who owns that which is industrially produced and then sold on to consumers. Legal reterritorialisation can be seen through the various sales of goods acts and contract laws that started to emerge, and the exploitation of chattel became underpinned by a strengthened significance of the free, unfettered contract, which became an increasingly significant legal instrument. It is through entering into contracts that labour could be exploited, and commodities exchanged, and it was the very legal instrument through which employers and employees could (re)territorialise, the emerging forms of ownership, and labour, connected to commodities. The contract is the very instrument that facilitates commercial exploitation of chattel as consumer products.

16 Hardt, 2010: 348.

Within this context it is the potential of the contract that is interesting. On the free market the contract is the founding legal instrument that allows the actors on the market to agree on the terms of the trade. Initially, the contract as an instrument is two-party oriented. It means it governs the terms of the trade, through e.g. offers and acceptance, between two autonomous actors on the free market. It is also object-centric as what is being traded is usually an object/commodity, seen as external from the market actors (people). This was very much the industrial logic pursued in order to accommodate the trade in industrial commodities. We will shortly see what happens when the contracts move from being two-party oriented, from being object-centric and when they become more process-oriented and how that is relevant for the construction of the commons. When we later arrive at multi-party agreements that happen on digital platforms like for instance the Creative Commons, where acceptance happens on a click-basis (contracts are "click-wrapped"), then the underlying assumptions of contract law of e.g. free autonomous actors on the market become questioned too.

5.1.3 Content: immaterial property

However, we need to briefly look at one more type of property, namely the immaterial one. We are still not quite sure which dominant form of property might be *the* dominant one today or which type of ownership has succeeded the industrial paradigm. Maybe they are several. However, many argue that it might be the finance or information-based immaterial property within advanced capitalism. Be it as it may. Hardt, as well as Negri, refer to it as *immaterial and biopolitical property production*. Among other things, they point to the fact that fewer people work in factories, that the labour market is more global than before, and that the type of goods being sold are increasingly less industrial and more immaterial or biopolitical in nature. The new type of good that currently seems to dominate, and that arguably might have dominated for quite some decades now, is based on "knowledge, code, language, *social relationships, affects*, and the like".[17] There seems to be "a tendency for immaterial or biopolitical production to emerge in the hegemonic position, which industry used to hold."[18] What these immaterial and biopolitical products are is difficult to outline. However, the (hyper)objects studied here are unquestionably one such example of, at least partly, immaterial and biopolitical products and within the legal rights connected to them they are often formulated as intellectual and intangible. I shall continue using the approach to artworks that has been presented in Chapter 3, and when commercialised the artworks are

17 (My emphasis), Hardt, 2010: 349.
18 Ibid.

packaged as immaterial products in the sense of how Hardt uses the term, even though they are not solely immaterial, as they are also packaged as commodities.

The traits that the hyperobjects in the guise of goods do have in common, and that Hardt also points to, is that they are based on and dependent on ideas, images and information. These products can be privatised, even if they are seen to be immaterial. However they always, or at least often, have a material aspect also. Certainly, they are controlled and governed by the institute of property. Conducting the same form of analysis that I undertook above, it is also here apparent that the "over spilling" or "colouring" of the two dominant forms of ownership and the creation of a hybrid form in the breaking point between two paradigms takes place. While it is possible to privatise and control certain aspects of the immaterial products as if they were industrial commodities, through legal constructions such as intellectual property rights, it is not simple or straightforward, or possible, to privatise the hyperobject in its entirety. The same actors are still present in the packaging process in more or less the same guises as when they emerged during the industrial paradigm: the large-scale factory, the labourer, the consumer... However, there are some other actors that remain unaccounted for in this round-up of usual suspects and that cannot be fitted as easily in the old industrial paradigm; those are the inventors, the artists, the hackers, the bloggers, the occupants, the public, the pirates, the communities, the future generations...

The difficulty, not to say impossibility, in safeguarding, enforcing and policing the ownership rights tied to hyperobjects as immaterial products is evident. In analysing this tendency we can once again not only see that the industrial paradigm is colouring the immaterial/biopolitical production, but that also the reverse is happening, namely that even "traditional" industrial production is now forced to adopt some of the emerging new traits such as informationalisation, dependence on knowledge/code, and also incorporation of aspects such as affects, experience and care. The notion of "experience"[19] in e.g. smart objects is treated as an additional trait to products, regardless of them being a car, a TV, a cup of coffee, a holiday, an event or any form of entertainment.

One of the specific aspects that becomes visible is that the personal experience is entangled with the object/commodity exposing the hyperobjectivity traits. Or expressed in the words of Morton, persons, land and things stick to each other and it becomes problematic when we are trying to legally keep them apart. Here it is warranted to briefly discuss two things

19 On the notion of experience see e.g. Zizek, 2009: 52: "[W]e primarily buy commodities neither on account of their utility nor as status symbols; we buy them to get the experience provided by them, we consume them in order to render our lives pleasurable and meaningful".

– the first is that the construct of immaterial products as governed by e.g. intellectual property law seems to be appropriating hyperobjects in general and artworks in particular, as being defined only as immaterial things. The second, that hyperobjects are therefore presented as merely intellectual and immaterial, with no tangible aspects other than in the form of the packaged commodity. Both of these reinforce the division and reaffirm the dichotomy between persons and things, and in extension, personhood and property in law.[20] What this oversees is the entanglement between the persons and the various forms of ownership, be they immovable, movable, or immaterial property.

5.2 Space

Following the discussion from above, what seems to be opening up is a space between the person and the thing, between personhood and property. The notion of the commons then, it could be claimed, develops through the notion of ownership towards the notion of a sphere or a space, physical as well as "virtual", that somehow binds persons and things, affecting quality of life, becoming a shared space, and this space is needed in order to lead a *good life*. This space is the first step towards the construction of the commons.

The thing with space is that it is everywhere. Everybody is talking about it yet nobody really seems to know, at least ever since the so called "spatial turn"[21] in law and elsewhere, what we have been referring to when we have been talking about *space*. In line with the general approach here let me then state briefly before I develop it further in this section, how I am employing the term space. My use of the term is in no way all encompassing, nor is it, necessarily, a mainstream approach. First of all. When I refer to space I am not referring to that which is generally referred to as "public space", although I do think that classical discussions on public space as carried out by e.g. Habermas are necessary. Here, space does not either, as Henri Lefebvre pointed out already in the opening lines of *Production of Space*, have a strictly geometrical meaning, or a meaning invoking the idea that it is simply an empty area or a vessel.[22] Far from being seen as an abstract public space or as a geometrical or an empty area, a *res existensa* as opposed to *res cogitans*, within the Cartesian western tradition,[23] my approach here is, if I had to label it, Spinozian. Or more accurate yet, Deleuzeoguattarian-Spinozian. The idea of space follows the idea of the *plane of immanence* in Deleuze/Guattari, and *body* in Spinoza, namely space

20 On personhood and property see e.g. Radin, 2009.
21 See generally Philippopoulos-Mihalopoulos, 2014.
22 Lefebvre, H. 1991.
23 Again, see the opening of Lefebvre, H. 1991.

as relational immanence, but with geometrical aspects to it. Or even space as "subversive property" as Sarah Keenan has labelled it which I will get to towards the end of this spatial section.

What does that mean? It means that space as employed here is not a strictly abstract concept, although it has abstract qualities. But it is also very much material, a surface on which spatial justice plays out. It constitutes conditions of life as it is always folded in or connected to the bodies that happen to be there.[24] However, and following Philippopoulos-Mihalopoulos, the surface onto which spatial justice unfolds is not flat, it is tilted, meaning that some objects take up more space, some weigh more, and that equally some are weaker, dependent on other constellations. So it is a monistic approach that is being undertaken here, understanding space as both abstract and material at once. Not as a metaphor but as a process of becoming that happens all the time. It has to do with subjectivity, as well as with the production and distribution of property as we shall shortly explore.

This approach to space, as Philippopoulos-Mihalopoulos claims, displaces the human from the centre.[25] While the discussion in the first section above regarding the Western understanding of property is very much human centric, my discussion regarding space attempts to displace the human from its centrality, at least for the benefit of the spatial.

5.2.1 Abstract public space: intersubjectivity

In *The Structural Transformation of the Public Sphere,* Habermas traces the constitution and the development of various versions of the public spheres. He begins with the Greek *polis* and its *agora,* a public space peopled by propertied, educated, free men that could take part in learned exchanges of ideas with each other. He ends up in the western European media age where advertising and journalism frame the public spaces in a wider sense and where debates on larger scale take place within a capitalist context.

The underlying principle of Habermas' study of the public sphere was firstly to demonstrate that often when the concept of public is being addressed; it is in fact the bourgeois public, very much dominated by bourgeois values and imperatives that is being referred to. His study sought to counterbalance such tendencies by introducing a wider notion of the public sphere that could be placed within the paradigm of the Marxist theory. Habermas did not focus on the governed individual overwhelmed by the administrated mass culture that Adorno and Horkheimer had been writing about in *Cultural Industry*[26] (and painting black when looking back at the rise of fascism),[27] but rather on "an account of intersubjective

24 Deleuzian reading of Spinozian bodies.
25 Philippopoulos-Mihalopoulos, 2014: 40.
26 Adorno and Horkheimer, 2007.
27 Deleuze, 1988.

communicative processes and their emancipatory potential".[28] Habermas was arguing that the public discourse, what he would later refer to as *communicative action,*[29] was equally relevant in the coordination of human life as were the state powers and the market economies.[30] The communicative action happens in the public sphere.

Habermas was also fascinated by how private individuals integrated and acted within the public spheres. In "The Public Sphere and Encyclopedia Article" Habermas wrote that the public "is the realm of our social life in which something approaching public opinion can be formed. Access is guaranteed to all citizens".[31] The public sphere is thus formed, he continues, when private individuals assemble to form a public body. That means that any communication that happens within the public sphere will always be connected to some of the fundamental rights, such as the right of assembly, right of information, freedom of speech and so forth. The public sphere requires the private individual for Habermas. Habermas did not equate "public", meaning state governed (*Öffentlichkeit*), with public in his sense, which is generated by individuals that communicate inside the public sphere. The public sphere that Habermas addressed is not an institution as such *but a space for communication.*

Habermas examined two types of social models in which the public sphere exists: *the liberal model of the public sphere* and *the public sphere in the social welfare state mass democracy*. The first model stems from the eighteenth century, which is the time around which, Habermas argues, the first liberal public sphere administrated by law with a demonstrable political function was constituted.[32] Later on, he arrives at the mass democratic welfare state, where he traces the rise of the capitalist media that affects and governs the public sphere. With the increasing importance of the commodity exchange, constitution-based states had been emerging where national constitutional laws were guaranteeing certain *individual rights.* The precondition for this, Habermas continues, was the developing of a market that was increasingly liberalised with a necessity for private people to be left to their own devices, free from state intervention, to independently act as *legal subjects* and later on, consumers. In that sense there was conversely a growing private sphere that came to be governed by the commercial trading laws. Laws were being enacted so that they would be adaptable for the market. That also meant that social relations assumed "the form of exchange relationships".[33] And here we return to the insight that the legal

28 Calhoun, 1992: 5
29 Habermas, 1985.
30 Calhoun, 1992: 6.
31 Habermas, 1974: 220–226.
32 See e.g. Habermas, 1992: 73.
33 Habermas, 1992: 74.

transactions were contract-based and the growing body of private law encouraged this. Here the public space and e.g. ownership rights, the market and the legal subject converge. All these three are private, but they converge in the public space.

Both the liberal market-based space and the welfare based space in the mass democracy therefore have traits that are both private (in that the public sphere is governed by private law) and public (in that it happens outside the traditional private sphere, the home, *oikos*). This public sphere still rests on the construction of the legal subject in general and fundamental rights and civil liberties in particular. States, as public governing bodies, are not allowed to meddle in the private affairs of people. Habermas clarifies this by stating that "the codifications guaranteed the institutions of private property and, in connection with it, the basic freedoms of contract, trade, and inheritance"[34] and that they remained free from state influences and interference. Thus, Habermas continues:

> The injunction-like character of liberal rights corresponded to the following ideas: these rights protected from state interference and encroachment those areas that in principle were the preserve of private people acting in accord with the general rules of the legal system.[35]

That means that these were negative rights that ensured a minimal protection of the individual from any intrusion from the state. With time, positive social rights[36] developed with a notion of a different type of state, one that was active and nurturing – and that meant that the *bourgeois* (owner of goods) became *citoyen* or *homme* (a human being among other human beings).[37] But this transition too soon transformed the human being, through capitalist media and the culture industry, from having been an homme into becoming a *consumer*.

Again, it is worth restating that contrary to Adorno/Horkheimer, when Habermas discusses culture dissemination in the public spheres of both the liberal and in the welfare model he does not paint an equally dire picture as Adorno/Horkheimer who depict it as part of the fully administrated culture industry, arguing that culture is more often than not only utilised in order to control and discipline people. Even though Habermas too recognises that culture can be an intricate and powerful aspect of the public sphere, he rather concentrates on the spaces in which it exists: first salons and later on, the media and various cultural institutions through

34 Habermas, 1992: 75.
35 Habermas, 1992: 223.
36 Although, as Gustafsson asks, is not the concept "social right" a paradox or an anomaly in itself? "Social" denoting something collective and in common while "right" denotes something individual, Gustafsson, 2002: 23.
37 Habermas, 1992: 225.

which art can be disseminated. The dissemination of culture happens in public, according to Habermas.

Culture dissemination, public sphere and their connection to the emergence of concepts of mass democracy, communicative action, contract, trade and, indeed, inheritance are very interesting here as naturally, all of those must be connected to the commons. While the notion of an abstract public space in this Habermasian sense and the intersubjectivity that happens there is the starting point in discussing space within this context, it must be further nuanced as it both renders the notion of space "immaterial", re-institutes the human in the centre as citizen or consumer, and relies on a notion of public that may be difficult to uphold in the era of the digital.

5.2.2 Material space: an empty container or a network-space

If we add materiality of space to space then what emerges is more than an abstract public sphere for intersubjective communication à la Habermas. Space then becomes a "place", or in more concrete terms a sort of geographical network, a container of people and objects in all their materiality, not just somewhere where abstract "communication" happens. In such a space objects have to be added to the analysis. In an intersubjective sphere there are only humans, and while they are connected and communicating, it is vastly anthropocentric. The human and the spatial are understood in an exclusory manner. In a geometrical network-space on the other hand, the human exists *together with yet separately from* the non-human i.e. space and in extension nature, dead matter, objects. To place this in a current setting, and if the digital aspect is added, the space itself is divided between analogue space (which can be both public and private) and virtual space (again both public and private). The object then that connects the analogue (living) human with its Other in the virtual space is the dead matter in the form of a *device*, such as a smart phone or a computer. All of these are seen as agents, or actors. As such it is not *as* anthropocentric.

In no particular order, some examples of this approach might be given. For instance, it could be argued that Bruno Latour's actor-network theory (ANT) exemplifies this approach. Within ANT non-human actors have been introduced into the network where humans exist among other (non-human) agents. The network constitutes a space, or a context, in which human and non-human actors are connected and cohabitate. The *Situationists* movement is another example of this type of space with e.g. the theory of the *dérive*, marked by the unplanned journeys conducted by a Benjaminian *flâneur* through space or more accurately through the landscapes, or even more accurately yet, through the urban landscapes. Also, here the notion of space is widened to include the non-human such as the landscape or the urban space that the human interacts with – often within a political context – nearing the discussion concerning e.g. the "right to the city" that was briefly touched upon in the Wikimedia Commons case above. This naturally can be further connected to the writings that span from Henri Lefebvre to those of David Harvey.

Lefebvre's ironic take on the production of space, as precisely commodification or reification of this type of network-space then certainly becomes relevant. So is this production of space to be understood as, well, a *commodification of space*? "Nature creates and does not produce"[38] writes Lefebvre. Production is connected to commodification. Because, in production there is a sense of labour, human made, intersubjective, that is captured as capitalist surplus. Nature's space is therefore not produced in Lefebvre while, following his reasoning, the urban space on the other hand and with it e.g. the right to the city are conversely produced. "Humanity, which is to say social practice, creates works and produces things".[39] With this approach, the dichotomy between the human and non-human is of course *produced* and upheld. Even though non-human actors are given agency in the network, they are still considered as *other than* human. In the production of network-space an intersubjective practice takes place where human beings produce things, products, and with them space. This space naturally soon becomes capitalist space, where it gains a more or less political meaning, but it is still nonetheless removed from, yet constitutive of, reality.[40] As such, this space can and does enable political activity as in Habermas, but it additionally reinforces the "triangulation between the spatial, the legal and the political".[41]

This approach extends out from Habermas as it is able to visualise and show that power struggles happen in the spatial and that the spatial is e.g. connected to the right to the city, that in turn is connected to, but still separated from, the human. Capitalist production is thus expressly shown within these connections between space-city-human. The difference between the approach to the network-space from the Habermasian abstract intersubjective-space above is that it has moved from the idealisation of the intersubjective *human* discourse and consent that happens through communicative action and highlights instead the struggle as well as the exercises of power that happen in and through the production of the network-space.

What the network-spaces, however, do not directly do is to address the notion of power, and with it, distribution of property. Power seems to be assumed to be either the "capitalist machine" or the "state". As such a verticality is constructed where the hegemonic power produces everything *downwards*, including space and property. What is not directly touched

38 Lefebvre, H. 1991: 70.
39 Lefebvre, H. 1991: 71.
40 Philippopoulos-Mihalopoulos, 2014: 31.
41 Philippopoulos-Mihalopoulos, 2014: 19.

upon is the idea of the body (or the object, or even hyperobject that I am exploring here) and its own power (*will-to-power* in Nietzsche, or *potentia* in Spinoza). Henri Lefebvre does show that bodies indeed also produce space: "each living body *is* space and *has* its space: it produces itself in space and it also produces that space"[42] which opens up for us to move towards the final approach to the space, namely the entangled space that "holds up" bodies and where they form a spatial assemblage, eventually a commons.

Of course the idea of the right to the city and more generally the notion of the urban commons has already been introduced in the Wikimedia Commons case above and I will return to it below also. What we can see so far is when we move from an abstract intersubjective idea of space then the Wikimedia Commons case seems irrelevant as the public space in an intersubjective sense is more connected to e.g. political manifestations and manifestations through e.g. protest. However, seen from this point of view and within the context of the right to the city then the case has another relevance as we can see how artworks (i.e. non-human entities, objects, things, products) placed in the public sphere also contribute to the political production of space. As such we can also see that the capitalist machine by utilising commercial intellectual property rights as was argued by the Swedish Supreme Court is in this way able to (re)appropriate at least the (re)production of space that happens online. However in this material sense we are still stuck in a dichotomical approach, we must divide: human–non human, physical space–virtual space, person(hood)–property, etc.

5.2.3 Relational space: a subversive property-space

Therefore, before we arrive at the discussion surrounding the commons we must visualise the space from this final perspective which reaches beyond dichotomies and manages to reveal the processes connected to the constant *becoming* space. In the becoming space, all of these parts in what appear to be stable dichotomies become challenged, converge and in the end they collapse. Therefore, the space becomes all the more material, and the justice aspects that happen in the struggle of bodies or hyperobjects to co-exist in space become revealed. We have thus entered the *posthuman* space, that is to say a decentred extension of the human that finds itself in assemblages with other bodies that are not just human. Or expressed more plainly, when space eventually becomes material, somewhere we quite literally can enter, or that can enter us, it becomes, as Philippopoulos-Mihalopoulos points out, a process. It is here that spatial justice emerges, that he defines as *the conflict between bodies that are moved by a desire to occupy*

42 Philippopoulos-Mihalopoulos, 2014: 45, see also Lefebvre, H. 1991: 70.
43 Philippopoulos-Mihalopoulos, 2014: 3.

the same space at the same time.[43]

This entangled posthuman space is much more directly connected to property than the previous two types of space, as e.g. pointed out by Sarah Keenan.[44] She shows that when revealing the relations where bodies are entangled with space, a type of property so far quite unknown to law is produced and revealed. This is what Keenan refers to as "subversive property". This type of property is constituted by the entanglement between persons and space. It must be touched upon before we arrive at the commons. In her analysis, Keenan shows how property is in fact a spatially contingent relation of belonging[45] and this can be added to the distribution of power as discussed by Henri Lefebvre. It is this very insight that is important to stress and arrive at here, particularly bearing in mind e.g. the Bruno Schulz case from above. There, it was made quite clear that how property was conceived was directly linked to material spatiality (territoriality) as well as the artist's subjectivity and belonging – as such property was constitutive of and inseparable from identity and belonging. It also showcases that the formation of community identity is equally dependent on this relationship between personhood, property and space which I will discuss further below when I arrive at Nancy's "being-in-common". Keenan notes:

> This analysis of property can be used to show that social properties like whiteness, Christianity, heterosexuality and other characteristics generally associated with membership of identity groups, can be understood as property in the same way as owning a car, a house or a patent can.[46]

In the Bruno Schulz case this was obvious. This insight cannot be taken lightly either, particularly in the context of this book. It also leads to one of Keenan's main conclusions, namely that seen like this, where property-space-persons are entangled a subversive type of property emerges, and it includes space that produces identity and belonging. This subversive property is constitutive of subjectivity, and as such it *holds up bodies* or produces subjectivity. In this manner space is always material, never separated from personhood or property, but rather it becomes, according to Keenan, "mobile identities" something that you "take with you"[47] She notes further:

> This spatial understanding of property as belonging and the idea of

44 Keenan, 2014.
45 Keenan, 2014: 5.
46 Keenan, 2014: 7.
47 Keenan, 2014: 30.

> subversive property involve a rethinking of the relation between space and the subject. If what is essential to property is the space that holds up particular relations of belonging, then it follows that space is not the inert backdrop to action undertaken by subjects. Rather, space is part of that action.[48]

What Keenan's analysis brings forth and reveals is of course that the concept of subversive property can be useful in exploring the question of how spaces of belonging and identities are produced, and how they are directly tied to property.[49] It furthermore illustrates one of the most important points of this chapter, namely that the commons emerges from an interplay between personhood and property. Space cannot be imagined without the production of property. And vice versa. But also, the property that is produced is subversive in type.

> Conceptualising property as a spatial formation also suggests the possibility of an alternative political agenda for property. For as property is spatially and temporally contingent, it is also malleable – it can be shifted by the subjects, objects and spaces that are involved in its constitution.[50]

The relational space that gives rise to subversive property is of course posthuman in nature as it understands the human as always entangled with space and property. The human forms an assemblage as any other assemblage, it becomes an object, a hyperobject, without any necessary prioritised central position. This insight is precisely the conclusion that now brings us to the commons. Through this entanglement of (private)property-(public) space-(post)human the lawscape emerges and we can now arrive at the concept of the commons.

5.3 Commons

Having followed and distinguished the particularities of ownership and spaces we now reach the commons, which is formed by revealing the in-between, the middle, that connects ownership, space and persons, or more precisely, where they all converge in a hyperobject.

As I will try to outline very briefly in this last section, a number of scholars have already addressed the issue of the commons from various perspectives. Mine begins in the entanglement between ownership-space-persons. Before I fully arrive at my approach to the idea of the commons

48 Keenan, 2014: 8.
49 Keenan, 2014: 65.
50 Ibid.

let me contextualise how I arrive there. In the beginning of this chapter I wrote that the general commitment to the commons here is to see it as a space, the in-between, the excess, which is created through the entanglement of personhood and property. Now when we have briefly and topographically moved through ownership and space I can develop that very commitment to the commons further by introducing how Hardt and Negri employ the term, a definition that will be the starting point here:

> By "the common" we mean, first of all, the common wealth of the material world – the air, the water, the fruits of the soil, and all nature's bounty – which in classic European political texts is often claimed to be the inheritance of the humanity as a whole, to be shared together. We consider the common also and more significantly those results of social production, [...] such as knowledges, languages, codes, information, affects and so forth. This notion of the common *does not position humanity separate from nature, as either its exploiter or its custodian, but focuses rather on the practices of interaction, care, and cohabitation, in a common world,* promoting the beneficial and limiting the detrimental forms of the common.[51]

I want to make the spatial in this definition more visible. But first.

Most current discussions concerning the commons, the way it is defined, constituted, governed and developed begin not with Hardt and Negri but rather, with a reading of Garrett Hardin's essay "The Tragedy of the Commons"[52] that I have already introduced. In that essay Hardin begins, famously, by envisioning a pasture, where animals graze, that is open to all shepherds. Such an open pasture eventually prompts the egotistic shepherds to overpopulate it and overuse it. The shepherds, driven by profit, he argues, and an unlimited access to the pasture that might benefit them leads to overgrazing, which in turn results in the destruction of an otherwise fertile land. A classical prisoner's dilemma. Hardin thus concludes in a much-quoted passage:

> Therein is the tragedy. Each man is locked into a system that compels him to increase his herd without limit—in a world that is limited. Ruin is the destination toward which all men rush, each pursuing his own best interest in a society that believes in the freedom of the commons. Freedom in a commons brings ruin to all.[53]

51 (My emphasis), Hardt and Negri, 2009: viii.
52 Hardin, 2009.
53 Hardin, 2009.

Hardin was by no means the first one to analyse the commons as a concept. As I have already mentioned it is a medieval concept, but it can be traced even further back to the non-exclusive ownership categories in Roman law (which I will show in Chapter 7).

After Hardin the next notable discussion about the commons happened in Elinor Ostrom's *Governing the Commons*,[54] which is of course the other seminal work concerning the study of the commons. In it she lists various other similar statements that invoke a tragedy of the commons, among them one by Aristotle:

> What is common to the greatest number has the least care bestowed upon it. Everyone thinks chiefly of his own, hardly at all of the common interest.

And she quotes Thomas Hobbes too:

> Men (in the state of nature) seek their own good and end up fighting one another.[55]

So let us begin there then, in the negative, in the tragedy of the commons.

5.3.1 Co-management: commons as resources

When Elinor Ostrom was awarded the Nobel Prize in Economy in 2009 for "her analysis of economic governance, especially the commons"[56] the commons as a viable economical concept was fully launched into the mainstream. She re-introduced it as an alternative for "economic governance", even though it had been presented as a non desirable one in Hardin's essay. Ostrom argued that Hardin only presented it in its "tragic" guise. As an ecologist, interested in controlling human population growth, Hardin was intent on discussing what will happen when humans destroy all their resources. He links in this way overpopulation and the fact the goods of the Earth will decrease as its population rises. His essay illustrates this particularly by focusing the analysis on fisheries. There, Hardin argues, a common resource can exist only insofar as the number of commoneers, i.e. number of people who exploit the commons, is limited. Then, and only then, can the common property be a beneficial resource. However, if the number of commoneers increases, or becomes unlimited, *then* the commons will crumble, he argues – mainly due to overexploitation and over population. Hardin presents this theory as a social or prisoner's dilemma, that is, if a

54 Ostrom, 1990.
55 Ostrom, 1990 (2011 edition): 2.
56 www.riksbank.se/en/Press-and-published/Notices/2009/Economics-prize-2009/

resource, such as e.g. fisheries is governed by a commons structure, it will eventually become overexploited and destroyed through extensive usage because the commoneers do not trust each other and are inherently egoistic.

Elinor Ostrom was one of the first scholars to challenge this conclusion by empirically showing that a commons does not necessarily have to lead to a tragedy. In fact, far from it being a place where resources are wasted in a free-for-all fashion, a place of "no law", she argues that the commons too can function as governance of resources even without the individual private right or state intervention. She discusses in particular already existing commons such as pastures in the Swiss village Törbel, some Turkish fisheries and access to irrigation water in Valencian *huertas*. Ostrom was one of the first economical theorists to challenge the prisoner's dilemma when it comes to the commons and provide a solution as to how the commons as a resource may be governed and managed as an institution. She makes a distinction between common *property* and common-*pool resources*. Common property, she argues, is a legal regime that governs a jointly owned legal set of rights. Common-pool resources, on the other hand are, according to her shared resource systems, economic goods, independent of property rights.[57] More specifically she explains that a common-pool resource, such as a lake or an ocean, an irrigation system, a fishing ground or a forest, are resources from which it is difficult to exclude or limit users once the resource is provided.[58]

Ostrom acknowledges from the outset that the traditional approach to the commons is to regard it in four ways, either as a tragedy, as a prisoner's dilemma, as a collective action, or as "Leviathan"/"privatisation". These approaches are often presented "as the only way" she argues. She presents her study as the "fifth" approach to the commons. One of the most interesting aspects of her study, that is relevant to point out here, is that she advocates various mixtures between public and private rights when it comes to managing common property resources. However, her particular findings from *Governing the Commons* are connected to what is usually (admittedly heavy-handedly) referred to as the natural commons i.e. commons connected to natural, and as such finite, resources. As we saw already in the introduction here, and if we are to uphold the dichotomy between the natural and cultural commons for a short while still, for pedagogic reasons, the resources in the cultural commons are not finite, at least not in the same sense as those stemming from the natural commons.

In *What is Literature*, Sartre for instance notes that an artistic creation, like a novel, is not completed until it has been communicated to others

57 Ostrom and Hess, 2007: 5.
58 Ostrom, 1990 (2011 edition): 497.

through reading, or connected to other machines, to phrase it in the words of Deleuze and Guattari. Therefore scarcity, prisoner's dilemmas, tragedy, and in extension enclosures and the exclusivity principles are foreign for artworks as resources in the commons. Hess/Ostrom write also in the introduction to *Understanding Knowledge as Commons* that most types of knowledge have traditionally been relatively nonsubtractive (infinite). They point out the obvious fact that the more people share knowledge, the greater the common good gets.[59]

Now to bring it back to the property-section above. Production of artworks in our time is obviously different from that in the industrial era. In fact, as I argued, most goods today, not only artworks, but also other more traditional "tangible" commodities, are today vastly dependent on the immaterial, i.e. knowledge, aesthetics, code, language, social relationships, affects, communication, sharing, and so on. None of those are scarce. Even when it comes to artwork packaged as a commodity, it still encompasses immaterial aspects such as knowledge and information that need to be communicated and shared. Artworks can thus be wholly or partly material (like a painting, or a pickled shark in a tank), but they do not have to be (like music, films, performance, dance). Suffice it to say here that artworks as hyperobjects are both immaterial products as they are based on ideas, skills and knowledge, but furthermore, and most importantly, they have material aspects also when they become property (commodity) or when they are entangled with space (e.g. right to the city) or people (e.g. production of subjectivity, identity, belonging through subversive property). Although it has been made possible to privatise and control artworks *as if* they were immaterial only through e.g. copyright, or even cultural heritage laws, it is now apparent that this dichotomy is no longer as simple or straightforward. Though scarcity and exclusivity have reigned over industrial commodities, it cannot be the case with the production that takes place in the knowledge society. At least not to the same extent.

We can discern here that the first wave approach to the commons is thus the one which begins with Hardin's "Tragedy of the Commons" and continues through to Ostrom's *Governing the Commons*, discussing the commons as management of finite or natural resources, or potentially also infinite intellectual resources. In the same tradition and in the work that Ostrom conducted towards the end of her life with Hess they broadened the concept of the resource to also include knowledge and immaterial works. However, the focus on commons as management of resources, either natural or intellectual, remained.

59 Ostrom and Hess, 2007: 5.

5.3.2 Relationality: beyond resource management

But the commons, as is already quite apparent, goes beyond the private–public, natural–cultural, dichotomy. Hardt and Negri have made an important contribution in the differentiation between the "common" and the "public", a distinction that is fitting to mention here in the context of commons as more than resource management. Whereas the term "community" (or indeed "public"), they write, is often used to denote a "moral unity that stands above the population" the "common" on the other hand does not refer to traditional notions of either the community or the public; it is based on *communication* among singularities and emerges through the collaborative social processes of production.[60] The notion of community is thus another ingredient that needs to be added to the commons.

Hardt and Negri write in *Commonwealth* that the concept of private, used in opposition to public, tends to often lump together all types of possessions. Therefore, they continue, the term public bears a connotation to hierarchical control as opposed to what is horizontally managed (NB not owned!) in common, through a community. For instance we manage our clean air in the natural commons, and we transfer through generations nursery rhymes, fairy tales, fables and other cultural heritage.[61] Whereas the concept of public, they claim, tends to amalgamate all the various intellectual and cultural expressions into some kind of public unity, the commons in their view on the other hand focuses also on the *alterity*, difference and singularities (each person's difference, each different community) that exist inside the public and that participate in the making of the commons.[62] In that case, the private is upheld too, at the same time as the community's rights in attribution, access and sharing are enabled. This means that the binary opposite public–private becomes problematic, as the two are part of one and the same thing – the commons.

The private singularities such as the individuals or the communities are thus seen as the building blocks in the edifice of the commons, and as such they cannot be ignored or destroyed when the commons is constructed. That is why the notion of the commons is far more appropriate than the public, or communitarian management, Hardt and Negri argue, as it does not demolish the individual-private entity (artist, artwork or indeed enterprise), nor does it impose a given, static notion of the community. It still enables the network and plurality-based activities to progress and continue in the commons. Using their reasoning we can begin to also argue, controversial as it may sound, that commons-based concepts could

60 All the quotations in this paragraph: Hardt and Negri, 2004: 204.
61 Mattei, in Bailey, Farrell and Mattei, 2013: 12.
62 Hardt and Negri, 2009: 203–204.

also safeguard e.g. copyright as a legal tool too. The individuality that copyright promotes is seen as an integral part of the commons and does not dissolve in favour of an often potentially paternalistic and homogenous "public". Hardt and Negri focus on the notion of the community instead, which is something that of course needs to be addressed when commons is discussed.

One of the more significant problems with the concept of community is that it is often presupposed as homogeneous or at least as an, at any given point, definable group. In the Bruno Schulz case we saw several instances where the definition of community was impossible to achieve, or at least where such community assumptions proved to be problematic. In Keenan's analysis as presented in the section above we saw how community and belonging can be intertwined with subversive property that holds up bodies. Jean-Luc Nancy's writings on community will be illustrative here. In *The Inoperative Community*[63] and *Being Singular Plural,*[64] he deals with the very question of what constitutes a heterogeneous community or a "We" and the components that could make it up.

In *Being Singular Plural,* Nancy argues that *being* as we understand it will always be a concept of "being-with", which means a collectivity of "Is" forming a co-existence into a "We". For Nancy, "being-with" does not necessarily constitute a traditional community or a public space in a Habermasian sense *per se* which is defined by enclosure forming an inside and an outside of an existing group. Nancy rather adds to Habermas by presenting various hybrids that allow for mutual entrances and exits into the community, without the necessity of enclosure, at least not as we are used to defining enclosure. In Nancy's study he discusses a "being-with" as a heterogeneous co-existence in an open-ended community. Nancy provides an alternative reinterpretation or a challenge of the concept of "community" as well as of the Cartesian subject in it. Consequently, Nancy does not only present an alternative way of viewing community, he also provides a complimentary understanding of how the individual, the subject, the "self", can be understood as a multi layered body and he develops his theory on the notion of *singularity* as opposed to individuality or subjectivity.

This particular understanding of community that Nancy presents is very helpful particularly in connection with the concept of haecceity which was introduced in Volume I. Connected, the two demonstrate how neither the individual, nor the community in which the individual or the legal subject exists are some unified, static concepts, but rather bodies that are constantly in a state of becoming. Here the notion of subversive property is

63 Nancy, 1991.
64 Nancy, 2000.

of course key, as it holds up these formations. Seen in that way, the participation in the commons is only one aspect of the unfinished project that is the individual and the communities in which individuals dwell entangled with space and property. Nancy, in the same vein as Deleuze and Guattari, also challenges the occidental idea of community arguing against imagining the community as being self-enclosed (or a tree with a singular origin, root, and so on). Instead he proposes imagining a "being-together" as a project of "being-in-common". Nancy argues that any community which attempts to become communal, in such an arborescent way "loses the in of being-in-common" and it loses the "with or the together that defines it".[65] Therefore, contrary to traditional models, Nancy dismisses a number of unifying ideas and "attempts to depict community as something that cannot be forced, but is instead a shared experience of finitude, which gives rise to an affirming 'Being-with'."[66]

Nostalgia towards an archaic community is a symptom of certain assumed ideas, Nancy argues, and such a homogenous community generates more or less imaginary concepts of the individuals in it. Historically these may or may not ever have existed. Such communities, if they indeed ever existed, have been replaced by a multi/pluralistic alterity, in Nancy.[67] It is the state of being-in-common, which is of interest here. The being-in-common adds to Habermas and Hardt/Negri. Nancy maintains that the being-in-common does not denote a uniformity that binds separate individuals; it is rather based on a "shared experience". That means that the being-in-common necessitates sharing existence and space, and here it is linked with the idea of the commons. Nancy's community thus "requires a new conception of the individual to understand this 'sharing' and, accordingly, for this 'being-in-common' to exist".[68] The classic concept of the liberal subject is in this theory replaced by the concept of a singular being and fits together in a scheme where individuality is approached as individuation, a project, a constant state of becoming, a verb, an event, a haecceity. Nancy's singular being confronts the notion of the in law, Enlightenment-based, often assumed, Cartesian individual, that is clearly definable within the external world, where there is a definable "inside" as well as an "outside" of the individual. Therefore, Nancy experiments with terminology such as "being self" and "being separated".[69]

It is this very relationality that constitutes the plural being-in-common. What Nancy achieves by way of the being-in-common is to radicalise the idea of equality, where he does not refer to "a class of belonging definable

65 Kellogg, 2005: 29.
66 Prestidge-King, 2005: 26.
67 Nancy, 1991: 9–10, Prestidge-King, 2005: 83.
68 Prestidge-King, 2005: 87.
69 Ibid. and Nancy, 1991: xxxvii.

with some common properties that should distinguish it from others".[70] On the contrary, an individual as well as community to which the individual (temporarily) belongs is for him based not on inclusion into an exclusive or enclosed group, but rather on sharing (*partage*) of the "emptiness of sense that is the being itself of the singularity together with the plurality, that no predicate can fill up".[71]

When applying Nancy's writings to the concept of being-in-common, the commons I wish to eventually place artworks as hyperobjects in emerges through the idea of being-in-common. It could even be referred to as "beingS-in-common" if we are to add an interobjective aspect to it. This second wave of the commons studies marked by relationality is here represented by Hardt/Negri who employ a biopolitical aspect to the commons, stressing the shared accomplishments that serve not only as resources but also as constituents of the self and the community. Adding on Nancy's idea of singular plural, also the concept of community is made more multi-layered. This leads us into the latest third wave of the commons studies, namely the posthuman approach to commoning, as a process, a constant becoming, that moves us closer to (spatial) justice.

5.3.4 Ecology: posthuman commoning

Finally we arrive at the third and latest wave of the commons research. This wave can be connected to the writings of Peter Sloterdijk[72] among others, where commons is understood as something far beyond a resource, or even more than a relational community, but rather as a collective phenomenon, as a lawscape or even an atmosphere, as an in-between of property-space-persons. Within this wave we can also place one of the latest jurisprudential theoretical developments that is often referred to as "ecology". Such line of reasoning is developed in e.g. *Earth Jurisprudence* by Peter Burdon[73] and as we have already established by Morton in *Hyperobjects*. Within the context of this book I attempt to show that these can certainly be connected to the Deleuzeoguattarian theory.

Commons as ecology means seeing the commons not as anthropocentric, not as a sphere where there are clear divisions between physical/intellectual; between human/non-human; between commons/commoneers. It means on the contrary seeing the commons quite literally as an ecology or an atmosphere of society in which such phenomena as activism or cooperative communes can also be included. In this sense the commons is something that can also include such "difficult to grasp amenities" as e.g.

70 Matteo, 2005.
71 Matteo, 2005: 331–332.
72 Sloterdijk, 1998; Sloterdijk, 1999; Sloterdijk 2004.
73 Burdon, 2014.

the attractiveness of a space, the "buzz" of a city, and so on.[74] In such an approach to the commons the living human being and the dead matter/object/resource converge, and become in the words of Bennett, living matter.[75]

Depicting the commons merely as a resource or as an object, divided from the human subject, and something that only waits for appropriation and exploitation by the human is problematic within this context.[76] That is of course a vastly anthropocentric view, that separates the human from its environments and surroundings, where that which is not human is seen as only there to be exploited by the human, as a utility or a resource. It is this very separation between the human and the non-human that I have tried to show so far in order to arrive at the final wave of the commons, which is also my own understanding of the commons. In a setting where hyper-objects roam the world, the human centrality has been if not refuted, at least questioned. What (or who!) is the commons then? Are we all commons in our own right? Do we carry the commons with and within us?

As has also become apparent – western law and jurisprudence have been affected and coloured by the idea of separation between the human and the non-human and therefore legal concepts have reflected this underlying assumption. Property: non-human only. Space: either public or private, external to humans. Rights: human only. Very well. But when persons, space and things become entangled in such a manner where it is impossible to tell them apart, and when the shared space, the in-between, the commons, is that which must be framed legally, then it appears as though no legal construct is able to envision and conceive of such a phenomenon.

One such insight is that most of these concepts have legally been formulated to accommodate for an industrial setting, where the property/resource/commodity is distinctly separated from the human/subject/consumer. This chapter thus arrives at the insight, that while there is an inheritance from earlier legal paradigms connected to the industrial society in law, we have to rethink and reconsider them in order to imagine a legal commons as a construction. Having that ambition also challenges us not to fetishise the commons, or assume that it is a resource *toute suite*. Or conversely a public sphere. When it comes to the commons, what must be understood now is that we are in the era of the posthuman and as such the person-space-things divide that we have come to rely on in law and elsewhere is now obsolete. And with that insight, we may have to grieve the loss of certain stable, or at least the appearance of stable, concepts, a loss that the new era has generated. But, in a world that is in crisis – old legal concepts simply cannot do.

74 Borch and Kornberger, 2015.
75 Bennett, 2009: 65.
76 Borch and Kornberger, 2015: 5.

Peter Burdon has for instance launched the term *earth jurisprudence*, that recognises human interconnectedness with nature and moves from the anthropocene, to the eco-central ideal of "earth community".[77] This is naturally in line not only with Morton's *Hyperobjects*, to which the subtitle is *Philosophy and Ecology After the End of the World* but also his two previous books *Ecology Without Nature* and *The Ecological Thought*. This also ties to Félix Guattari's works outside of Deleuze, for instance the essay "Three Ecologies"[78] or his other writings on *ecosophy* that I will return to in Chapter 8. What they all have in common is that they displace the human as we saw above, at least from its centrality. I shall explain before connecting it to this final and third approach to the commons.

We inherited from the Enlightenment the idea of human centrality. From then on, the human being has been seen as the supreme thinking species, at the top of evolution's so called pyramid But then with modernity this species became shattered, fragmented, marred with neurosis, and because of its hedonistic desire for self-preservation it systematically started destroying everything around itself, not just nature, but also culture, other life forms, and finally, itself. In the wake and aftermath of the wars and crises that have taken place from the turn of the twentith century onwards the legal concepts that we today call (human) rights have been developed, specifically designed for the species homo sapiens. The notion of *human* rights was, and still is, connected to the legal subject. The legal subject, as we saw in e.g. the Richard Prince case above, is very bureaucratic in nature, German at least in its modern origin and connected to the legal state.

The modern project therefore strengthened the idea of the human being as the central subject in law that must be protected because of its supreme status, as well as because of its shortcomings. What was at the same time also strengthened was that it was this particular life form, homo sapiens, human being that was given the privileged legal subjectivity and therewith rights over other life forms and resources. The thought of providing a rights status or agency to e.g. nature, animals, culture, *also* has ever since been a foreign idea for us. Rights, as we have come to know and understand them today, are created by the human for the benefit of the human, in order to preserve the species, protect it from itself.

Let me take a brief detour to exemplify precisely this. The discussion as to whether or not the human being ought to be the only life form that is granted legal privileges and rights was highlighted in a case recently with the so called *monkey selfie*. The case is about an image that was created when a monkey quite literally snapped the camera from the natural photographer David Slater and took a picture of itself. The question that arose was whether Slater could be seen as the copyright

77 See e.g. Burdon, 2015.

78 Guattari, 2005.

holder of the image taken by the monkey. He argued that even if it was in fact so that the monkey by sheer curiosity had happened to snap the camera, that he himself nonetheless must be considered as the author of this work, as he had made all the settings in the camera, and created the very scenario that was eventually caught on camera. Slater argued that the photographer does not always have to be the one that operates the camera, in order to be seen as the author. Furthermore the snap by the monkey was incidental – had it not been for the human being, we would not have had the image. When Slater later tried to register the copyright in the United States, the American Copyright Office refused to grant registration claiming: "The Office will not register works produced by nature, animals or plants".

A similar question was raised in 2012 when the river Whanganui in New Zealand was deemed to be a legal entity and given a so called *legal voice*. After negotiations with local Māori people it was recognised as a legal person in law, equal to e.g. a company. Another instance of natural entities being granted legal standing was the formulation in the Ecuadorian constitution that grants rights to rivers, forests and other natural entities or when an Indian court recently gave sacred rivers Ganges and Yamuna human status. That the human being, and only human being, ought to be seen as the exclusive bearer of rights, and as such a subject in law, is no longer an unquestioned fact.

But in view of what we have discussed so far, maybe it does not even matter who is granted the status of a subject if everyone is seen as a hyper-object. Thus the dichotomy between the human subject and the non-human object (animal, nature, culture, and in turn the dehumanised Other human beings) has collapsed now and we are in a crisis. Ecological crisis. Financial crisis. Legal crisis. Ethical crisis. From this, by the anthropocene created big bang, the hyperobjects emerge. We are familiar with the hyperobjects by now, they are massively distributed in time and space, impossible to capture, see or describe, like e.g. global warming, radio active plutonium, artworks, *people*. These objects quite literally stick to us, they are viscous, dispersed, non-local, and we can never capture them in their entirety. So how do we envision the commons now when everything is entangled?

We have entered the era of interobjectivity, where every object can stick to any other object, forming interobjective assemblages, and where objects always exist in relation to each other. Constantly mutated. Therefore, it is useless making a distinction, legal or otherwise between the object and the subject, human and nature, commons and the commoneers. We are all entangled. The hyperobjects were created by the human beings' dominance on Earth but they are now here to stay and they walk among us. They are stuck to us, we carry them with us, in and on our bodies. The human subject, with its roots in the Enlightenment died during the twentieth century, and we have now all become mutated objects: *hyperobjects*.

So once again, what is the commons in the era of the hyperobjects and after the death of the subject? How can culture be administrated in a legal commons with this insight? Do we need the old constructions of ownership, space, individual rights in order for the concept of the commons to be envisioned in law today? Who should in that case the rights to the commons be given to? Us? Only us? The animals? Nature? Culture? Them? And in that case what kind of rights to the commons are we talking about? Individual rights? Community rights? Can we then still talk about *human* rights with a clean conscience?

Rosi Braidotti asked maybe the obvious question in this context, namely what is *human* anyway in "human rights"?[79] Because if we assume that the human is the Cartesian subject that we once inherited from the ideals of the Enlightenment, well then, many of the so called homo sapiens probably fell outside this definition anyway. If the human is understood in that way, as rational, white, male, propertied, citizen, then probably many (most!) of us never attained a human status. Thus, Braidotti wonders cynically: *When were we ever human?* Or as Costas Douzinas often points out, (human, individual) rights were only ever the ideological gloss on the underlying capitalist empire. That is: an illusion. So here we are, all entangled with the hyperobjects around us. Can we regulate the commons? Do old concepts even apply? What happens with the human now? We worry that the world might end, but guess what, according to Morton we do not have to worry: it already has, we are already post-anthropocene. So we keep looking to the law now, expecting that it can breathe a new life in all of this. Can the idea of the commons breathe life into a new posthuman reality?

This is the beginning of the construction of the commons in law. The insight that property-space-persons are entangled in assemblages. That the human has been decentralised and that the posthuman hyperobject has emerged. To be able to create such a concept as the commons in this setting we must first square off with the old legal principles such as human-based intellectual property rights and the governing empire of global capitalism, which I will do in the next two chapters.

79 Braidotti, 2013b.

Chapter 6

Intellectual property law

Commons and schizophrenic capitalism

The book *Tabula Picta: Painting and Writing in Medieval Law*, examines the medieval notion of *tabula picta*, that spans all the way back to Roman law. In it, the author Marta Madero poses the question: to whom does a painted tablet belong?[1] Is the owner the person who painted the image on the wooden tablet or the person who owns the tablet itself? In extension she also poses the question, who owns writing? Is it the person who owns the parchment or the person who wrote the text? Connecting some founding ideas of property rights to materiality of the artwork Madero is precisely exploring the origins of what today is framed within the scope of intellectual property rights. We have already so far deconstructed a number of founding assumptions that underpin intellectual property law, and in this chapter I aim to study them closer, particularly in order to connect them to the Deleuzeoguattarian notion of "schizophrenic capitalism" and later on in the next chapter the Deleuzeoguattarian forms of possession. These will open up the more concrete discussion on constructing a notion of the commons in law.

Madero's study is relevant in many ways here, both as a legal historical exploration and examination of medieval law connected to ownership of artworks, that explores the *longue duré* of the principles of intellectual property law, as well as it reintroduces the discussions concerning the implications of materiality when it comes to ownership of the immaterial works. But, before I get to materiality in intellectual property law, some contextualising words. So far I have engaged very little or obliquely with practical intellectual property law. I have instead placed e.g. copyright law in a wider legal philosophical framework within the contexts of this study in order to open up a discussion connecting a rhizomatic approach to jurisprudence and commons. Until now, intellectual property law has served as an example of the legal enclosures and assumptions that hinder the conception of the cultural commons in law. However, in this chapter, I want to more directly turn to the construct of intellectual property law

1 Madero, 2010.

itself, and how it has historically been put into play in terms of the issues concerning e.g. ownership and (im)materiality of art.

A similar approach to intellectual property law construction, however concerning not the creative works *per se*, but patent law and inventions instead, has been conducted by Alain Pottage and Brad Sherman. In their study *Figures of Invention: A History of Modern Patent Law*[2] they re-evaluate the sometimes ostracised aspect of immovable from modern patent law. They focus particularly on the medium in and through which the invention is made visible and how the materiality of the medium, as it were, matters.[3] Like Madero, they too place their study in a legal historical context, but equally at the same time provide new insights into current proprietary structures that surround modern intellectual property law.

Why is this relevant? How is it relevant for the commons? In order to in earnest construct a workable legal concept of the cultural commons, we need to address what I in the previous chapter referred to as the old constructions, and here I am particularly focusing on global intellectual property law and its ownership structures. We know that intellectual property is proprietary in nature and that it functions within global advanced capitalism. We also know that the opposite is true, namely that global advanced capitalism in turn supports, drives and enables the intellectual property construct as it looks today. Intellectual property law is today global, more or less fully harmonised. This harmonisation has been enabled mainly by the so called TRIPS agreement.[4] Let us first look at the global nature of intellectual property law before we connect it firstly to capitalism and then to the materiality of artworks and later still to the concept of the commons.

6.1 The global aspect: TRIPS

It is often claimed that unlike prior international intellectual property agreements negotiated under the auspices of e.g the World Intellectual Property Organization (WIPO), TRIPS has teeth.[5] Attempts to achieve global harmonisation of intellectual property regimes are nothing new. Ever since the 1880s and The 1883 Paris Convention for the Protection of Intellectual Property and The 1886 Berne Convention for the Protection of Literary and Artistic Works there have been international conventions regulating this area of law on an international level. These two

2 Pottage and Sherman, 2010.

3 Matter matters, as it were.

4 Agreement on Trade-Related Aspects of Intellectual Property Rights (TRIPS). Annex 1C of the Marrakesh Agreement Establishing the World Trade Organization, signed in Marrakesh, Morocco on 15 April 1994.

5 Helfer, 2004: 1.

conventions, *Paris* and *Berne* respectively, were placed under WIPO (a United Nations agency) in 1967. In the UN capacity WIPO does not have any direct mechanism for the enforcement of the two conventions or intellectual property rights on a global level. With the TRIPS agreement this hitherto weak enforcement possibility changed as TRIPS was brought under the umbrella of the World Trade Organisation (WTO). Apart from a couple of countries in the Middle East and Africa, the rest of the countries in the world have now all signed TRIPS, including the USA, Russia and China that have generally been reluctant regarding signing and agreeing to the terms of the previous conventions. Another interesting aspect is that all developing countries are also signatories of TRIPS.

This means that under TRIPS also the countries in the so called Global South are signatories. As such they are given the same burdens as the countries in the Global North. Also, since the developed countries are usually the owners of intellectual property and the developing countries are often the *users*, there is a built-in North–South divide that is perpetuated through this mechanism. This has been pointed out and criticised by the so called Access to Knowledge movement or A2K:

> To a large extent, the "North–South" divide has merely become a leitmotif for a new transnational IP discourse framed more broadly as access to knowledge, or "A2K". This discourse, among other things, offers a counter narrative that has systematically challenged the established IP orthodoxy, which has represented ever-stronger IP rights as a source of inescapable virtues for economic growth.[6]

It is this orthodoxy of intellectual property rights that is leaning towards an increasingly monolithic legal framework created by the international harmonization. It has given rise to a global regime with a basic intellectual property regulation that is more or less the same all over the world. This harmonization is, however, not neutral. This may seem like a controversial statement, but in my view it is not controversial, even if it can be criticised. There are of course national divergences and there are intellectual property law principles that differ depending on jurisdictions. However, with the TRIPS agreement, especially from a theoretical point of view, the differences in the various national intellectual property regulations are marginal, not to say technical. Therefore it can be said that the TRIPS agreement represents a radical shift in terms of global intellectual property law in at least three ways according to Amy Kapczynski.

a) Although treaties on intellectual property are not new (and indeed

6 Okediji, 2008: 4.

are remarkably old), before TRIPS, such treaties were generally overseen by WIPO. WIPO had no enforcement capability and countries could choose to join treaties in a "à la carte" fashion.

b) As TRIPS is part of the WTO, a country is not able to join the WTO unless it adheres to the TRIPS agreement. WTO has a dispute resolution system and any violations of the TRIPS are punishable, and

c) Intellectual property standards incorporated in the TRIPS are far more expansive than many of those that were in force in certain countries before the TRIPS, particularly in the developing countries. TRIPS requires for instance the member state to impose criminal penalties for pirated copyright goods.[7]

It has therefore been claimed, rightly so in my view, that the strong TRIPS agreement, with unprecedented enforcement possibilities, or with teeth, as Laurence Helfer refers to it, promotes an intellectual property right concept that is increasingly privatised, and where individual rights are premiered over public interest, faire use etc. This is where the TRIPS agreement is linked to the concept of the commons in this context. So far, the most serious type of critique that has been delivered against TRIPS' encroachment on other values that are not neo-liberal in nature have been for instance from the public health[8] point of view concerning e.g. access to medication, particularly in the developing countries.

Globally, there appears to be a tug of war, or a dichotomy, which I want to explore in this chapter, between the private commercial intellectual property rights and the public, open access to the goods and content that fall under the scope of these rights. Theoretically, this very tension where the public and the private, and the open and the closed are pitted against one another is what hinders the construction of the commons. Here, I am thus exploring new ways of addressing these issues. By utilising the Deleuzian and Deleuzeoguattarian theory of possessions in Chapter 7, it will become possible to envision another type of legal approach to these matters. It does not necessarily have to do with inventing new solutions; rather, it has to do with visualising the possibilities, which may be already there. But let me discuss the orthodoxy first.

The argument that I shall be advancing in this chapter is a very common one, and therefore I hope, straightforward. Intellectual property law as we know it is part of the global capitalist machine, to paraphrase Deleuze and

7 Kapczynski, in Krikorian and Kapczynski, 2010: 25.

8 See e.g.'t Hoen; Shashikant; Gombe and Love; dos Santos Pinheiro: all in Krikorian and Kapczynski, 2010, see also the report from the UN High Commissioner for Human Rights The Impact of the Agreement on Trade-Related Aspects of Intellectual Property Rights on Human Rights, Report of the High Commissioner, U.N. ESCOR, 52nd Sess., U.N. Doc. E/CN.4/Sub.2/2001/13 (2001).

Guattari, that reterritorialises any lines of flight that might be moving us towards a commons construction. More clearly. If we assume that artworks at some point exist (a priori *or* a posteriori) in the commons, they will directly be excluded from the commons by the proprietary enclosure and exclusivity mechanisms governed by the private intellectual property law. This is not innocuous either, because as it has already been established in so many studies, ownership of intellectual property works also entails ownership and control of information, knowledge and as such constitutes an exercise of power.

In the now classic article "A Politics of Intellectual Property; Environmentalism on the Net?" James Boyle claimed for instance that the more we move towards a world in which the message, rather than the medium, is the focus of conceptual and economic interest, the more central intellectual property becomes as a means of the exercise of power.[9] Already in 1997 he made the claim that in the information age, ownership and control of information are the most important forms of power.[10] Additionally, he claimed further that this, as a statement, was so well accepted, that it has even become a cliché, and that one could "get away with saying in a *law review article* without footnote support".[11] This of course bears on the much wider biopolitical question namely how can we ever speak of a democratic power balance if ownership and control of information is part of the capitalist machine and as such not fairly distributed? That in turn borders on Foucault's discussion in *Discipline and Punish*,[12] something which Deleuze too commented upon. Deleuze wrote in the essay "Postscript on the Societies of Control":

> In the societies of control [...] what is important is no longer either a signature or a number, but a code: the code is a password, while on the other hand disciplinary societies are regulated by *watchwords* (as much as from the point of view of integration as from that of resistance). The numerical language of control is made of codes that mark access to information, or reject it. We no longer find ourselves dealing with mass/individual pair. Individuals have become *"dividuals"* and masses, samples, data, markets or *"banks"*. [...] The disciplinary man was a discontinuous producer of energy, but the man of control is undulatory, in orbit, in a continuous network.[13]

9 Boyle, 1997.
10 Boyle, 1997.
11 Ironically I provide a footnote to that very statement, (emphasis in original), Boyle, 1997: 87.
12 Foucault, 1991.
13 Deleuze, 1992: 5.

It is an insightful observation, particularly bearing in mind that it was written in the beginning of the 1990s, where concepts as e.g. Big Data could only be conceived as figments of imagination. The argument is especially interesting as Deleuze is pointing out that in the society of control – arguably a society that very much resembles the digital knowledge society, which is also enabled by the global intellectual property construct – we have moved beyond the mass/individual pairings and individuals have quite literally become dividuals, banks of data (Big Data!), spaces of and for mass information. Certainly, I am stressing a similar line of reasoning here in terms of the artwork as hyperobject, as a bank of data that has latched onto the human being, making itself as well as the human an information carrying organism, a posthuman, controlled and governed by data. As such, the human as hyperobject is inscribed in the capitalist machine, always already part of it, and not separate or outside it. This chapter's analytical endeavour must therefore begin and be grounded in the circumstances of today, that is in a society governed by the old concepts but fully embedded in the posthuman digital knowledge society and the knowledge economy.

6.2 Schizophrenia: intellectual property v. capitalism

Today, we find intellectual property legislation as a sophisticated legal construct, one that has been around for at least 600 years.[14] It governs knowledge, power, information, the creative expressions and output, and per default, economy and democracy. However, the idea here is not to chart the evolution of intellectual property or indeed copyright law in order to arrive at the concept of the cultural commons. Rather, the intent is to use the theoretical approach laid out in Chapters 2 and 3 where rhizomatic jurisprudence and artworks as hyperobjects were presented, and to add on the concept of the commons that was introduced in the previous chapter, in order to read intellectual property law rhizomatically within global advanced capitalism and the digital knowledge economy. It also allows the analysis to follow the lines of flight and processes of deterritorialisation and movement of global intellectual property law. The purpose is not to present a critique of current intellectual property law per se, but to follow its potentiality and connectability, specifically towards the concept of the cultural commons. This can mean at points having to look back at the legal history of intellectual property law but not in order to describe the evolution of it, but rather to reveal the existing creative

14 Counting from the first Venetian privileges of the fifteenth century, that are commonly accepted as the first forms of IP law. There are other instances of intellectual property-like laws that date back thousands of years BC also, but it is generally accepted that the Venetian privileges were the predecessors to the modern intellectual property laws.

potential that is (always) already there within the current legal construct. And while doing that we need to keep connecting intellectual property law to (the schizophrenic, as we soon shall see) capitalism.

As has been established so far, the big project that Deleuze and Guattari collaborated on was *Capitalism and Schizophrenia*, or their elaboration on the schizophrenic nature of capitalism. Let us start there then. Charles Ramond summarises, aptly in my view, the Deleuzeoguattarian approach to capitalism and its schizophrenic nature in the following manner:

> This unexpected association of "capitalism", "schizophrenia" and "revolution" shows indisputably the authors' recognition of there being a positive dimension to capitalism. The point at which the authors realise that their position with regards to capitalism is "*ambiguous*" becomes quite clear from that which has been stressed.[15]

Ramond directs our attention towards this unexpected association that Deleuze/Guattari make between capitalism and schizophrenia. They, Ramond claims, seem to have a position vis-à-vis capitalism that can only be described as ambiguous. In the article "Deleuzian Capitalism" Frédéric Vandenberghe seems to be arriving at a similar conclusion:

> Needless to say that I am not claiming that Deleuze's libertarian critique of capitalism was anti-critical or phony from the start and that Deleuze is somehow the Giddens of the 1970s: a neo-liberal disguised as a libertarian, or Thatcher on LSD. What I am claiming is, rather, that capitalism has *progressively integrated the critique of capitalism into its mode of functioning*, with the result that capitalism appears stronger than ever, whereas the critique of capitalism seems rather disarmed.[16]

Or as William E. Connolly explains it elsewhere:

> To put it another way, we still don't know what capitalism can become, even though its density and fragility give us reason to *worry about the worst.* Deleuze pursues this issue through a multi-tiered conception of time as becoming, with periodic forks in climate, asteroid showers, religious movements, new instruments of investment, technological

15 (my translation and my emphasis), "Cette association inattendue du 'capitalisme' de la 'schizophrénie' et de la 'revolution' indique incontestablement la reconnaissance par les auteurs d'une dimension positive du capitalisme. [...] On voit bien, dans l'expression que j'ai soulignée, à quel point les auteurs se rendent compte que leur position vis à vis capitalisme peut elle-même être considérée comme 'ambiguë'." Ramond, in Campagnolo, Ramond and de Saint-Victor, 2010: 110.

16 Vandenberghe, 2008: 879.

> developments, invasions, and state priorities, etc. engendering *a capitalist assemblage in which we can intervene but never master.* To the extent either Marx or Habermas was tempted by the mastery project, *Deleuze breaks with each.*[17]

Intellectual property law rests on the same common structural feature as capital, namely that it is constructed (and understood) as capital and property that can be possessed with a corresponding private rights construction – intellectual property rights qua individual rights, part of private law. Acquiring copyrights means acquiring rights *as property*, that has already been established a number of times during the course of this book. However, if we follow the Deleuzeoguattarian analysis of capitalism it becomes obvious that capitalism in itself is not as binary and as structured, or striated, as law (pretends to be). This means that, being schizophrenic, capitalism for Deleuze and Guattari does not necessarily pose the idea of property and the idea of public interest as each other's opposites, because within the capitalist sphere they are both one and the same: commodities. In fact, also within the free market there is a constant connection that happens between the goods and, as Hardt and Negri put it, bodies, actions, ideas, knowledges, fantasies, images, etc. That does not mean that capitalism is unproblematic, it just means that it too is far more complicated than usually described, and not necessarily adverse to a concept of the commons. Capitalism functions both as a territorialising and a deterritorialising machine. Hence its schizophrenic nature. Hence Deleuze and Guattari's ambiguous relationship to it.

The capitalist reterritorialisation of information and code is particularly interesting to comment on in the context of intellectual property law and the commons. This has been dubbed by Boyle as the second enclosure movement. Boyle refers to the first enclosure of the commons, which according to him took place in England between the fifteenth and ninetieth centuries, encompassing a long historical "process of fencing off common land and turning it into private property". With the advent of global intellectual property rights "once again things that were formally thought of as either common property or uncommodifiable are being covered with new, or newly extended, property rights."[18] The enclosure of the intellectual commons is thus a consequence of what Boyle refers to as expansion of intellectual property rights and the private paradigm that have taken over resources previously held in common. The territorialising intellectual property law thus grounds or striates the capitalist project too, slows it down, delimits its alternatives. This is so established by now that *I*

17 (My emphasis throughout), Connolly, 2008.
18 Boyle, 2003: 33–34 (first quote) and 37 (second quote).

too could now get away with saying that in an academic book without footnote support.[19]

Schizophrenic capitalism has proven that it is quite able to cope with and adapt more easily to societal changes, while (dogmatic/positive) law always seems to treat lines of flight that occur as un-imagined encounters that each time appear to upset the entire legal system anew. This leads to a "fundamental conflict between the efficiency with which markets spread information and the incentives to acquire information"[20] or "[t]here is always something that flees and escapes the [law], something that is not controllable, or at least not yet controlled".[21]

6.2.1 Type of ownership: privilege...

The two legislative strategies that have been employed so far in order to construct ownership of the artwork have been to construct it as either a *privilege* or a *right*. The two are obviously vastly different, and both affect ownership and control in their own particular ways. It is however probably not merely an exercise in semantics when asking whether a possession in one's creation is formulated as a privilege or a right. It goes back to the very question posed by Madero that I started this chapter with. Who owns the painted tablet?

As we know, the first regulations of intellectual creations came in the form of privileges. The rights construction is a comparatively recent one and originally, an Anglo-Saxon, model. Tom W. Bell argues that while intellectual property certainly has some property-like attributes that still the *privilege* construct might be a far more correct description of what it actually entails (a privilege to enclose what was previously in the commons), and that the legal concept should in that vein be called intellectual *privilege* as opposed to intellectual property *right*.[22] Bell's use of the concept of privilege is a critique of the Hohfeldian use of the term "privilege". Bell suggests that Hohfeld's use of the term mistakenly makes a connection between a privilege and a *liberty*.[23] While his may be an interesting theoretical exercise in itself I shall leave it at that here. Interestingly, and as indirectly picked up by Jessica Litman, when privilege is discussed in this context, it is usually the author's privileges and not the

19 But as I am not of the same confident nature as James Boyle, do see e.g.: Boyle, 1997–98, 2003 and all of Lessig's works quoted in this book!

20 Grossman and Stiglitz, 1980.

21 The word in brackets that I have replaced by "law" was "society" in the original quote by Vandenberghe, 2008: 878.

22 Bell, 2007.

23 Bell, 2007.

public's privilege to information and access that are being referred to.[24] Litman writes:

> The detailed bright lines have evolved, through accident of technological change, into all-inclusive categories of infringers with tiny pock-marks of express exemptions and *privileges*, and undefined and largely unacknowledged free zones of people-who-are-technically-infringing-but-will-never-get-sued, like your next-door neighbor who duplicates his wife's authorized copy of Windows ® rather than buying his own from the computer store.[25]

Keeping in mind that Litman wrote this in 1996 she can be forgiven for thinking (perhaps naively) that the phenomenon of "people-who-are-technically-infringing-but-will-never-get-sued" was going to be everlasting. In the age of Digital Millennium Act, IPRED[26] and their national peers, we now *know* that rights owners do not have any "pangs of consciousness", when it comes to suing the private infringers, i.e. their own consumers.[27] Thus, when privilege versus *rights* is discussed then the concept of privilege is not strong enough in comparison with commercial rights constructions that can provide strong enforcement possibilities and incentives that can generate direct and indirect revenue. And when privilege as befalling the *public* and not the *owner* is discussed then it is too strong of a grant as it, conversely, does not allow for the abovementioned type of enforcement, as the ownership of property is not clean, it comes with a burden of public privilege.

Privilege, as such, can therefore not be understood as a clear concept. A privilege in intellectual works must be first and foremost understood as a concept that spans over several different interests, the artist, the public, the industry, the state etc. Somebody must grant the privilege at the expense of someone else, as Lord Macaulay phrased it "[f]or the sake of the good we must submit to the evil; but the evil ought not to last a day longer than is necessary for the purpose of securing the good."[28] Lord Macaulay clearly

24 Litman, 1996.

25 (My emphasis), Litman, 1996: 42.

26 Directive 2004/48/EC of the European Parliament and of the Council of 29 April 2004 on the enforcement of intellectual property rights (also known as IPR Enforcement Directive or IPRED).

27 A fairly recent example from the film industry involves Voltage Pictures who in May 2010 initiated a lawsuit against 5000 John Doe defendants for illegally distributing the film The Hurt Locker. Voltage Pictures then amended their original complaint in April 2011 bringing the total number of defendants to around 24 500 (24 595.2 to be exact). By the end of 2011 more than 250 000 individuals had been sued for similar alleged acts. DeBriyn, 2012.

28 See Gordon, 1988-1989.

expressed that with the current copyright construction in mind; however one might attempt to structure it, some evil will always need to be endured. The question is whether this "evil" that Lord Macaulay is referring to is the privilege or the rights construct, or something else. The fact that the notion of property has migrated into the privilege realm means that the demarcation between a privilege and rights-based copyright is blurred.

6.2.2 ...or right?

Chapter 5 above made a connection between the Lockean notion of acquisition of property and the rights-based construction in law. To recapitulate briefly, I presented the Lockean idea of there being a "natural" connection between object-labour-ownership. Thus, the person who invests labour into something becomes the owner of the said object. And as a consequence then, many argue that the justification for intellectual property rests on a similar notion of the author/inventor being entitled to the exclusive right in the work/invention, because mental labour was invested in its creation.[29] This Lockean idea of course requires a cognitive division between the body and the mind and as such a reasoning that people are entitled to own what they put labour into (through property rights) and intellectual labour into (through intellectual property rights). This dichotomy is of course problematic in a Deleuzeoguattarian setting where an assemblage always involves an immanence of both.

In that vein, and by applying Hardt/Negri to immaterial property it was argued that while it clearly is possible to privatise and materialise also intellectual intangible works within the institute of property, it is often a somewhat forced endeavour, especially in the context of the digital spheres and the hyperobjects that are always elsewhere. Yet the idea of holding as property that which a person, or a group of persons for that matter, produces by their own initiative, intelligence and industry cannot be fully negated. The rights construction that underpins intellectual law today seems to be fully enabled to subordinate under the capitalist machine. The problem with the capitalist machine on the other hand, is that it empowers the private interest to such an extent that the public interest in its turn gets negated, the public sphere shrinks, and so the legal construction of intellectual property rights becomes increasingly powerless to balance the public against the private.

This is particularly true when, as Hardt and Negri very well point out, capitalism becomes biopolitical[30] or, as I have referred to it here, advanced.[31] Here I am making an even more violent claim, namely that

29 See e.g. Craig, 2011.
30 Hardt and Negri, 2009: 131.
31 See e.g. Käll, 2017.

capitalism is becoming (or probably always was) not only schizophrenic but also *nomadic* in Deleuzeoguattarian terms. The exclusive rights construction that allows ownership of intellectual production forms part of such a process. With a rights construction-based intellectual property law (which is territorializing, through e.g. national laws) the nomadic capitalist machine (which is deterritorialising), is enabled to encroach (through e.g. the TRIPS agreement, striate and reterritorialise) that which we are looking for here, namely the (global) commons. Slavoj Zizek develops such a line of reasoning further. He writes that privatisation involves an iterant violent act that overtakes three types of commons, namely:

- *the commons of culture,* the immediately socialized forms of 'cognitive' capital, primarily language, our means of communication and education, but also the shared infrastructure of public transport, electricity, the postal system, and so on;
- *the commons of external nature,* threatened by pollution and exploitation (from oil to rain forests and the natural habitat itself);
- *the commons of internal nature* (the biogenetic inheritance of humanity); with the new biogenetic technology, the creation of a New Man in the literal sense of changing human nature becomes a realistic prospect.[32]

Zizek links the "inappropriateness of the notion of *private property* to [...] 'intellectual property'".[33] What Zizek describes here is not an indication of the biopolitics of capitalism but a *nomadology* of capitalism, the new wave of capitalism, the capitalism that keeps evolving rhizomatically through and with the given societal lines of flight. In the knowledge economy capital ownership of knowledge has been enabled by the exclusive rights construct, particularly the intellectual property rights. This means that Zizek's and Hardt/Negri's readings can be nuanced with Deleuzeoguattarian (re/de)territorialisation. Reading law as a territorialising machine adds to the schizophrenic nature of the biopolitics and then the nomadism of capitalism.

6.2.3 Right and privilege

In order to continue the discussion concerning the right and privilege balance, or lack thereof, I am exploring the Deleuzeoguattarian link between right and privilege in the commons. I have already established that there seems to exist an underlying assumption in intellectual property law that an intellectual creation is a type of *invention* where creators are seen as inventors, creating works *ex nihilo.* Boyle distinguishes this paradigmic

32 (Emphasis in original), Zizek, 2009: 91.
33 (Emphasis in origina), Ibid.

conception of the idea of invention with the idea of *information* and the notion of developing intellectual creations that are based on already existing works (and as such not inventing anything *ex nihilo*). This was particularly clear from the Richard Prince case above, where nothing new was, strictly speaking, created. Lewis Hyde comments on the creative effort in a similar manner, first providing a quote from Rimbaud, that I take the liberty to re-quote here:

> Right now I'm debauching myself as much as possible. Why? I want to be a poet, and I'm working to make myself a *seer*… It's a matter of getting to the unknown by the derangement of *all the senses*… The suffering is tremendous, but one must be strong, to be born a poet, and know that's what I am. It's not at all my fault. It's wrong to say: *I think*. One should say: *I am thought*…
>
> I is someone else. Too bad for the wood that discovers it's a violin…!

Hyde then reads this passage as the inversion of the Cartesian "I think therefore I am", and in the inversion a "non-I", or rather "another-I" is revealed. This "another-I" is also more-than-human in nature as it seems to be referring to dead matter, things, too. The violin that discovers… The creator thus becomes a vessel carrying everything that already exists. Or in Picasso's more poignant words, the creator becomes a thief as "All artists borrow; great artists steal."[34] This means that Rimbaud's utterance represents Boyle's idea of *information*. We never invent anything, we just gather information, or conversely we are gathered as information (again Big Data). This was also obvious from the Prince case. Why is that interesting for this analysis? First of all, it is important to understand that the notion of the *ex nihilo* creation, which is the pervasive and perverted assumption that underpins current intellectual property law, is problematic. Scholars such as Boyle have already established how this is the case. Second of all, is that the juxtaposition of the two models *invention* and *information*, the I and the another-I, the human and the more-than-human, as each other's opposites has also become problematic.

When fusing the *invention* and the *information* strands, connected by the notion of the concept of the author as not (only) a unit, a legal subject, but *something else* – and as we have seen so far – a hyperobject, it also becomes clear how the notions of right and privilege converge. An author that does not think, *but that is thought*, an author that does not invent, *but that steals*,

34 Hyde, 2012: 202. As a matter of fact, it is disputed to whom this quote really can be attributed and there are a number of variations of it. Some claim that T.S. Elliot said "Immature poets imitate; mature poets steal"; and that it was Picasso who said that "Good artists copy. Great artists steal." Or it might have been Stravinsky who said "Lesser artists borrow; great artists steal." For more variations see Quote Investigator: http://quoteinvestigator.com/2013/03/06/artists-steal/

an author that is not human but a (hyper)object, relational to any other hyperobject requires both private rights and public access privileges in order to create. Both a right and a privilege. This very movement of entanglement must be acknowledged in intellectual property law in order to create a commons concept.

6.3 Embodiment: content v. container[35]

Let us then return to Madero's *Tabula Picta* and the question posed therein, namely who owns a painting, the person who painted it or the person who owns and has provided the artist with the wooden tablet? The one who provided the immaterial (creation) or the one that provided the material (tablet). We are going to keep exploring this idea, keeping in mind the notion of the artwork as a hyperobject (remember: viscous, non-local, subject to temporal undulation, phasing, interobjective). What is now interesting to discuss is how the construction of the ownership concepts for such hyperobjects converge in both material and immaterial things, where both the painting and the tablet are relevant. Reading the medieval legal codes Madero was able to show that rather than assuming a binary reasoning the "medieval file of the *tabula picta* evidenced how the legal categories constantly reformulated the classification based on variable and crossed opposites; and the plurality of those rationales signalled that materiality was not a given".[36] Finding an unexpected relationship between materials and *species* in medieval law, Madero's study opens up for further legal studies of the hyperobjects, its materialities and connections to *species*: to be one, to take root, to unite, to blend, to mix, to prevail.[37] How does that connect to intellectual property law and commons as discussed here?

The intellectual property discourse concerning artworks often relies on two concepts namely the (immaterial) content and (material) carrier. Even if the two are not always uncomplicated to differentiate it could be said that the first one, the *content*, is assumed to be that which is being expressed and is as such immaterial and the second one, the *carrier* or the form, is assumed to refer to how that is being expressed or communicated, and through which channels, and as such it provides the materiality. The dichotomy *content v. carrier* may appear to be a new one, but the dichotomies *content v. form*, or *expression v. form*, are certainly ancient. In this section I want to push this even further to the idea of the container, that we saw in Henri Lefebvre, pp. 129 aa in connection to space, i.e. container in the sense of a network or an "empty" space that contains people and objects, in order to add on the spatial to the discussion.

35 Lefebvre, H. 1991.
36 Madero, 2010: 3.
37 Madero, 2010: 3.

This can be broached by beginning in a classical concept in intellectual property law – namely the so called *first sale doctrine.* In order to balance the public and the private rights, the stipulation of first sale means that once a copy or an embodiment of a work has been sold (classical example is a copy of a book), the person who purchased the material object (the book) may in their turn sell it, lend it to friends etc., but it does not mean that the purchaser of the book can do the same with the underlying copyright in let us say the novel that has been embodied in the book form. Thus a dichotomy between content and carrier is created and upheld. This creates a space almost akin to public domain that exists between the material object and the immaterial copyright. Hyde writes:

> "First sale" is a limitation on an owner's exclusive right such that once you have bought a book (or CD, or video disc, or map…) you may do almost anything with it that you want. You may return to it multiple times, read it to your child, copy bits into a journal, give it to a friend, loan it to a student, sell it to a stranger…. You may not print and sell copies, that is true, but all these other things you may do. The right of first sale creates an *object specific,* down-stream public domain; the copyright owner's control ends at the point of purchase.[38]

However when the first-sale rights are taken into a domain where works are digital both in terms of content and in terms of carrier, as is e.g. the case with music, then the dichotomy becomes problematic. Many business models today focus for instance specifically on streaming, that is an alternative to downloading, where the content is provided to the user in a manner that is more similar to broadcasting, rather than the idea of purchasing a physical commodity-thing in which the content is contained. It is a matter of making content available on an on-demand basis rather than on a download-to-own basis. This can be exemplified by Spotify and iTunes business models. The Spotify business model is an on-demand streaming one while the iTunes model is a download-to-own one. When it comes to content streamed through Spotify, the consumer is never given the opportunity to shift format of the content, e.g. move it from the Spotify platform onto a physical carrier in order to for instance lend it to somebody else. In iTunes on the other hand the consumer purchases a copy, and the first sale doctrine kicks in. This was clarified by the ECJ in the so called *UsedSoft v Oracle* case.[39] There, it was put forward that regardless of whether the content had been "embodied" in a digital or an analogue carrier, the first sale doctrine would be applicable. Interestingly, and as a

38 Hyde, 2012: 66.

39 C/128-11 UsedSoft, see also Capitol Records, LLC v. ReDigi Inc., Redigi [USA] and C-419/13 Art & Allposters International.

matter of a short divergence, in *UsedSoft* the "content" that was discussed was in fact a contract for digital services, where providing services through a database was seen as a packaged copy formulated in copyright law, as "content". That the contract itself has become content clearly shows the collapse of the industrial dichotomy between the contract and the product (or carrier). When the contract becomes the very good that is being traded, or more accurately the *service*, then the carrier becomes unnecessary. It also means that what is protected is an ongoing service, a process, and not a finished, finite, "expression" – which of course also challenges the dichotomy form-expression. And so on…

But to bring it back in the context of this study. In a hyperobject setting where the content and the expression of the artwork converge and when both the content and the carrier get mixed up and become in a way one and the same, this dichotomy has fully collapsed. The difference made between expression and form thus becomes equally impossible to uphold. In order to merge the two in a legal concept of a commons we need to do this exercise and show how content and carrier, or expression and form, may be approached in a spatial setting of networks, becoming a lawscape.

6.3.1 Content-carrier entanglement: Dominium and object extinction

In medieval and Roman law, the issue of ownership of a written or painted object always came down to the determination of *dominium*.[40] However, if the object was somehow extinguished, e.g. if it was lost, then the dominium became extinguished too. Today of course, in the digital setting, as well as when artworks are approached as hyperobjects, it is no longer possible to describe the content either as object-centric or as fully immaterial. It becomes increasingly difficult to enclose artworks, as well as to keep the underlying intellectual property from being infringed upon. Let me schematically show the development of object centricity using music as an example (see Table 6.1).

To illustrate this further, let us look at two other examples provided by Hyde. He describes the electronic publication of Lewis Carroll's 1865 book *Alice in Wonderland* (in the public domain, outside the scope of copyright), that comes with a copyright notice that prohibits (enforced with digital rights management) the copying, printing, lending of the book, but also precludes the book from being *given to someone else* and *read aloud*.[41] Hyde's second example is the electronic version of the US Constitution (again, in the public domain) offered on sale via Amazon.com, which makes it

40 Madero, 2010: 15.
41 Hyde, 2012: 67.

Table 6.1

	Content	*Carrier*	*Object-centric?*
Concert/live public performance	Preformed	Live	No
Music on a long play disk	Physically inscribed on object	Long play disk + stereo	Yes
Music on cassette	Physically inscribed on object	Cassette + Walkman	Yes
Music on CD	Physically inscribed on object	CD + CD player	Yes
Digital download: peer-to-peer	File	Downloaded immaterial file + computer	No but can be downloaded on a carrier such as a CD
Digital download: bit torrent	Parts of file	Downloaded immaterial part of file + computer or portable devise such as mobile phone or tablet	No but can be downloaded on a carrier such as a CD
Digital streaming: e.g. Spotify	File	Streamed immaterial file + computer or portable devise such as mobile phone or tablet	No, cannot be downloaded, but portable

impossible for readers to print it more than twice a year and directly expresses that hacking of the code enforcing this restriction is illegal.[42] To link it with the second enclosure movement:

> [I]ntellectual property rights have become *broader* (covering more kinds of information, *deeper* (giving rights holders greater power), and *more punitive* (imposing greater penalties on infringers). Supplemental measures have also been introduced to increase the technological control of rights holders and to counter the way digital technologies facilitate copying. Anticircumvention laws have been introduced [...]. This shift has been called a '*second enclosure movement*' [...][43]

Therefore, and as a consequence of the second enclosure movement and through e.g. digital rights management all intellectual works have been placed predominantly within the property paradigm. Property is here defined as the right of a single individual to be the gatekeeper with respect to a resource and to act autocratically with respect to decisions about its

42 Hyde, 2012: 67.
43 (My emphases throughout), Kapczynski, in Krikorian and Kapczynski, 2010: 24.

use. This vision of property is sustained by the notion that only the individual owner, and not the state, community, or nonowners, may make decisions about the price or terms of transaction of that property.[44]

Amy Kapczynski refers to this type of property and ownership as a *despotic dominion*, quoting Peter Drahos, as a type of "*dominum* over the abstract object of intellectual property [which goes a long way toward maintaining the] *imperium*."[45] Seen from a Deleuzeoguattarian point of view it is a construct that territorialises and striates the smooth space of the content in a digital setting. As such it can be detrimental to the exploitation of works commercially in the long run, particularly if access to information is seen as an ingredient in the creation of content as opposed to approaching content as being created *ex nihilo* and embodied in a material copy. Nonetheless, there is large potential here regarding the creation of a legal concept of the commons. And as it is becoming all the more apparent, Deleuze and Guattari's theory provides us with the appropriate tools to unleash this potential in a manner than transcends binary opposites between open–closed, market–state, even capitalism–state, freedom–fetter, content–carrier, etc. As Jeffery Atteberry writes:

> Perfectly aware of the potentially duplicitous character of bourgeois freedom, Gilles Deleuze and Félix Guattari have described the process of capital's development in terms of a 'generalised decoding flows' and a dynamic of 'deterritorilization'. The current informationalist regime and the discourses attending to it – including that of the A2K movement – fit nicely within Deleuze and Guattari's paradigm. The informationalist mode of production represents a new order of decoded flows. The freeing of information promises to restructure the relations of production, replacing vertically integrated structures of production within horizontally networked ones.[46]

So what conclusion can be drawn here in terms of the intellectual property construct, the materiality of the artwork as hyperobject and the creation of a cultural commons? As we have moved through centuries from the *tabula* in Justinian code and arrived at the digital *tablet* today where once again the content and carrier converge, we can more clearly see that objects governed by intellectual property are in no way only immaterial or "intellectual" in nature. The insights of the medieval jurists might come in handy in understanding the materiality of intellectual property law today that also demonstrates the collapse of certain taken for granted dichotomies.

44 Krikorian and Kapczynski, 2010: 26–27.

45 Ibid. p. 26. Quote taken from Drahos, 1995: 16.

46 Atteberry, in Krikorian and Kapczynski, 2010: 341. Atteberry is quoting Deleuze and Guattari, 2004: 224 in his quote.

However, in the collapse of the dichotomies, a sphere for the commons has been revealed. Before we leave this chapter let us finally move away from the content and return to the concept of the author in intellectual property law.

6.3.2 Corporality: community v. author

I have already started to unpack the notion of the author in the Richard Prince case above. First I discussed the so called "death of the author" in modern and contemporary art, and the idea of the fetishised image of the author as transmitted through current constructs of legal subjectivity and copyright law as flawed or at least difficult to apply today. I began to deconstruct the romantic notion of the author in order to show that under the construction of an "individual" there lies, in the words of Deleuze a "dividual" – a legion. I want to open up the notion of the author as transmitted through copyright law to a community, which is the final section to be addressed before we move on to the construction of the commons.

In order to that I want to connect intellectual property law and its constructs to cultural heritage law. Before that is done, a quick disclaimer. It may perhaps be understood as transgressive to draw copyright and cultural heritage law together in order to make a point about the connection between the notion of the author and the notion of the community. As the one (intellectual property law) is usually placed inside a private law paradigm and the other (cultural heritage law) inside a public international law paradigm, it may appear as the two have different rationales and are as such incommensurable. However, as might already be clear from the approach to jurisprudence so far, and from particularly a Deleuzeo-guattarian reading, what is generally (or dogmatically) considered a transgression may in fact form a "becoming" within this setting. That being said, in order to make the point about the author and community without too many transgressive sidesteps I use a very classical example where the two meet namely in claims for intellectual property from indigenous peoples regarding protection of traditional knowledge and cultural expressions. It is precisely in this instance where intellectual property law and cultural heritage law meet and converge.

I will not dwell on defining traditional knowledge or traditional cultural expressions of indigenous peoples more than how they are addressed in the UN Declaration on the Rights of Indigenous Peoples from 2007 (DRIPS), namely:

> Art. 31
>
> 1. Indigenous peoples have the right to maintain, control, protect and develop their cultural heritage, traditional knowledge and traditional cultural expressions, as well as the manifestations of

> their sciences, technologies and cultures, including human and genetic resources, seeds, medicines, knowledge of the properties of fauna and flora, oral traditions, literatures, designs, sports and traditional games and visual and performing arts. They also have the right to maintain, control, protect and develop their intellectual property over such cultural heritage, traditional knowledge, and traditional cultural expressions.[47]

Clearly, as stated in art. 31, traditional cultural expressions and traditional knowledge may very well be able to fall or be claimed under an intellectual property construction such as copyright, trademark or patent right. However, when the above quoted section in DRIPS is studied we can also see that it covers a wider field than what would traditionally be captured by intellectual property law, such as e.g. the practices of a community. The question that I briefly then want to explore here is how a private property right granted to an individual corresponds to a communal right granted to an entire community.

There are a number of issues that could be raised here. The first one is, if we are briefly to return to the discussion raised in the beginning of this chapter, namely the western nature of the intellectual property construct. We can pose the question whether it is at all appropriate to apply intellectual property law on non-western indigenous knowledge and traditions. With the TRIPS agreement, as we saw above, a North–South divide has been implemented in the global intellectual property regime, where the western paradigm of course dominates. If and when indigenous communities want to attempt to claim intellectual property then they have to do so by fitting in their claim within a western discourse and legal construct, for instance they have to designate an individual "author" or "inventor" of any traditional knowledge or cultural expression at hand. Of course this is not necessarily how creative and intellectual production happens in many indigenous communities. The idea of individual expression is not necessarily prevailing in (m)any of these communities.

And while the idea of a communal intellectual property right is still foreign for e.g. copyright law today, many indigenous communities are turning precisely to intellectual property rights in order to gain protection for their traditional knowledge and cultural expressions. This is done by e.g. registering traditional patterns as trademarks, or writing down oral stories or folklore so that they become fixed and as such subject to copyright. However, turning communal traditional expressions and knowledge into private and individual intellectual property assets is not straightforward of course, as the construct of intellectual property does not directly lend itself to these types of communal interests.

47 UN Declaration on the Rights of Indigenous Peoples 2007 (DRIPS).

Another issue is the duration of intellectual property rights that is limited in time. The cultural expressions of indigenous communities often go back further in time than the general duration of e.g. copyright that is 70 years after the death of the author. Here, the death of the author does not refer to the philosophical idea as raised by Foucault and Barthes and discussed in the Richard Prince case above, but quite literally, the death of the author who is/was the initial holder of the copyright.

However, and as has become more apparent throughout the discussion here, these constructs of individual expression and definable author are of course problematic within the western context too as we have seen. When the author and the artwork are revealed to be hyperobjects and vastly more spatiotemporal in nature than assumed in intellectual property law, then the aspect of community within the author is revealed. It is this very space, the in-between the author and the community where the potential for a commons construction happens.

This also bears on the discussions concerning cultural appropriation that indigenous communities have been fighting against. Their cultural expressions and traditional knowledge are of course connected to a wider claim than the possibility to commercially exploit their own cultural output. It of course has to do with broader political aspirations and rights to e.g. self determination and legal recognition as a community. Here, we reach another cul-de-sac because whereas within the construct of intellectual property law there appears to be a fetishisation of the individual; in cultural heritage law conversely we seem to be creating an equally problematic fetishisation of the community. So how do we in that case define community? Geographically? Culturally? Legally? *Genetically*?

6.3.3 Community in public domain

What I am exploring here is the space that is being opened up between the notion of a community and the construction of the individual author or inventor. In *Communitas* Roberto Esposito[48] traces the origins of community, claiming that community is what binds people together either through property or through an obligation/debt.[49] This is a different conception of community than the ones presented in Chapter 5 by e.g. Nancy (the heterogeneous being-in-common) or by Keenan (the construction of a community belonging in and through subversive property). And as we know, in for instance international public law and in cultural heritage law, particularly where the notion of community is more prevailing than in intellectual property law, community is distinct from other collective nouns such as that of the "state" or the "nation". A community, or a people, is instead seen as a

48 Esposito, 2010.
49 Esposito, 2010: 6.

group that is bound by a common cultural identity (as opposed to a political identity for nations, and legal identity for states).[50]

The notion of community in intellectual property law is thus still a rather foreign concept, and is only perhaps obliquely touched upon through for instance the constructs of the public domain or the public interest. The public however, appears to be a much looser collection of people than a "community". The idea of the "public domain" for instance as imagined in intellectual property law rather appears to be any collection of people that is not the author him/herself. Let us stay with the word "domain" for a second. The word refers to both a territory as well as to a ruler or government, but it can also have a more abstract meaning connoting a sphere of knowledge or some other activity. Etymologically it comes from the Latin word *dominus*, that means both master and owner. It is also used to denote a ruler or a saviour such as e.g. Jesus Christ. It refers to a communal or a public territory, that can be both physical and abstract.

If we follow the term back in history by connecting it to intellectual property law and intellectual property resources it too goes back to Roman law. In the next chapter I will in more detail explore the various "public" non-exclusive ownership constructs that stem from precisely this legal tradition and their relevance for the construct of the commons However, the notion of the public domain is also, more pertinently, a concept within current intellectual property law. This is one of the limitations on intellectual property rights, where everything that is not within the scope of an intellectual property provision, will be in the public domain. So for instance, public domain encompasses all works that are no longer in term (for copyright 70 years after the death of the author), or if it is a matter of an idea that has not been "expressed", or if it is a discovery and not invention in patent law, etc. A classic example of works in the public domain are Shakespeare's works. But it could also be a question of works where the rights holder has given up or renounced their rights, a classic example here is when the inventor of the polio vaccine Jonas Salk refused to patent his invention, even though he could. As the story goes, when asked why he refused to patent, he replied rhetorically "Would you patent the sun?" meaning that this was a public good that should not be kept in his private control. Other examples of content considered to be in the public domain are traditional knowledge and practises. Which of course brings us back to where we started this section, namely in the intersection of the community and the individual.

It is precisely within the discussion concerning what is public domain and what is not that the tension between the community and the individual

50 Professor Fiona Macmillan developed this argument during her course The Legal Protection of Cultural Heritage (Protezione giuridica del patrimonio culturale) (II semestre) at Univeristà Degli Studi Roma Tre, Rome 2016.

claims become particularly visible. In order to create, the authors have to use knowledge and inspiration considered to be common, in the public domain, open to everybody to engage with and according to the rationale of intellectual property laws *appropriate*, and turn it into private property. Naturally, and as we have seen throughout the course of this book, it also means that creation seldom happens *ex nihilo*, but rather by, as the Newtonian saying goes, "standing upon the shoulders of giants" that came before us.

Therefore, the sphere of the public domain that marks the borders of the intellectual property construct has not only to do how with how intellectual property can be commercially exploited and for how long. Content that is created, invented, designed and placed within the enclosure of private intellectual property rights already contains common knowledges, traditions, practices, it already contains a collection or constellation of available information about the community from which it stems. As such it is connected to the formation of a community, identity, belonging and knowledge about who we are, or who we could be, it holds up our bodies, as Keenan has expressed it. This connects the contents with the intellectual property constructs to the rights and interests not only of the current communities but also of future generations. Furthermore, it is of course as such also connected to democracy, access to information, production of knowledge, creation of lifestyles, etc. Arguably, this is particularly apparent today, in the digital knowledge society. This means that at the borders of intellectual property rights, where we meet the public domain, there is information and knowledge needed for everybody in order to form communities, identities, belongings etc.

Which brings us to the end of this chapter. Can it still really be said that cultural heritage law has nothing in common with intellectual property law? Can it still be said that ownership of artworks ought to befall individuals alone? Stating that the old concepts such as heritage and property, individual and community are completely separate, means accepting certain assumptions, such as for instance that content is created out of nothing, invented by a single author/genius, who is granted property rights in such a creation through a Lockean understanding of work and value creation. Throughout this chapter I have tried to explicitly open up these assumptions on which the rationale of intellectual property rests, in order partly to show the connection to e.g. cultural heritage and traditional knowledge, but also in order to reveal the spaces that opened up when various old dichotomies began to collapse such as the material–immaterial, content–carrier, etc. When the collapse of these dichotomies occurs, the possibility of imagining the commons is simultaneously revealed, as it is precisely such dichotomical reasoning that has so far hindered the conception of the commons in law, as was established in Chapter 2.

In the next chapter, I will continue to discuss precisely this and connect the notion of schizophrenic capitalism, the deterritorialised (intellectual property) law, to the Deleuzeoguattarian models of possession in order to arrive at a legal formulation of the commons. Some final remarks here. This chapter began by stating that intellectual property law is now global, driven by the capitalist machine, and enforced through e.g. the TRIPS agreement as part of the WTO structure. After that I demonstrated that capitalism as power is "schizophrenic" and nomadic while (dogmatic/positive) intellectual property law is territorialising and static. Which means that the capitalist machine does not have to rely on simplified dichotomies in order to understand the exploitation of the artwork, while law relies on these dichotomies heavily, even when they can no longer be upheld. By showing the collapse of the dichotomies of right–privilege, content–carrier, public–private domain, community–individual, a critique of the static intellectual property law can be brought forward. Through this critique the collapse of the dichotomies opens up a potential, or a space, that law can fill through the construct of the commons. It is with that insight we now move into the penultimate chapter, where the legal concept of the cultural commons will be articulated.

Part 4

Legal Commons

Chapter 7

Ownership

Possessed

Commons constructions and initiatives through which access to artworks and creative content is enabled are evidently not a particularly new phenomenon. We have seen how the notion of sharing within commons-like-settings already has existed for many a century. However, it was not until the advent of the digital economy when many of the engagements with the content and sharing started to happen online that the notion of the *cultural* commons entered the discussion in earnest. For the last couple of decades legal research has grappled with the commons phenomenon, cultural or otherwise.[1] How to strike a fair balance between that which is open and available for anyone by its very nature and that which is private, and enclosed, without simultaneously creating a *tragedy of the commons* that Garrett Hardin so appropriately warned us about in the 1960s. What we are thus now arriving at are the different "solutions" or "compromises" that have recently been presented in the guise of *commons initiatives* where attempts to make the rights of the individual creator more flexible have been made, in order to benefit from a more open access and encourage sharing of works. This has been done in order to achieve a more democratic distribution of culture and in extension, knowledge. Some of these projects even offer the possibility for the rights owners to abandon all or most of their copyrights for the "common good".

1 See generally Borch and Kornberger, 2015; and Finchett-Maddock, 2016. It is, furthermore, impossible to account for all the books, articles, conferences, workshops and discussions on the topic of the (cultural) commons that have been going on in the last couple of years, here in a note. Throughout this book I have been referring to some of the most notable ones such as the books written by e.g. Lessig and Vaidhyanathan that in their turn refer to many other projects. But commons is not solely discussed as a "critical" issue, also within the field of more dogmatic studies as well as in course books, these types of discussion have not been circumvented, see e.g. Cornish, 2004, Bailey, Farrell and Mattei, 2013.

The most noteworthy commons initiative from the last decades is probably the one carried out under the umbrella name *Creative Commons*.[2] Creative Commons serves as an example of a typical commons project from the twenty-first century. I want to focus on Creative Commons here as it is the largest and the most established initiative and as such it also serves as a representative for many other commons initiatives in general. The discussion about creating such an initiative as the Creative Commons commenced when it became apparent that in the digital sphere it was increasingly difficult to draw a line between where creative inspiration stopped and where infringement of intellectual property began. It was pointed out and argued that intellectual property law in many ways *impedes creativity*. Simultaneously, it was claimed that it, intellectual property law, as such, *does not afford appropriate protection to the artist*.

This chapter will be further embedded in the Deleuzeoguattarian theory. Using the concept of the commons I arrived at in Chapter 5, forming namely as an ecology, where person-space-property are entangled, a sphere where bodies or hyperobjects are formed relationally. I will also return to one of the case studies presented in Chapter 4, in order to tie it more concretely to the idea of the commons. I want to do so particularly through the Deleuzeoguattarian forms of possession, the *sedentary* and *nomadic* models. In essence, this chapter fuses the theoretical approaches with the empirical base in order to arrive at the final discussion on the *legal*[3] concept of the cultural commons.

7.1 The Deleuzian forms of possession

The concept of the commons adopted herein is a posthumanist one, and as we have seen not presented in the sense of the opposite of private or as equal to public. Lawrence Lessig commented on the commons in the following manner:

> Commons may be rare. They may evoke tragedies. They may be hard to sustain. And at times, they certainly may interfere with the efficient use of important resources. But *commons also produce something of value*. [...] They are *environments* that commit themselves to being open.[4]

It is precisely the environmental, spatial, that makes commons a lawscape and an *ecology* as I am exploring it here. What is relevant to delve deeper into at this point are the Deleuzeoguattarian modes of possession that can

2 http://creativecommons.org/ Other noteworthy commons projects that can be mentioned in passing are iCommons, Wikimedia Commons and Science Commons. The last one is a project under the larger umbrella of the Creative Commons.

3 Here I propose we read "legal" as "statutory".

4 (My emphases throughout), Lessig, 2001: 85.

potentially handle this idea of the commons, this particular relational constellation of the private and the public entangled with property and personhood that come together in a space that is the commons. In keeping with the Deleuzeoguattarian theory, we saw in Volume I how jurisprudence can conceive of the commons in this way, and now it is being suggested that one might approach and even construct the legal concept of cultural commons by further applying Deleuze/Guattari particularly their modes of possession. This can more precisely be done by employing the possession forms that emanate from the rhizome theory, namely the already mentioned sedentary model and the nomadic model. Within such a setting possession ought not to be equated with "ownership". Rather, the modes of possession are used by Deleuze/Guattari in a more flexible manner, where to possess does not necessarily, or at all, mean "to own".

It is therefore imperative to look at the Deleuzeoguattarian modes of possession in more detail as well as joining these two concepts with the discussion concerning the commons. As I already stated, I stay with the commitment to the commons that I put forward in Chapter 5. To be more precise, I followed the development of the commons from the idea of it being a resource and commoning being resource management à la Hess and Ostrom; through to a more radical understanding à la Hardt and Negri of the commons as a network, relational, immaterial and as encompassing affect and non-human actors, where commoning needs to reach beyond the idea of mere resource distribution; and finally I arrived at an idea of the commons as a relational posthuman ecology à la Burdon/Morton/Nancy and commoning as a verb, a process always encompassing a shared, relational space between hyperobjects and (subversive) property, with an open ended production of subjectivity, a being-in-common.

That does not mean that the two earlier types of commons are irrelevant. Hess and Ostrom presented for instance a number of goods or resources that may be managed (and not necessarily owned) in the commons. In their analysis, they argue that the easier it is to make a good exclusive the more difficult it will be to incorporate within the commons. What firstly needs to be established from that point of entrance, and one of the reasons Ostrom's commons concept is not enough, is the insight that the (cultural) commons spans over much more than resource categories presented by her, and later her and Hess. Another aspect from Hess and Ostrom is also necessary to point out in order to continue this discussion. While it may be easier to govern what they refer to as the "public goods", "common-pool resources" and "toll or club goods" in a commons setting those are not the only categories of goods, to use their terminology, that are relevant to consider for a legal concept of the commons. I have already attempted to show that when it comes to cultural resources Ostrom's fourth type of goods, namely private goods, or perhaps more accurately physical private goods, which she claims is not fit for governance within commons, also has to be very much taken into consideration and placed inside the commons discourse as it is being carried out here. The example that I have put forward is for instance the Schulz mural. It is doubtlessly a physical object, at least once it was private, *but* at the same time it also embodies an immaterial potential and is constitutive of a community. Regardless of its corporality and physicality it is still part of the commons in this sense. The mural, even though it appears as physical and private in nature, when understood as a hyperobject, the assumption that a physical (private) good can strictly speaking only ever be in one place at a time is nuanced. Seen as a hyperobject that is constantly entangled with other hyperobjects it instantly creates the in-between-space that acts as a commons. That means that the fact that even though an artwork may be private, physical or seemingly easy to enclose, it does not for that matter mean that a commons-based interaction with it should per default be ruled out. The concept of the cultural commons here, it cannot be stressed strongly enough, does not *only* concern the digital, immaterial, or dematerialised, cultural works, it also very much concerns the physical works and spaces such as paintings, cultural landscapes or museums. This was shown in Chapters 3 and 4 through putting into play the notion of the hyperobject and its five traits. Therefore, when it comes to artworks as hyperobjects, in their tangible as well as their intangible guises, the concept of the cultural commons can prove to be the answer to many a (legal) dilemma. And we can only arrive there through e.g. Hess and Ostrom.

But we must reach further. The Deleuzeoguattarian method that I propose be used in this endeavour has already so far opened up the notion of jurisprudence and what it can and could do (Chapter 2), the notion of the artwork (Chapter 3), the notion of what is framed as a problem (Chapter 4), the significance of understanding property and space as connected to the commons (Chapter 5) and the notions of intellectual property and capitalism (Chapter 6), and what they all can or could do – i.e. the Deleuzeoguattarian method has revealed inherent potentialities. Now finally, let us move to the constructive exercise in envisioning the legal concept of the cultural commons through the Deleuzeoguattarian modes of possession. I will now begin by looking at the possession modes and how they are conceived of in theory, then I look at two existing commons initiatives and how they have been packaged legally, and then finally I arrive at the legal commons.

7.1.1 The sedentary and nomadic forms of possession

Stable or territorialised relations constitute that which Deleuze and Guattari refer to as the *sedentary model of possession*. Edward Mussawir argues that in law the sedentary possession model is based on the principle of "seisin" – namely possession as not that of actively "seizing" but rather one of "being seated", "set down", "sitting down" or even "presiding" over.[5] In law, the idea of seisin stems from feudal fiefdom, when the king was the one who could own and divide land, while the subjects had tenure in fiefs. This sedentary model is thus built on the assumption of *enclosure;* in order to possess for instance realty, or any other type of space or property for that matter, certain plots (of space) have to be enclosed. Chattel within the sedentary model is, as we have seen above in for instance Chapter 5, then tied to and belongs to the person who owns the space/land or, later on in the industrial setting, labour. Mussawir develops this further as he writes "one cannot possess without dividing up a field into plots as closed or exclusionary spaces."[6] This notion of enclosure, and fencing off, needed in order to possess is thus in Deleuze/Guattari connected to the sedentary type of possession.

The sedentary model of possession is in turn contrasted to the second form of possession, namely, *the nomadic model.* Contrary to the focus on enclosure and exclusivity (that is relevant for *rivalrous* or finite resources) that are both tightly connected to the sedentary model, the nomadic model conversely does not imply any such exclusion or stable territory-based possession.[7] Mussawir writes:

> Under the nomadic model, however, possession implies a different kind of relation that *cannot sustain any of these elements of establishment, exclusion and lack.* Since possession does not imply division, exclusions or stable territory, one requires other factors altogether [...][8]

This "lack of lack" as it were shall be revisited further on below in order to show how it adds to the legal concept of the commons. Mussawir, for the purpose of understanding the two Deleuzeoguattarian models, maps them out and presents four main characteristics to each model. He then uses the four characteristics in order to analyse the territorial possession of the indigenous people of Australia. Here however, I propose that a similar type of theoretical approach may be used when the legal concept of the cultural commons is being discussed. I argue that as the notion of space is territorial, possession of land and landscapes are therefore quite commensurable in the discussion about the commons. Ownership and access to indigenous land is therefore, strange as it may sound, a very similar, not to say the same phenomenon, as ownership and access to artworks.

5 Mussawir, 2011: 107.
6 Ibid.
7 Mussawir, 2011: 107 aa.
8 (My emphasis), Ibid p. 107.

Mussawir presents the two Deleuzeoguattarian models of possession in the following manner:

The sedentary model

1 Space is divided in order to be possessed,
2 What you possess is always a plot/lot/portion (closed space), for example a *house,*
3 You possess only by remaining the same person (that is, as an *in*dividual), and
4 Possession implies exclusion and displacement.

The nomadic model

1 Space is possessed without being divided,
2 What you possess is always flows/movements/intensities (open space), for example *the ocean* or *the desert,*
3 You possess only by being plural (that is, as a multiplicity, a community or a pack), and
4 Possession implies population and flight.[9]

I shall attempt to demonstrate the versatility, usefulness, and ultimately, creativity of the two models of possession that Mussawir has drawn up from Deleuze/Guattari. In order to apply Deleuze/Guattari such models as the one drawn up by Mussawir can prove to be very helpful.

So far, the legal concept of the commons has been approached as spatial plateaus that are created out of the interaction between rhizomatic jurisprudence (law) and capital (property), and lines of flight (space), that occur particularly within cultural creation (personhood). Or, yet more precisely, this attempt here approaches the commons as *spatial flows* between all of these. This fluid approach and the interobjectivity that happens in the commons understood as ecology takes place in a society that is always nomadic and leaking (*en fuite*), and as such it constantly becomes more, for the lack of a better word, concrete, when we can draw on everything that has been presented so far. Or put differently, I can now show how this is not a metaphor.

Mussawir questions what he refers to as the Deleuzian critique of the legal rights-construction connected to possessions; something that he claims has almost become a knee-jerk reaction within critical legal thinking, that is – to criticise the individual rights-construction. He argues that it is not as simple as dismissing rights-constructions *altogether* as "ideological

9 (My emphasis), Mussawir, 2011: 107–108.

appropriation. As examples of *res communes* resources from Roman law she mentions the oceans and the air mantle, since they were impossible for anyone to own.[18] We of course know today that it is quite possible, and in fact a common legal practice, to both "own" and "exclusively control" such things (hyperobjects!) as the ocean and the air mantle. We have here explored, through the notion of hyperobject the fluidity and liquidity of artworks, as such they can be compared to, and are in fact expressly compared to, oceans and air. But is there an impossibility argument at play here? What we have seen in modern environmental laws within global capitalist structures e.g. trade in exhaust fumes and the quotas "owned" by each nation state, and the accompanying legal constructs, the claim that things or hyperobjects that were previously assumed to be impossible to own, at least since Roman law, is thus if not refuted, at least strongly challenged.

3 ***Res publicae*** – things belonging to the public and open to the public by operation of law
The classic examples of *res publicae* for Roman law, according to Rose, were roads, harbours, ports, bridges, rivers that flowed year-round, and lands immediately adjacent thereto.[19] This category is clearly very interesting for the inventory of ownership rights categories that can conceive of the commons. The notion of (safe) harbours and ports are now natural phenomena within the digital spheres, as are of course, pirates. Take for instance the Pirate Bay as an illegal harbour for access to liquid cultural content. As a phenomenon it certainly makes one wonder how much of a metaphor the name Pirate Bay really is. Or the safe harbours proposed to be created in French museums for cultural heritage artefacts that are seen to be under threat in war-torn Syria, that were discussed in Chapter 3. Also the notion of the "public" is a key term that we have been exploring through the construct of the "public domain" in intellectual property law, and also wider in terms of public- or state-governed resources. While I have already presented a critique of only seeing the commons as a public resource, the concept of res publicae can be claimed to be one additional rights category that can begin to connect the landscape and the law, arriving of course at lawscape.

4 ***Res universitatis*** – property belonging to a (public) group in its corporate capacity
The standard "owner" for the Roman *res universitatis* was the city or a municipality, and its belongings were such public facilities as theatres

18 Rose, 2003: 93.
19 Rose, 2003: 96.

and race-courses; but both private and public groups could own this type of property which also included lands or other income-bearing properties. The chief limitation on *res universitatis* in Roman law was that, at least in theory, the relevant corporate bodies required the authorisation of the state.[20] The modern term for university obviously stems from this category, connecting the "ownership" of knowledge and spaces in which knowledge is produced, accessed and shared, with the group or community that is seen as its custodian, namely the students and the professors. The aspect of production, sharing and access to knowledge has already been put forward mainly through the discussions concerning digital platforms for sharing of content.

5 ***Res divini juris*** – things that are unowned by any human being because they are sacred, holy or religious
The last category presented by Rose, and one that may appear as the strangest at least within the secular legal traditions that have their roots in the Enlightenment is the so called *res divini juris*. This is an ownership category that may have fallen into oblivion since the Enlightenment and the development of a secular society, but one that might be interesting to keep in mind when discussing the commons. Rose claims that these are things classed under the religious rubric in Roman law as e.g. temples, tombs, religious statuary. All of these objects were considered to belong to no one because they were dedicated to the service of the gods, or because an offense to them was considered to be offensive to the gods. Such things were a class of *res nullius* but although they are physically capable of appropriation, they are still unowned; the impediment to propertisation is not natural but divine.[21] This category is also very interesting in terms of cultural heritage and cultural sites that encompass precisely the idea of these things being holy and the objects almost divine. In cultural heritage disputes it is not uncommon to see conflicts stemming from the appropriation of religious objects, e.g. the use of Tiki the Maōri religious symbol as a trademark for surfboards. But also places such as museums could be discussed under the banner of res divini juiris. Are these considered to be sacred places or are they fully secular within the Enlightenment traditions?

Rose devotes attention to the commons and how it may be connected to these categories in Roman law. Addressing artworks as hyperobjects as I do here and as such attributing them with something of a viscous or liquid

20 Rose, 2003: 105.
21 Rose, 2003: 108–109.

character[22] and considering the sphere in which artworks exist and move in, with which they interact as *oceans*[23] further connects this discussion to Deleuze and Guattari's concept of smooth spaces. There seems to be a strong case for this particular connection read through the Roman law categories. This discussion also provides us with an entrance into the legal concept of the cultural commons as a possession but not something that is owned in the manner of *exclusive* individual rights. What can be shown through Rose, is that there is already a long standing legal tradition of classing possessions in non-exclusive ownership categories.

This is done here by way of Deleuze and Guattari's sedentary and nomadic models of possession, the smooth and striated spaces, that can be justified through connecting them to Roman law. But before I present the legal concept of cultural commons proper, I want to briefly look at how some commons constructions have been framed using legal instruments (mainly the contract) without any prior existence of an underlying legal construct of the commons per se, particularly such initiatives as the Creative Commons.

7.3 Possession and commons

7.3.1 *Commons (1): multi-party initiative-based Creative Commons*

In recent years the initiative-based alternatives to copyright have proven to be vastly popular as an addition to intellectual property law. First it was the various open source[24] movements and the Linux system in coding. But later it spread to other areas too. Both licence models and business models that enable access and sharing of intellectual works have since been constructed as commons, underpinned by various *contract solutions* where certain aspects of copyright (or other intellectual property rights) are negotiated within more flexible (often non-exclusive) models in order to contractually construct a commons type solution. Licences (optional, compulsory, as well as statutory) have for instance been used in order to facilitate mass-utilisation where single rights clearances would have been far too cumbersome and/or costly to achieve. This is e.g. the case when it comes to background music for live broadcasting.[25] Here I focus on the initiative Creative Commons, which is a hybrid of both a licence model *and* a business model. Creative Commons is a non-profit initiative, and is formally an NGO. It has been widely accepted and established.

22 Dahlberg, 2011: 265.
23 Ibid.
24 See e.g. Open Source initiative, http://opensource.org/
25 See e.g. European Convention on Transfrontier Television (2002).

Driven by the copyleft[26] and open source movements, the Creative Commons was founded by Lawrence Lessig in 2001. Taking on board some of the most renowned experts in intellectual property law and cyber law, as for instance James Boyle, the project was born as both an alternative *and* a supplement to copyright law. Having written, criticised and commented upon the restrictive nature of copyright law, Creative Commons, helmed by Lessig, became a hub where creative content could under rather flexible terms be accessed and shared. The initiative provides various ready-made licences that users can sign on to and then apply to their works. It provides six different licence types ranging from non-restrictive to more heavily restricted. All licences are *non-exclusive*, which means that the rights owners ultimately retain their copyright and the works are not abandoned or left in the public domain. This has many similarities to the Roman law categories of ownership discussed above. The following is stated in the so-called "baseline rights" for the Creative Commons:

> Every license will help you: retain your copyright; announce that other people's fair use, first sale, and free expression rights are not affected by the license. Every license requires licensees to get your permission to do any of the things you choose to restrict; to keep any copyright notice intact on all copies of your work; to link to your license from copies of the work; not to alter the terms of the license… Every license allows licensees, provided they live up to your conditions, to copy the work; to distribute it; to display or perform it publicly; to make digital public performances of it; to shift the work into another format as a verbatim copy. Every license applies worldwide; lasts for the duration of the work's copyright; is not revocable.[27]

The Creative Commons licences are thus six different types of worldwide, royalty-free, non-exclusive, perpetual (or for the duration of copyright) licences, that can be more or less restricted, depending on the wishes of the original creator, and that the creators freely can choose from. Looking

26 "Copyleft is a play on the word copyright to describe the practice of using copyright law to offer the right to distribute copies and modified versions of a work and requiring that the same rights be preserved in modified versions of the work. In other words, copyleft is a general method for making a program (or other works) free (libre), and requiring all modified and extended versions of the program to be free as well. This free does not necessarily mean free of cost (gratis), but free as in freely available to be modified. Copyleft is a form of licensing and can be used to maintain copyright conditions for works such as computer software, documents, and art." http://en.wikipedia.org/wiki/Copyleft

27 http://wiki.creativecommons.org/Baseline_Rights

closer at the six licence types offered by the Creative Commons one finds the following options:

1 **Attribution** (CC BY) – allows others to *distribute, remix, tweak, and build upon the work, even commercially,* as long as they credit the original creation. According to the Creative Commons, this is the most accommodating of licences offered and they are recommended for maximum dissemination and use of licensed materials.

2 **Attribution ShareAlike** (CC BY-SA) – allows others to *remix, tweak, and build upon the work even for commercial purposes, as long as they credit the original creator and licence their new creations under the identical terms.* According to Creative Commons, this licence is often compared to the "copyleft" free and open source software licences. All new works based on the original work will carry the same licence, so any derivatives will also allow commercial use. This is the licence used by Wikipedia, and is recommended for materials that would benefit from incorporating content from Wikipedia and similarly licensed projects.

3 **Attribution No Derivatives** (CC BY-ND) – allows for *redistribution, commercial and non-commercial use, as long as it is passed along unchanged and in whole, with credit to the original creator.*

4 **Attribution Non-Commercial** (CC BY-NC) – allows others to *remix, tweak, and build upon the original work non-commercially,* and although their new works must also acknowledge the original creator and be non-commercial, they do not have to license their derivative works on the same terms.

5 **Attribution Non-Commercial Share Alike** (CC BY-NC-SA) – allows others to *remix, tweak, and build upon the original work non-commercially, as long as they credit the original creator and license their new creations under the identical terms.*

6 **Attribution Non-Commercial No Derivatives** (CC BY-NC-ND) – This licence is the most restrictive of the six main licences, only allowing others to *download the original works and share them with*

others as long as they credit the original creator, but they cannot change them in any way or use them commercially.[28]

Clearly, and as already pointed out by e.g. Maritza Schaeffer, the Creative Commons licensing regime does not propose any outrageous or revolutionary additions or changes to copyright law.[29] It offers a ready-made licence structure, within the already given possibilities of copyright law. The licences potentially cut down costs that the users would have had, had they needed to e.g. draft and negotiate their own terms. It is a mix of the copyright regime (all rights reserved) and the open source model (no, or very few, rights reserved).

The initiative has spread around the world and many have adopted its licensing scheme. Creative Commons has hundreds of millions of licences and it is used not just by individual creators, but also by enormous organisations such as Google, Flickr, Al Jazeera, The World Bank, Wikipedia, Whitehouse.gov, etc.[30] This further demonstrates how the idea of the commons is now nothing new, revolutionary, radical or even foreign to creators, users, the market or the "law". It is, as it is often referred in an American setting, "bi-partisan". I will return to that in a moment. So far suffice it to say, that the digital knowledge society *requires* these types of solutions when it comes to access to content, regardless of political orientation. That is a statement that has been so rehashed in recent decades by people like Lawrence Lessig, it has almost become trite.

However, what we are able to do now that was not possible in the beginning of the 00s is both to assess where the commons initiatives such as the Creative Commons currently stand, and how we can reach further in developing the concept of the commons also legally. It goes without saying that Creative Commons is a tremendously successful and important

28 (The Creative Commons licence text has not been fully copied, and all emphases are my own) Creative Commons Licences, http://creativecommons.org/about/licenses/meet-the-licenses. See also generally Schaeffer, 2008–2009.

29 Schaeffer, 2008-2009: 387.

30 http://creativecommons.org/who-uses-cc

initiative, one that truly (re)introduced the notion and the commons into everyday use and demonstrated how it can fully function as an addition to the global copyright laws. Still, for all its popularity, it has its downsides too, and it has equally been subject to some substantial critique.[31]

Hyde comments for instance that when it comes to the Creative Commons authors who do not wish to be owners at all and who would like to put their work altogether into the public domain must invent complicated schemes as e.g. a licence to the public at large (and even that may not work: these licences can be considered to be too general, and the rights would forcefully revert back to the original owners).[32]

This is not the only type of critique directed towards the Creative Commons either. The type of critique presented more generally states that the Creative Commons initiative stifles creativity because it removes the incentive to create content (as it undermines the strong individual copyright, and in extension the exploitation possibility). This is an idea that builds on the tragedy of the commons argument that assumes that when something is not within the individual ownership sphere, as a resource it will eventually perish. Another often reoccurring type of critique asserts that Creative Commons forces the creators to give up some or all of their rights in order to participate in the commons project, that in turn creates an "ideological fuzziness". Schaeffer provides yet another aspect to the critique, namely, she queries whether a Creative Commons licence is truly of any use when it comes to tangible works and for that which she calls "visual art".[33] While the quality of critique directed towards the Creative Commons as an initiative has varied, this particular point that Schaeffer raises, which questions the Creative Commons licences' applicability on tangible works is a particularly pertinent one within the context here as I have argued that also physical and visual works must be included in the commons.

In fact, in the beginning of this chapter it was pointed out how vital it is that we precisely not forget the tangible, physical aspects of the artwork when we are discussing the commons concept. Having examined the Creative Commons licence structure Schaeffer arrives at the following conclusion vis-à-vis commons and tangible works:

> Despite the two examples in which the licenses would likely work well for today's artists-works in a digital media and works created by appropriation artists-overall *there is not a general need for the licenses in the visual art realm* from the perspective of the artist. Creative Commons

31 Dusollier, 2006; Pallas Loren, 2007; Elkin-Koren, 2005.

32 Hyde, 2012: 58.

33 She is using the definition of "visual art" provided in the US Copyright Act 17 U.S.C. § 101 etseq. (1976).

> licenses *tip the balance in favor of the user, rather than the artist*, since it is the user who benefits from the work being licensed freely under the specified terms. Unless artists *intend to benefit from spreading a message or gaining popularity specifically through use of the internet*, or use Creative Commons as a branding point, *there is not an obvious benefit or incentive* to use the licenses for their works of art.[34]

Keeping e.g. the Richard Prince case in mind, as she is expressly mentioning appropriation artists, this statement becomes interesting. Would a commons structure per this reasoning tip the balance away from the artist in favour of the user (or the used)?

Another critique is that the entire Creative Commons initiative is based on a very particular underlying licence structure. It is thus dependent on the *contract* as a legal concept in order to function. Dusollier writes that the contract dependence exactly makes the Creative Commons rely on "private ordering", the same order as the copyright driven capitalist industries rely on. "This reliance on private ordering means results from an ambiguity that is at the core of the Creative Commons project and might even reinforce the rampant commodification process that is at work in copyright today."[35] Niva Elkin-Koren addressed the same issue in the article "What Contracts Cannot Do: The Limits of Private Ordering in Facilitating a Creative Commons" where she claims that:

> [R]eliance on contracts alone is risky. It entails support of strong copyrights and freedom of contract. It requires adjusting the law of contract, allowing enforcement against third parties. The legal regime that would validate Creative Commons' licenses would also enforce contracts that restrict access to creative works.[36]

Dusollier arrives at a similar conclusion in the article "The Master's Tools v. The Master's House: Creative Commons v. Copyright". She writes that "[i]n sum, if the interest pursued by the creator is the hope for remuneration, the Creative Commons scheme is not very helpful."[37] I do not agree with the general conclusions presented by either Dusollier or Schaeffer that claim that there is no obvious benefit or incentive for (visual) artists to be part of a commons project in general and the Creative Commons in particular, or that the creator should not hope for any remuneration, other than perhaps free promotion. It is safe to say that the organisations listed above as using Creative Commons licences such as e.g.

34 (My emphases throughout), Schaeffer, 2008–2009: 401.
35 (My emphasis), Dusollier, 2006: 292.
36 Elkin-Koren, 2005.
37 Dusollier, 2006.

Google nonetheless manage to receive remuneration for their activities. Granted, this may not be the same when it comes to smaller or less established artists or companies, but the principle that I aim to show here is that the commons construction does not preclude profit and remuneration, *as such.*

That is not to say that the Creative Commons scheme is unproblematic, it is. I believe that what the two articles found to be particularly problematic here is not the idea or concept of the commons itself but rather the way the Creative Commons is structured. I claim that the benefits and incentives of a commons are not merely restricted to the augmenting of knowledge and participation in democracy, but that there may also be some financial benefits directly connected to the commons within the structures of the sharing economy that in fact go hand in hand with global advanced capitalism, particularly when the schizophrenic and nomadic nature of it has been revealed. Within such a structure, the commons is part of the revolutionary nomadic forms of possession and as such forms a type of subversive property, but it is also part of the capitalist machine – as such it is bi-partisan.

7.3.2 Commons (2): individual contract-based cultural commons

I want to now briefly return to one of the cases from Chapter 4, and expressly add on the dimension of commons that is not necessarily referred to as commons, by looking at an individual contract-based solution that happened there. I want to do so in order to show how a commons can be created on a smaller scale too, or without necessarily even calling it a commons. Also, we can see that a commons solution that is not a digital platform like the Creative Commons could also be created. Here too, the commons solution was created through the institute of the contract. I am referring to the settlement in the Schulz case and the long term agreement[38] that emanated therefrom.

We have already gone through the facts concerning the Schulz case, namely, to remind ourselves briefly, that Yad Vashem was interested in the find that Benjamin Geissler and his team had made in Drohobych, and that Yad Vashem representatives subsequently took five pieces of Schulz' mural to Israel. What was also briefly mentioned in Chapter 4 is that an agreement was reached between the state of Ukraine and Yad Vashem that the Schulz pieces would from then on be kept in Israel on a long term loan but that Yad Vashem would expressly acknowledge that the pieces belong

38 Many of the facts presented here come from a legal analysis conducted by a Ukrainian lawyer which was reported to professor Thomas Hoeren, Humbolt University, Germany. The analysis was then forwarded to Mr. Benjamin Geissler, who in his turn forwarded it to me. The analysis is from here on referred to as the Hoeren report.

to the cultural heritage of the Ukraine. There was a string of agreements entered into, in fact.

The first agreement (A1) that I have come across is the oral consent to remove the pieces of the mural from the site, given to Yad Vashem representatives. This consent was given by the people in whose house the mural was found.[39] According to the official information provided by Yad Vashem (press release by Iris Rosenburg, 29 May 2001) one member of their foundation (Mark Schrabermann) was responsible for removing the pieces of the mural and taking them to Israel. This was done, further, with another consent (A2) given by the city council (Aleksej Radzievskij, Taras Metuk and the head of the Cultural Centre for the City of Drohobych).[40] These two (oral) agreements were then challenged by the state of Ukraine that asserted that regardless of the two consents given, the consenting instances (owners of the house and the city council respectively) did not have the required authority to give this type of consent on matters concerning exportation of any items of cultural heritage found on Ukrainian soil.

The Ukrainian Law on the Protection of Cultural Heritage (LPCH) supports this claim. According to 1 art. § 1 of LPCH, anything excavated from Ukrainian soil must be deemed to be cultural heritage of the Ukraine. According to §§ 5 aa cultural heritage may only be removed with consent by certain bodies of authority that are the sole competent bodies that may give consent. The competent bodies of authority that deal with the protection of the cultural works are named as following:

> According to §5 para 1. No 25: the supreme authority of administration. In this case it would have been the Minister of Culture, and
>
> According to §6 para 1. No 16: the district authorities. In this case it would have been the district capital – here, Lvov.

Relying on this regulation the state of Ukraine challenged the two consents that had been given, claiming that they lack the required authority. Since none of the two consents for removal had been given in due procedure, they argued that the oral agreements that were entered into were thus invalid and void. A person, or people, who are convicted of removal of pieces of cultural heritage from Ukrainian territory without due consent for removal commits the criminal offence of smuggling, according to § 201 of the Ukrainian Criminal Code.

39 I have not been able to find out whether there was any consideration given to the house owners for this to take place, or whether money changed hands.

40 Hoeren report. Same here, I have not been able to find out whether there was any consideration given to the city council of Drohobych for this to take place, or whether money changed hands.

In the aftermath of the removal of the pieces, the last and most interesting agreement was entered into, namely the already mentioned final long-term agreement (A3), between the state of Ukraine and Yad Vashem. This agreement acknowledges that the pieces of the mural are in fact Ukrainian cultural heritage, currently held in Israel on a long-term loan. The interesting legal question is whether this subsequent agreement that arose post facto, after the pieces had been removed from Ukraine to Israel, but which was nevertheless entered into with due competence, could make up for the initial lack of appropriate consent and authorisation. Another interesting question is whether by entering this agreement a cultural commons was inadvertently created.

The Ukrainian Committee that signed the long term agreement comprised the head of the civil service in matters of transfer (or migration) of the cultural treasures – Vladislav Kornienko, First Secretary of the Embassy of Ukraine in Israel and Museum Director Vladimir Ilarianov Zenovij Bervetzkuj. According to § 5 Paragraph 1 of the LPCH No. 25 these are indeed the competent bodies that have the authority to give permission for removal. Arguably, an agreement with the relevant authority was entered into this time. However, it can be argued that the initial removal of the five pieces of the mural and their transfer to Israel could not be pardoned by this subsequent act and was still not covered by A3 and thus potentially remains illegal or even void. Perhaps then, the agreement between the Ukraine and Yad Vashem only concerns the retention of the pieces of the mural in Israel, and not their removal and transfer out of the country which would in that case still remain illegal in terms of consent given with due competence.

A further complication with the agreement between Yad Vashem and Ukraine is that it may be in conflict with the Ukrainian Constitution. According to art. 9 of the Ukrainian Constitution all international agreements that are entered into must be in accordance with the Constitution. The agreement at hand (A3) may be in conflict with §53 of the Ukrainian Constitution. According to §53 para 5 the state guarantees the protection of historical and cultural heritage, *ipso facto*, the state must ensure that the historical and cultural heritage located outside of Ukraine, be returned to the Ukraine. This is a constitutional obligation that the Ukraine has. By entering into this agreement it dispensed of its cultural heritage without any compensations. It means that since the state acts as a guarantor in terms of preservation of Ukrainian heritage, it is responsible for it not to be taken out of the country without due consent and/or if it is outside the country for it to be returned. When the Ukrainian constitution is read in that manner, it can be argued that a contract that allows Ukrainian cultural heritage to remain in another country for an unspecified period of time, which the A3 indeed does, due to the consecutive automatic renewal periods inscribed therein, such a provision may be in conflict with this principle of the Ukrainian Constitution that stipulates the return of cultural heritage.

There is also an exception to this particular rule and that is if entrance into these types of agreement has been done in pursuit of a "higher purpose". It is very difficult to define what constitutes such a higher purpose. It could be e.g. the security and safekeeping of national heritage that cannot be done within the source country and that transfer out of the country serves a higher purpose and as such makes up for the removal of the cultural heritage. The safeguarding can in those cases override the home territory principle. Yad Vashem does moreover acknowledge openly, as already stated, (in A3) that the five pieces of the mural are part of Ukrainian cultural heritage. Yad Vashem's status as a cultural and memorial institution also means that they do have the means and knowledge to keep the pieces of the mural safe and provide for any and all necessary restoration and up-keep. All this could possibly mean that the higher purpose that the Ukrainian Constitution requires has been met.[41]

Further still, the fact that Ukrainian law, in accordance with the UNESCO conventions, deems the mural to belong to the cultural heritage of the Ukraine, is not at all unproblematic. We have seen that Poland too is asserting rights in the works left behind by Schulz, arguing that he ultimately was born on Polish territory, and that he was a Polish citizen who, significantly, wrote in Polish and was Polish. This fact may also challenge the long-term agreement with Yad Vashem, as it is, after all, not entirely straight forward whose (national/religious/communal/cultural) heritage the mural ultimately can be ascribed to. At least not in the sense where a closed, homogeneous community is assumed. Therefore, the fact that Yad Vashem acknowledges that the pieces that they hold are Ukrainian cultural heritage may not necessarily have any bearing.

Another problem with the A3 agreement is that it is not sufficiently defined particularly regarding the terms concerning the return of the mural, but also regarding the automatic extensions of the term and the penalties that are included within the agreement. All these clauses appear uncertain and not sufficiently defined. This taken together means that there is a risk that the pieces will never be returned to the Ukraine, even after the term of the agreement has expired. In fact, the term of the agreement could carry on in perpetuity, since there is no real expiration of the term.

It could be argued that this uncomfortable contractual solution to the problem concerning the dispute of the belonging of Bruno Schulz' mural may have an unexpected potential in the realm of the commons. However, it has a very much sedentary approach to this work. As we saw earlier, our traditional understandings of the laws of persons and the laws of things

41 As a matter of fact, before Geissler's find, and before Schulz garnered new attention, there are claims that many of his works had already been destroyed in the Ukraine, such as for instance certain oil paintings (Goldfarb, 2013).

have not only fundamentally been questioned with the Schulz case, it also demonstrates the difficulty in circumventing the lock-ins created with various forms of contractual agreements, where the object of cultural heritage is assumed to be separable from e.g. the community, or the territory or the person(s). It is therefore necessary to include the various res concepts from Roman law and the Deleuzeoguattarian forms of possession in order to understand (the shortcomings) of the contracts that were entered into as a way of circumventing legal difficulty in terms of belonging, and the legal issues that this case gave rise to.

The approach to possession and access in this case is clearly based on a sedentary form of reasoning where in order to possess we have to: divide and exclude. Certain plots have to be assigned to certain individuals, and the individual has to be one and the same person or a legal subject, i.e. a definable (unified) entity such as a nation state, or a cultural institution, or a private person. A more itinerant community concept (e.g. the Jews in diaspora) is not captured here. To possess within the sedentary model of possession the notions of exclusion and displacement are thus always perpetuated. All of these are present in the Schulz case and the agreements entered into along the way, particularly in the final agreement (A3) that the state of Ukraine entered with Yad Vashem.

Since Schulz' mural could not be grasped, or understood by any statutory law directly, the work had to be captured, striated, territorialised and set down by a legal instrument that is the contract, even if, conversely, it means that the work has to remain constantly fragmented, divided and displaced. With the contract solution used here, within a sedentary reasoning, in terms of at least the A3, a settlement was reached and it appeased the question as to who would, from then on, possess which piece and where they should be kept. Therefore, yes, it could be argued that a type of commons was created here.

The sedentary reasoning relied here is simultaneously made difficult by the fact that the artist's belonging cannot be framed and contextualised easily, that his territorial belonging is contested and is in constant flux. At this point we could return to the elusive concept of *res divini juris*. Rose exemplifies the concept in the following manner:

> It is the canon, the classics, the ancient works whose long life has contributed to their status as rare, extraordinary – and also a little wild, never quite capable of complete domestication even by the most erudite pedant. And lest we forget that all things godlike may be accompanied by lesser gods (or even false ones) and their representations, we might wish to include here too the iconography of modern commercial culture, the Mickeys and Minnies and Scarletts.[42]

42 (My emphasis), Rose, 2003: 109.

Rose is referring to the music of Bach, the Mona Lisa and the modern day Disney icons as potential *res divini juris* of our time. Fair enough perhaps. And while Schulz' mural arguably has not reached the status of these works (yet?), maybe it could. And as such there are still aspects of this category from Roman law that challenge the sedentary contract at hand, which governs the possession of and access to Schulz' mural. Rose also provides some potential examples from the realm of nature, and the natural commons as being res divini juris:

> [T]he great wilderness parks, deserts and seashores, with their sense of the sublime and the vast, may in some ways fill the role of res divini juris. Such places suggest to the visitor the majesty of creation, the vastness of space, the untamedness of something outside human capacity to grasp. If there is a role for res divini juris as tangible public property in our modern jurisprudence, surely this is one place where it resides.[43]

The interesting aspect with Schulz's mural is that it is so connected to physical space. It was quite literally part of a house. It is being reconstructed by Benjamin Geissler as a virtual space within a physical space, as a 360° experience that one enters into. Far from being dead matter, it is a space, an in-between that emerges when property, persons and space are entangled, one that can be entered, but also one that has been reterritorialised, grounded, by the legal instrument of the contract. But can it really be pinned down, striated, territorialised, made to fit within the reasoning of the sedentary modes of possession? Both the example of the Creative Commons – an initiative named as a "commons", and the settlement agreement in the Schulz case – not named as a commons per se, are representative of attempts at creating commons solutions. They are also examples of why contract-based solutions do not always work, and why a legal platform for the commons is needed.

7.3.3 Commons (3): the legal concept of cultural commons

Deleuze/Guattari write in *A Thousand Plateaus* that "the nomads do not precede the sedentaries; rather, nomadism is a movement, a becoming that affects sedentaries, just as sedentisation is a stoppage that settles the nomads."[44] When Deleuze/Guattari discuss the nomadic space they do so in connection to their basic principle of smooth, heterogeneous space. The nomadic space and the nomadic forms of possession cannot simply be

43 (Emphasis in original), Ibid.

44 Deleuze and Guattari, 2011: 475.

presented in opposition to striated space and the sedentary forms of possession either. Thus, they write:

> [W]e must remind ourselves that the two spaces in fact exist only in mixture: smooth space is constantly being translated, transversed into striated space; striated space is constantly being reversed, returned to smooth space [....] and the two can happen simultaneously.[45]

It is this very continuity, the constant movement from one form to another, the unfinished transitions from one form to the other, that must be understood and it is imperative that it be kept in mind when discussing the concept of the commons. The concept of the commons (natural as well as cultural, if we are to return to that damning dichotomy) can never be approached as a static concept. Yet at times, it becomes striated too. As society develops, it too becomes subject to lines of flight, that move it, force it into new nomadic territories, and so on, as we have seen with e.g. the Creative Commons initiative. Even though it initially and most probably was a result of nomadic lines of flight and became a smooth space at one point in its own right that fled the striated space of copyright law, it too became striated with time.

Deleuze/Guattari claim that the distinction between the two types of spaces is that in the smooth space we encounter "free action" while in the striated space we encounter "work". The combination between free action and work when it comes to the production of artworks is particularly obvious, and this theoretical framework therefore allows for both free action and work/property in the cultural commons. With the Creative Commons project in particular it can be shown how commons initiatives can both challenge and exist within capitalist structures. This is entirely in line with the mixture of smooth and striated spaces that Deleuze/Guattari present, particularly within global advanced capitalism:

> *world capitalism,* a new smooth space is produced in which capital reaches its "absolute" speed, based on mechanic components rather than the human component of labor. The multinationals fabricate a kind of deterritorialized smooth space in which points of occupation as well as poles of exchange become quite independent of the classical paths to striation. What is really new are always new forms of turnover.[46]

I have especially discussed the TRIPS agreement as the legal construct that harmonises and governs the global turnover of intellectual property. The

45 Deleuze and Guattari, 2011: 524.
46 (Emphasis in original), Deleuze and Guattari, 2011: 524.

current intellectual property regime can thus very well be read within the concept of "world capitalism" as Deleuze/Guattari describe it. Thus, when discussing the concept of the commons within this regime, it is imperative that the deterritorialising nature of capital on a global scale be kept in mind:

> The present day accelerated forms of the circulation of capital are making the distinctions between constant and variable capital, and even fixed and circulating capital, increasingly relative; the essential thing is instead the distinction between *striated capital* and *smooth capital*, and the way in which the former gives rise to the latter through complexes that cut across territories and states, and even the different types of States.[47]

Accordingly we arrive, through the nomadic and sedentary forms of possession, smooth and striated spaces, to smooth and striated capital. This particular distinction applied to current (intellectual property) law is very pertinent as it allows us to see some inherent characters that exist within the artwork packaged as commodity – namely the striated capital within sedentary forms of possession (e.g. commodity based type of exploitation) and smooth capital with nomadic forms of possession (e.g. global, knowledge-based, network-based forms of management of artworks, commons, and ultimately *hyperobjects*). How then can it all converge into a legal concept of cultural commons?

We have seen, since Chapter 2, where rhizomatic jurisprudence was presented, that legal concepts within the Deleuzeoguattarian theoretical matrix gain certain potential that in turn caters for these particular movements from smooth to striated, from sedentary to nomadic (and vice versa). In fact, Deleuze/Guattari go from the section where they treat smooth and striated capital into a section that they call "The Aesthetic Model: Nomad Art".[48] However, the nomad art that is referred to by them is not nomadic – i.e. non-static, not-striated, fluid, continuous, etc. – but literarily they are referring to the art created by ancient people that led *nomadic lifestyles*. They write:

> On one side, Egypt had its Hyksos, Asia Minor its Hittites, China its Turco-Mongols; and on the other, the Hebrews had their Habiru, the Germans, the Celts, and Romans their Goths, the Arabs their Bedouins. The nomads have a specificity that is too hastily reduced to its consequences, by including them in the empires or counting them among the migrants, assimilating them to one or the other, denying

47 (Emphasis in original), Deleuze and Guattari, 2011: 543.
48 Ibid.

> them their own 'will' to art. [...] Moreover, it does not have that role in the guise of a 'will'; it only has a becoming, it invents a 'becoming-artist'.[49]

By using the example of Creative Commons and the Schulz agreement I have on the other hand, or perhaps even further still, attempted to show the nomadic (and migrant) tendencies in the artworks as hyperobjects. The particular becoming that I am interested in and that I will try to finally arrive at is the very becoming of the legal concept of the cultural commons. How does a concept of commons *become* law? In order to answer that, let us just be reminded how Deleuze/Guattari end their own penultimate chapter, before they reach their conclusion of *A Thousand Plateaus*, by writing:

> Even the most striated city gives rise to smooth spaces: to live in the city as a nomad, or as a cave dweller. Movements, speed and slowness, are sometimes enough to reconstruct a smooth space. Of course, smooth spaces are not in themselves liberatory. But the struggle is changed or displaced in them, and life reconstitutes its stakes, confronts new obstacles, invents new paces, switches adversaries. Never believe that a smooth space will suffice to save us.[50]

A legal concept of the cultural commons will not suffice to save us. However, it can be given a platform in law by way of Deleuzeoguattarian theory and their ambiguity towards schizophrenic capitalism and the societal flows. This reasoning opens up a potential, an alternative, a framework that can theoretically introduce the cultural commons into rhizomatic jurisprudence. For that to be done the artwork's qualities as a hyperobject must be acknowledged.

Furthermore, approaching the commons as an ecology, a lawscape, means displacing it from the paradox or prisoner's dilemma discussions. Seen as such it becomes pragmatic, or bi-partisan, in nature (politically speaking):

> Almost the entire range of liberal traditions, from laissez faire to progressive liberalism or social democracy, can find information based cooperation attractive. The left, too, can find in these practices one way out of the dead end that state socialism proved to be. Libertarianism, of both right-wing, market-oriented, and left-wing, anarchistic varieties, likewise finds attractive narratives to tell about cooperation in the networked commons. Adherents to this broad range of views can then, as a practical matter, ally with market actors who eschew political views

49 Deleuze and Guattari, 2011: 476.
50 Deleuze and Guattari, 2011: 551.

> altogether and who are focused on survival, innovation, and growth in an increasingly competitive global economy where learning and adaptation are imperative. Needless to say some of this congruence is temporary and ad hoc. Some, however, represents a real change in conditions and intellectual alignments.[51]

And put yet in another way in the words of Lawrence Lessig:

> The struggle against these changes is not the traditional struggle between Left and Right or between conservative and liberal. To question assumptions about the scope of "property" is not to question property. *I am fanatically pro-market,* in the market's proper sphere. I don't doubt the important and valuable role played by property in most, maybe just about all, contexts. This is not an argument about commerce *versus* something else. The innovation that I defend is commercial and noncommercial alike; the arguments I draw upon to defend it are as strongly tied to the Right as to the Left.[52]

This can also be done from a legal side, to imagine a legal concept in this way, as an ecology, that the entire ideological range can find attractive. The Deleuzian and Deleuzeoguattarian theory has demonstrated how it is not a question of Either (inflexible copyright, market, right) Or (public, state governed, left) but *both,* or *and, and…* This type of reasoning as we have seen throughout this book is not only suited to but required for the construction of such a concept as the cultural commons in law. Atteberry writes about this in conjunction with the Access to Knowledge movement:

> The solution to this problem of the continued colonialist distribution of wealth, therefore, will not be found simply in a *cultural* commons, although *a cultural* commons will surely have an important role to play. When faced with the dynamic of deterritorialization, Deleuze and Guattari ask, could it be that the revolutionary path is to 'go further still, that is, in the movement of the market, of decoding and deterritorialization? For perhaps the flows are not yet deterritorialized enough'. The questions for the A2K movement then become what function the *cultural* commons serve in the globalized economy, and how might we accelerate the process that it promises by finding ways to resist its potential neo-colonial reterritorializations?[53]

51 Benkler, in Krikorian and Kapczynski, 2010: 231.

52 (My emphasis), Lessig, 2001: 6.

53 (My emphasis, quote modified), Atteberry in Krikorian and Kapczynski, 2010. The quote has been modified here, the words "cultural" in italics have replaced Atteberry's original "informational".

The final section of this chapter conclusively merges the theoretical approach to the A2K movement that has been challenging the construction of intellectual property. Already in 2002, and soon after the adaptation of the Doha Declaration that resulted in TRIPS, there came an influential report from the UK Commission on Intellectual Property Rights (CIPR). Even though it was a national report, it had a significant impact, because the commission consisted of international members, also including members from developing countries, experts, representatives from the industry and academia. This was the first time a "one size fits all" in terms of intellectual property rights and management of these rights was called into question:

> [I]n terms of its content, the CIPR report captured very accurately the growing trend of opinion that distanced itself from both a maximalist discourse that promoted the absolute benefits of intellectual property and a discourse that was unequivocally critical of intellectual property as a matter of principle. It thus recognized both the benefits and costs of intellectual property protection, emphasizing the need to ensure that the costs do not outweigh the benefits [...][54]

This book has certainly been a theoretical exercise that has attempted to show just that, a critical approach to intellectual property law and how intellectual property law still is, simultaneously and adamantly, able to recognise the benefits of a construct of the commons. Particularly legally, the concept of cultural commons as an addition to current intellectual property legislation has been discussed, but other than on a contractual or a licence-level, a full step is yet to be taken towards a full-scale commons concept in law. However, the A2K movement itself, as well as the discussions in terms of reforms of current intellectual property rights are not new.

The time is now ripe to *seriously* discuss a construction of a legal concept of the cultural commons. Yet, other than on the so called policy levels, or initiative levels, such as e.g. Creative Commons, or on an individual level such as the Schulz settlement, and various other initiatives that govern access to art,[55] the issues concerning a legal framework of the cultural commons have so far not been discussed expressly. That being said, the

54 Abdel Latif, in Krikorian and Kapczynski, 2010: 102.

55 e.g. the Andy Warhol Foundation that can also be seen as a commons in that sense. The Andy Warhol Foundation takes a nuanced stand in terms of who is allowed access to the works that Warhol left behind (including the tangible paintings). Their stand illustrates precisely these types of hybrid initiatives that allow for both access and revenue. The Andy Warhol Foundation's motto is: "We're Lessig when it comes to artists and scholars [and] Disney when it comes to commercial use." It means that certain interests are not on a par, and there is nothing that says that they cannot be treated differently in terms of access.

policy and initiative driven projects can now be evaluated and lessons from those projects can be borne in mind when discussing legal alternatives. When placing it in a setting of rhizomatic jurisprudence, where the artwork is seen as a hyperobject, the commons as an ecology, and intellectual property law as part of schizophrenic capitalism the solution becomes apparent. This book has attempted to show the theoretical possibility and potential to successfully fuse a legal concept of the cultural commons with intellectual property law, as well as with the free market and global capitalism.

One of the theoretical breakthroughs that the Deleuzeoguattarian theory provides here is what I referred to on p. 181 as the "lack of lack". On a most basic level it can be read in as denoting the unlimited nature of the intellectual products (they are not finite, non rivalrous), and on a theoretical level it can be connected to nomadic form of possession, and smooth capital. The way in which nomadic forms of possession of hyperobjects can be grasped legally, that traditionally envisions possessions to be based on sedentary principles, is by understanding and approaching law in its rhizomatic guise and understanding the smooth attributes of capital and the potentialities the rhizomatic readings of law open up to. Hyperobjects are in constant flux, in various states of becomings, nomadic, multiplying, spreading, like viruses, between objects. The process has to avoid falling into the trap of the regime of arborescent conjunctions, the "either…or", concepts that fundamentally hinder the creation of a legal concept of the cultural commons.

> *So in order to create legal pathways which facilitate that art can be communicated, accessed and shared, could legal thinking formulate a conception of the commons and could the concept of the cultural commons be introduced, applied and given a platform in law?*

Yes, provided we adopt a Deleuzeoguattarian approach to law, by approaching the artwork as a hyperobject, by understanding the legal concept of the cultural commons as an ecology and by allowing for the lines of flight that move it all, by traversing smooth and striated spaces, *by engaging in rhizomatic jurisprudence.*

Chapter 8

Exit

Atmosphere

Conclusively and on a final note. Yes, the concept of the cultural commons has become increasingly important for legal studies. Within this field, however, as has been shown throughout this book it is a concept that has been widely contested: sometimes presented as a sphere for creativity, democratic access and freedom of speech, and at others as a concept that denies property rights and (mis)appropriates the public domain. In this book my aim has been to precisely take up the cultural commons as a concept, not as a metaphor and not as an abstract notion, but rather to connect it to spaces such as museums and urban landscapes. I arrived in Chapter 7 at the legal cultural commons where I argued that by reading it through the Deleuzeoguattarian forms of possession and non-exclusivity ownership concepts from Roman law, the commons in law can be envisioned as a *lawscape* that can quite literally be entered and engaged with.

In this book I have chosen to focus largely on artwork in the context of copyright and cultural heritage regimes. To do that I have had to draw on the works of Deleuze and Guattari in order to open up the concepts of jurisprudence and examine the realm of the commons as a potential space for overcoming the still very entrenched dichotomy between the owner and the consumer of culture, between the public and the private regimes of governance. Challenging these dichotomies, it has been the productive and the creative potential of law itself that has emerged. One of my approaches has been to showcase the commons on an empirical basis in order to arrive at it within a legal framework, which is able to accommodate a multitude of interests and values.

I have here engaged with the concept of lawscape in a manner that precisely moves the ontological question of law (what is it?) to the more situated one (where is it?). Where is the law that governs the cultural commons? Is it always already here or must we construct it *ex nihilo*? This is a rhetorical question, of course. Because we now know that we are in the lawscape, we walk in it.[1] How come we do not see it then? Has it already

1 Philippopoulos-Mihalopoulos, 2014: 39.

become *atmosphere*? And if so, has it turned invisible? So as a final note in this last chapter, I want to dedicate some pages to this discussion – the argument being the following, the idea that the cultural commons in law must not be constructed – it must be made visible.

8.1 Visualising the lawscape: cultural commons as an e-scape

Rip, mix, burn. After all it's your *art*.[2] This is a modified version of Apple Inc.'s advertisement slogan. I have placed the word "art" in italics instead of the original "music". The original slogan reads: "Rip, mix, burn. After all it's your music". Lawrence Lessig addressed this already in his book *Future of Ideas* from 2001. The slogan "Rip. Mix. Burn" was used to promote an iTunes desktop CD burning capability. It was seen as a controversial slogan by some as it seemed to be advocating or at least referring to piracy. However the terms and conditions for use of this very iTunes desktop together with intellectual property laws and digital rights management solutions that bundled it made it, as Lessig wisely pointed out, impossible to in fact rip, mix or burn. Lessig writes:

> Try to "rip, mix, [and] burn" Disney's *102 Dalmatians* and it's your computer that will get ripped, not the content. Software, or *code,* protects this content, and Apple's machine protects this code. It may be your music, but it's not your film. Film you can rip, mix, and burn only as Hollywood allows. *It* controls that creativity—it, and the law that backs it up.

Lawrence Lessig claims that the first instinct when battling infringement of copyright on a large scale has been to wage the so-called "copyright war" against infringement and infringers. The second response was to create alterations within the digital architectures of the networks, to build digital rights management and content IDs in order to lock down distribution of cultural content that tries to get beyond the permissions granted by the rights owners. This second wave response came with a renewed optimism for the private realm and the rights owners, as the first wave response had not provided satisfactory decrease of infringing activities. It proved difficult, not to say impossible, to achieve perfectly controlled and controllable re-use of content in the digital spheres. As we know, infringing activities continued even after these digital control measures were put in place.

2 See Lessig, 2001: 9-11. On Wikipedia, the slogan is described in the following manner: "'Rip. Mix. Burn.' (2001) used". See also: http://en.wikipedia.org/wiki/List_of_Apple_Inc._slogans

Lessig therefore argues that the only way to understand and approach access to and sharing of art is to find the right mix between what he calls *law, norms, market* and *architecture.* He defines law as statute, norms as rules that exist "outside" the legal sphere, market as the free liberal market, and with architecture he refers to the architecture of internet – both technical and legal – that creates and enables the online digital environment. But now when we have reached the end of this book we know that making a distinction between law and its so called outside is not as simple as that. And, as we also know now, however much we are inside the law, we still need an outside in order to conceive of new possibilities and legal constructions.[3] Going back to Lessig's writings from the early 2000s, but placing it in this context, it is warranted to ask whether we can create a rupture needed in order to make the legal cultural commons visible? A rupture that will make the lawscape reappear, again.

Ever since Lessig wrote *Code and Other Laws of Cyberspace*[4] in 1999 and as late as in May 2013 in his inaugural lecture,[5] when he was made honorary doctor at Lund University, he has been addressing these four modalities, law, norms, market and architecture, that he claims all need to be accounted for when we are discussing improvement of law particularly in terms of the cultural commons. Lessig argues that without all of the four modalities put together laws do not, and perhaps cannot, function in the knowledge society. Only by understanding the interaction and connections between all four can we improve the law. Thus, according to Lessig, we need to understand them all equally well, and in order to that, we must also, sometimes, step outside the law.

In this book, I have attempted to go one step further than that. In the second chapter I began by challenging the notions of an inside and an outside of law. This distinction, it has been argued, is unnecessary, as long as law, *whatever law now is,* can be connected to anything that is deemed to be both "inside" *and* "outside" it. When Lessig lists law, norms, market, and architecture as four *different* modalities he assumes that there exist such occurrences as a definable law, norm, market, and architecture, and that they can be analysed, separated, and even found. He is probably at least partially right in claiming that assemblages like these appear at times, and that these four may form plateaus in the Deleuzeoguattarian terminology, but in claiming that, it will also always be *problematic* to draw an ontological line between the four, to find their limits and borders, to denote where the one ends, and conversely where the other begins. And it brings us back to the ontological question. Such reasoning will always lead us into treacherous binary reasoning, back into the world of paradoxes and hostile

3 Philippopoulos-Mihalopoulos, 2014: 1.
4 Lessig, 1999, and second edition Lessig, 2006.
5 Lessig, Inaugural Lecture, Lund University 30 May 2013.

binary opposites. I have throughout this book endeavoured to show that even if we multiply binary reasoning, and make quadruple modalities, like Lessig proposes that we do, we will have not gone far enough in the project of *going beyond* the idea of a closed off law, and as such we will not be able to *see the potential of law* nor will the commons ever appear as the lawscape it is. Reasoning entirely like Lessig suggests we do, means that there are possibilities that will always be deemed to fall outside the law, to exist in one of the three other modalities, and as such to also fall outside the legal reach and its possibilities. But, if law is approached like a rhizome, as suggested here, then suddenly all the modalities are seen as always already inside the law. As such, the idea of the commons is already there, but as it may be argued, invisible.

That being said, connecting these four modalities to the global commons initiatives that have been taking place in various guises since the beginning of the twenty-first century is important. Lessig himself, and the Creative Commons initiative in particular, have been pivotal in this process, but as we have entered a new decade, it is warranted to ask what do the Creative Commons-like initiatives of the future look like? Can Creative Commons itself continue to exist and manage to reinvent itself?[6] Should commons, creative or otherwise, be governed by contract or inscribed in law?

Lessig argues that when we did not seize the opportunity ten or 15 years ago to legislate, with the momentum of for instance Creative Commons and other global and local digital openness initiatives, to regulate the commons in law and/or reform copyright law more radically now, it might be too late. I do not agree with this conclusion. I suggest here that now is *precisely the right time* to discuss this and to make the commons in law visible. Why? Because now is the first time we can evaluate the commons initiatives that have been running for over fifteen years in various contract-based guises, and imagine new ones. We could also add on to our empirical base various protest-based or e.g. Occupy initiatives that have been turned into commons, like for instance the Teatro Valle in Rome. I have not discussed these specifically here, but it is important to note that these solutions have been particularly driven by the austerity that has emanated from the crises currently taking place around the world.

Lessig argues that if we ever want to conceive of a commons we must imagine a system where professionals that create content can be compensated, but where amateurs, at the same time are allowed to be inspired, to

6 From time to time the Creative Commons reaches out globally through various channels including Twitter (https://twitter.com/creativecommons) to the public and their supporters to donate funds in order for the initiative to be able to continue. This means that the future existence of the project, at least in its current guise, is by no means guaranteed.

create and share, without being burdened by regulation.[7] This is where the legal concept of the cultural commons fits right in. Within the context of this book, and particularly when we have established the artwork as a hyperobject, I have shown that it is now impossible to divide the professionals from the amateurs. They are entangled. As such this is the first justification for the commons.

Lessig argues further that the solution lies in finding the perfect balance between the four modalities. I would like to argue that the solution may lie in finding a possibility within law that *connects it* to norms, market and architecture at any given point, as well as makes it able to shift connections as any of the other modalities, *now known or hereafter devised*, (to use a common copyright licence language) change. This is not just semantics; it is a radically different approach from what Lessig is arguing for. This approach denies an inside-outside of law reasoning, but rather calls for a spatial understanding of law where the four modalities are already connected in the lawscape.

Using Deleuzeoguattarian theory I have argued that it is possible to conceive of the concept of the cultural commons as an ecology, and how, understood as such, there is no direct need to refer to an "outside" of law or the commons: together they are the lawscape. I have claimed that this connectedness and connectability is not something that needs to be *invented* – it needs only to be made visible. When Lessig claims that the lessons of *Code Is Law* have not been learned, the notion of law in his context can be challenged, as well as the claim that code *is* law. Not challenged it in the sense to say that code *is not* law, but challenge it within the framework of this approach here, namely that *what law is* might be irrelevant, as long as we understand that it can be connected to everything that affects it. Code is law, and law is law – a machine, a rhizome, *always already, something else.*

This is not a semantic claim either. This is the very *potential* of law, it being able to adapt to the deterritorialising and fluid (and fleeing) tendencies of society. We live in a connected world that constantly communicates and is dependent on communication (in all its guises). The commons forms a central part in this connected existence, and there, it is obvious, law has to accommodate for all kinds of connections. There are of course many problems with the digital spheres. We have been reading about them and studying them for over two decades now. I have attempted to present some of these problems. Lessig notes for instance that with the arrival of the internet there was a lot to worry about, and digitisation has brought with it plenty of bad, despite much of the good it has given us. Ditto about the law. In the context of copyright both Lessig and many other scholars with him have for a long time claimed that we have been

7 Lessig, Inaugural Lecture, Lund University, 30 May 2013.

regulating in the last couple of decades as if the digital spheres did not exist. This very stance has meant that sharing became piracy – i.e. infringement of intellectual property rights. This in turn resulted in large-scale litigations as for instance in the Napster case. In the short term, these legislations managed to destroy organisations such as Napster, but in the long term – it resulted in a multitude of Napster-like entities, Pirate Bay being the last prominent one among them. To use a now tired but still surprisingly potent anecdote, when Galileo Galilei was forced to recant his belief that the Earth moves around the sun in front of the Inquisition, he is supposed to have followed up the recantation by uttering the words: *Eppur si muove /And yet it moves*. The same can be said about current approaches to law, art and commons. The digital spheres it is safe to say, not only exist, they now also *leak*. So, regardless of how many underlying sharing structures have already been recanted, taken down, and more recently, how many underlying structures that enable leaks have been disabled, and regardless of how many law professors recant the possibilities of law – the digital spheres are here to stay, *whether we like it or not*. This invites a more potent discussion on the commons, where it can finally be shown that law-art-commons are entangled.

Deleuzian and Deleuzeoguattarian theory together with the notion of the lawscape has therefore been utilised to describe societies and laws that are constantly moving, fleeing, *and leaking* and where entities, bodies, are more connected than we have previously assumed. This must be acknowledged in jurisprudence as well as in the everyday practices of law. Such a fundamental acknowledgement is called for. There will be connectedness, sharing, there will be a sharing economy: the industrial society is over, the ideals of the Enlightenment gone. And this tendency ought not to be fought by law. If the sharing of artworks during the last 20 years has happened via digital platforms (legal as well as illegal), then the sharing of the future, it can be argued, now happens with information. It is no longer just a matter that concerns the so called cultural content, it has spread to also include wider types of information, data, (more or less "fake") news and knowledge that is being shared and where further regulation may no doubt be called for. But we now also know that any regulation territorialises societal changes and lines of flight, and we must be aware of that. This can be concluded, by connecting the nature of the digital sphere to the liquidity of Deleuzeoguattarian smooth spaces and the viscosity of Mortonian hyperobjects. Interestingly, it is precisely where we have ended up here, in the sharing of the future, which also provides an answer as to why the Deleuzeoguattarian theory may now be more pertinent than it ever has been before... Because, we have long enough now tried to e-scape the changes that the fluid digital sphere brought about by building legal dams towards the tidal wave of the viscous information that has been coming at us, *and yet*, it leaks.

8.2 Cultural commons in times of crisis: an ecology

Lastly, once we have reached not only the potential but also the peril of the digital spheres they can now be connected to a more general discussion in terms of access and distribution of resources in the knowledge economy within the context of the still very much on-going global crisis. In the first sentence of *Commonwealth*,[8] Hardt and Negri claim that crises such as war, suffering, misery and exploitation, increasingly characterise our globalising world.[9] Our particular crisis, if we now have to ascribe a date to it in a Deleuzeoguattarian manner, can be marked by the year 2008, and it has brought on a paradigm shift of its own, where the questions of sharing and accessing *both* natural *and* intellectual resources have been raised. In our crisis, there seems to be a shortage of both.

This book has in fact in been written with that very backdrop, a time of crisis: financial crisis, environmental crisis, employment crisis, technological crisis, legal crisis, *intellectual property crisis, cultural heritage crisis*... The crisis particularly hit the global cultural and entertainment industries early on. It has certainly also affected, and still affects, law. First it appeared as though we were entering the end of times.[10] Then it appeared as if the only way to exit the crisis was to *reclaim* what had been lost, the causes,[11] the struggles, the influences, the territories, the streets, the spaces, the squares, the realms of power... To do that, law on a global level had to be approached differently, as a bio political governance, as a war machine. So law slowly, and perhaps unbeknownst to many of us, became something else, it became a territory, a machine, and then a lawscape, and now lastly, an atmosphere. Invisible to the naked eye. As such we have to re-imagine jurisprudence and law in order to visualise it, and in order to pose different questions concerning the role of law in connecting art and commons.

As I have attempted to show in this book, issues surrounding ownership of culture must not only be connected to intellectual property law but cultural heritage law too. The disputes surrounding ownership of cultural heritage have so far been approached as direct consequences of colonial pasts, marked by acts of plunder, looting, stealing, and (mis)appropriation[12] of cultural items. Since the processes of decolonisation, the return and repatriation of cultural heritage to countries of origin (having often been taken to the colonial countries) has been an act of acknowledgement of the now new states' national identity, belonging, sovereignty, as well as a direct measure in terms of building the national subjectivity of the decolonised states, now free from colonial influence. At the same time,

8 Hardt and Negri, 2009.
9 Ibid p. vii.
10 Zizek, 2011.
11 Zizek, 2009.
12 Macmillan, 2013.

also the minorities, indigenous peoples, and other more fluent groups within all nation states, have been acknowledged as communities whose cultural heritage must be safeguarded. I have tried to address the notions of community, property and belonging together throughout this book, and now I have arrived at the urgency of continuing these discussions when it comes to ownership of that which is often referred to as cultural heritage.

Today however, we are facing different types of problems connected to heritage, not necessarily those tied to colonisation but rather those connected to the internal destruction or dispersal of a people's own national heritage. Here the definitions of community are vital. Lately, we have for instance seen the *internal* destruction, abduction or illegal export of cultural items where national insurgent groups, rebels and/or terrorists have deliberately and systematically destroyed national cultural heritage. The issue is thus not one of cultural heritage items having been taken, relocated or (mis)appropriated by an occupant, colonial power or external enemy, but rather that internal belligerent groups have understood certain artefacts as testaments of a past or a community belonging that does not conform with their own ideology. An example of this is of course the destruction of the cultural site Palmyra in Syria, where the terrorist group Islamic State has destroyed some of the most significant ancient artefacts, sites and buildings, claiming that these are idols from a pre-Islamic, pagan tradition. Where such cultural heritage has not been destroyed, it has been dispersed, looted and illegally sold off to undisclosed buyers around the world in order to finance the on-going war and the existence of, here, the Islamic State. Whether they like it or not, the cultural heritage of Palmyra thus still holds up the body of the IS. This has of course also led to a systematic destruction and severe impoverishment of Syrian heritage both deemed as national as well as of having a great significance to other communities and the entire human kind.

From that, another ownership issue previously not directly encountered has sprung up, namely how to deal with the legal definition of "national" heritage. This has become increasingly relevant recently particularly in view of the protection, administration and location of the objects that are not deemed "national" in a traditional sense. The Bruno Schulz case that was discussed here at length is a more than typical example. These are artefacts that do not conform to a traditional idea of a monolithic nation-state but that are still tied to a state somehow e.g. through the state's history. Ownership of this category of cultural heritage still remains legally uncertain and unexplored. One way of dealing with these issues has been as we have seen to as far as possible at least make the disputed works available digitally.

This is where technology and the digital become connected to cultural heritage and where intellectual property and cultural heritage converge in a legal concept of the cultural commons. When it comes to technology, however, there is an optimism in it being able to create these types of solutions. But this optimism seems to forget that technology is not always something that will advance access, or create solutions. Take for instance the so called *disruptive technology* that has inherently challenged legal as well as technical structures, forcing them both to change. Some earlier disruptive technologies are of course the tape recorder (first wave), file sharing systems (second wave). A more recent one is perhaps the 3D printer (third wave).

It is an interesting phenomenon that we are witnessing the cultural content that just recently migrated online to the digital sphere (within the context of the second wave of disruptive technology, such as digitization and file sharing), is now experiencing a reverse movement, namely migrating back to the material world with the third wave of disruptive technology such as e.g. 3D printers. How might that affect the cultural commons and how ought for instance the internet of things (when regular, previously merely physical objects become embedded in electronics, software, connected – "smart") be regulated? And if printing out an image from the online sphere – like e.g. Richard Prince did with the Instagram portraits, how will this then affect the commons and with it both intellectual property and cultural heritage laws?

And it will become more and more difficult to make these assessments the more advanced the technology becomes, and the more entangled it becomes with our daily lives, all the way through to our body. Increasingly we rely on our social media, on apps, on more or less artificial body parts: the smart objects have become part of our bodies. It also means that it is no longer a sci-fi statement to claim that the technology, and with it smart devices, have merged into our bodies. We exist both online and off line. In the book *The 4th Revolution: How the Infosphere is Reshaping Human Reality*, and as we saw in Chapter 4 above, Floridi writes that in the infosphere we have all become *inforgs:* information carrying organisms. Our lives as human beings have now merged into an *onlife* that exists both on and off line. Part of that life is also made up by the creative content that we create as well as interact with.

So, the new existence, onlife as well as the objects connected to the internet of things are here to stay. Which means that the posthuman entanglement between the human and the object becomes a hyperobject, which we have discussed throughout this book. This is now a material reality. When it comes to law it is increasingly difficult to continue to focus on legal concepts that solely rely on dichotomies where property ownership is divided from personhood, where exclusivity principles or assumptions about the individual are divided from the ideas of the community, and so on. And we do have to take these matters seriously. The borders between the cultural, or the artificial, and the natural have now also collapsed, the body and the object have converged.

In such a setting the cultural commons, just becomes *commons*, part of our onlife. Law, art, commons, have through this process, become quite literally body-machines, entangled with the human body, nature, its entire so called context. We have been able to see this by applying the concepts of hyperobjects and rhizomatic jurisprudence. In this merger (intellectual property, cultural heritage) law becomes connected to ethics too, and thus reaches beyond humanism as the ideas of humanism, as inherited from the Enlightenment, have now collapsed. And as Ihab Hassan poignantly put it: "Humanism may be coming to an end as humanism transforms itself into something one must helplessly call *posthumanism*"[13]

This means that legally, after the current crisis, when law has become an ecology of existence, the humanist, anthropocentric reasoning that places the human being in the centre may have to be released, or at least questioned and discussed. We have seen how anthropocentrism is constantly re-created within law through e.g. the relentless use of and reliance on dichotomies such as immaterial–material, body–technology, personhood–property, etc. Maybe one of the strongest arguments advanced in posthumanist studies is this very insight, namely that bodies are relational, constantly converging and with that it becomes increasingly impossible to draw lines between bodies. In line with Deleuzian readings of Spinozian philosophy, it also becomes rather apparent that we can no longer discern nor know what a body (or a hyperobject) can do. Through technological advancements as well as via the market driven schizophrenic capitalism that has been able to follow and capitalise on the technological lines of flight, it has now almost become impossible to draw a line between the human body, the human intellect, capital and the spaces in which they co-exist. That is why it is equally impossible to speak of such things as "intellectual" property or "cultural" heritage. All bodies become entangled with hyperobjects and as such all become more or less material, they become a space, an ecology, the lawscape has reappeared. This entanglement is the very ethical core that the discussion of law, art and commons now must latch on to.

8.3 Not one but several ecologies: on an apocalyptic note

I have now reached the end of this book. It is the result of a process that began about 16 years ago when I as a 19-year-old law student listened to a professor, that later became my doctoral supervisor. He gave a lecture on the Frankfurt School within our jurisprudence course. It was September 2001. 9/11 had happened about two weeks before that lecture. We, as the rest of the world, were still in a confused daze. He never mentioned what

13 Hassan, 1977.

was happening outside the university in his lectures, but he spoke about Marxist jurisprudence and connected it to the critique of ideology. From there he arrived at the concept of the cultural industry in the writings of the Frankfurt School as they are known vernacularly, the Institute of Social Research as they were formally called. He explained how the Frankfurt School thinkers saw culture as administrated, as very much part of the ideology used to govern people, and how the commodified, mass-produced artworks, Adorno and Horkheimer the two frontrunners of this intellectual enclave had claimed, would eventually lead to fascism. I have spent 16 years coming to terms with that claim.

On 5 December 2016 Alex Ross wrote an article in the New Yorker called "The Frankfurt School Knew Trump Was Coming".[14] In that article Ross makes the poignant claim that the election of the 45th American president saw as victor somebody who is as much a "pop-culture phenomenon as he is a political one." Did Adorno and Horkheimer have a point? When Walter Benjamin, also a part of their group, famously claimed that "There is no document of culture which is not at the same time a document of barbarism", maybe were they, after all, onto something? In the post industrial digital sphere where what they called culture industry has changed and been turned into an all encompassing space where the human and the cultural object converge, and where the two have become entangled in a hyperobject, then there might be an aspect to culture that my study has failed to see. And it goes back to the argument I heard the first time at that lecture, end of September 2001, that culture when it has passed through the capitalist system can, whether we like it or not, also be (used as) ideology.

In the collection of essays "Authoritarian Personality"[15] Adorno and Horkheimer assembled texts tracing the becoming of a potentially fascistic individual and in that process, they claimed, the administrated culture that has become commodified plays a pivotal role. The argument of this book has been to reveal the importance of the artwork in precisely the reverse, in freeing individuals by allowing us to engage in democratic society, in the construction of identity, community, belonging through the artwork. As such a legal construction of the commons, it has been claimed, is not only necessary – it is vital. While the findings of the Frankfurt School for a long time now have been largely dismissed as elitist and not understanding contemporary and subversive art, we seem to be experiencing a return to their lines of reasoning. However, this time from a different vantage point. So, what if this construction of a legal commons that I have argued for also could enable ideological, as well as we have seen through this book *bodily* and biopolitical, governance of people that will eventually lead to the

14 Ross, 2016.
15 Adorno et. al, 1993.

creation of fascistic individuals? Would a legal commons counteract or reinforce the creation of such individuals? I dare not answer that question here, more than paraphrasing Deleuze and Guattari – the commons will not save us.

What I dare say, however, is that I have been engaging in what Guattari refers to in the essay "The Three Ecologies" as ecosophy, that is the three ecological registers: the environment, social relations and human subjectivity.[16] When we are connecting law, art and commons these three ecological registers have been borne in mind. But that does not answer the question regarding the movement of subjectivity towards fascism through an administrated construct of the commons. Guattari writes:

> At every level, individual or collective, in everyday life as well as the reinvention of democracy (concerning town planning, artistic creation, sport, etc.) it is a question in each instance of looking into what would be the dispositives of the production of subjectivity, which tends towards an individual and/or collective resingularization, rather than that of mass-media manufacture, which is synonymous with distress and despair.[17]

Guattari thus gives an explanation that the production of subjectivity can happen in several ecological registers, some are synonymous with resingularisation and democracy, and some with mass-media manufacture, distress and despair. In these (post?) apocalyptic times we should then understand that commons is not a messianic concept, but rather a space where the bodies of law and art meet and converge. As to which ethical or ecological register then prevails, that is a question of spatial justice. In there, as Ugo Mattei once put it, "You don't define bene comune [commons], you fight for them!"[18] So the pragmatic answer, without refuting the Frankfurt School, is that we must continue to fight for the *ethical* commons, even if and when the commons has been inscribed in law.

To bring together, on a very final note, the merger of pop culture, politics, struggle and law. I want to do that by pointing to the very latest development in the Richard Prince case concerning *New Portraits* and his prints of "borrowed" Instagram images that have also been discussed at length here. During the US election campaign in November 2016 Prince screen grabbed an Instagram image from the account belonging to Ivanka Trump. The image, depicting Trump having her hair and make up done by her styling team, was included in the *New Portrait* series and put on sale.

16 Guattari, 2005: 19–20.

17 Guattari, 2005: 23.

18 www.youtube.com/watch?v=aAi4wwirTYU (2:04-2:07). See also Bailey in Bailey, Farrell and Mattei, 2013: 112.

Trump, herself an enthusiastic art collector, bought the print for USD 36 000. After the subsequent election of her father, Prince wrote on his Twitter regarding the Ivanka Trump portrait: "This is not my work. I did not make it. I deny. I denounce. This is fake art." Parodying the turn of phrase used by Donald Trump when addressing the so called "fake news" on his Twitter just before that – Prince thus denounced the Ivanka portrait as his. He claimed that he did that as a moral commitment. He also returned the money Trump had paid for her portrait. Thus, the relentless nature of art, politics, struggle, information, and so on, keeps multiplying, keeps finding new assemblages in which to exist, keeps being entangled with personhood, property, subjectivity, democracy, identity, belonging and so on. We can no longer pretend that they can be separated. We can no longer claim that they are completely administrated as commodities, or that they are not commodities. They are at the same time property as they are constitutive of our subjectivity, personhood. Hyperobjects. They stick to us.

Which of course brings us to the end of this book. The end of this walk that began in London that early September day at Charing Cross station and ended precisely here. We have traversed the lawscape. And now here we are. In the posthuman, post apocalyptic state of matters. We have seen how we have become more-than human, entangled with the hyperobjects around us. The fetishised idea of the artwork as something unique, special, sublime, can no longer be upheld. We now know that the artwork is just another hyperobject, another space, another (undead, cyborgian) body that struggles to occupy space with every-body else.

This begs the final question: If we so far have been fetishising the artwork and regulating in such a manner, and with the world now marred with crisis, underpinned by poverty, war, natural disasters, apocalyptic sentiment – is the creation of a legal concept of the commons the very rupture we have been looking for that will take us away from a fetish towards ethical productions of subjectivity?

Bibliography

Publications

Aderet, Ofer. 2012. Israel Court Orders Kafka Manuscripts Be Transferred to National Library, *Haaretz*, 14 October, available at: www.haaretz.com/jewish/news/israel-court-orders-kafka-manuscripts-be-transferred-to-national-library.premium-1.469870

Adorno, Theodor W. et al. 1993. *The Authoritarian Personality*, Norton [originally published 1950]

Adorno, Theodor W. 1998. *Aesthetic Theory (Theory and History of Literature)*, (trans.) Robert Hullot-Kantor, Minneapolis, MN: University of Minnesota Press [posthumously published in 1970, written between 1961 and 1969]

Adorno, Theodor W. and Horkheimer, Max. 2007. *Dialectic of Enlightenment*, (trans.) John Hummings, London: Verso [originally published in 1944]

Agamben, Giorgio. 2004. *The Open: Man and Animal*, (trans.) Kevin Attel, Stanford University Press

Anon. (n.d.) *Internet Encyclopedia of Philosophy*, available at: www.iep.utm.edu/deleuze/

Dyrk, Ashton. 2013. *Using Deleuze: The Cinema Books, Film Studies and Effect*, open access, available at: http://etd.ohiolink.edu/send-pdf.cgi/Ashton%20Dyrk.pdf?bgsu1151342833, pp. 58–59

Åslund, Åsa. 2008. *Allemansrätten och Marknyttjande: Studier av ett rättsinstitut*, Lindköping University, Sweden

Bailey, Saki, Farrell, Gilda and Mattei, Ugo (eds). 2013. *Protecting Future Generations Through Commons, Trends in Social Cohesion*, No. 26, Council of Europe Publishing

Bandle, Anne Laure and Phammatter, Marie. 2015 Conference Presentation, 'Museum Selfies: Engaging with Museum Collections or Infringing Copyright?', Access to Material and Immaterial Goods: The Relationship between Intellectual Property and its Physical Embodiment, Luzern University, 23 and 24 January

Barad, Karen. 2007. *Meeting the Universe Halfway: Quantum Physics and the Entanglement of Matter and Meaning*, Duke University Press

Barr, Olivia. 2016. *A Jurisprudence of Movement: Common Law, Walking, Unsettling Place*, Routledge

Barthes, Roland. 1967. "Death of the Author", (trans.) Richard Howard, available at: https://writing.upenn.edu/~taransky/Barthes.pdf

Bauman, Ken. 2011. "The Beginner's Guide to Deleuze", available at: http://htmlgiant.com/random/the-beginners-guide-to-deleuze/

Bell, Tom W. 2007. "Copyright as Intellectual Property Privilege", in *Syracuse Law Review*, 58

Benjamin, Walter. 2007. *Illuminations: Essays and reflections*, (ed. and intro.) Hanna Arendt, (trans.) Harcourt, Brace, Jovanivich, Inc., NY: Schocken Books [originally published in Zeitschrift für Sozialforschung, in 1935]

Bennett, Jane. 2009. *Vibrant Matter: A Political Ecology of Things*, Duke University Press

Berendt, John. 2005. *The City of Falling Angels*, The Penguin Press

Bertacchini, Enrico, Bravo, Giangiacomo, Marrelli, Massimo and Santagata, Walter (eds). 2012. *Cultural Commons: New Perspectives on the Production and Evolution of Culture*, Edward Elgar

Björling, Erik. 2016. "The Expression of Legal Argumentation: Towards a Methodology for Narrative Studies of Discourses of subsumption'", *International Journal of Legal Discourse*, 1, 1: 117–132

Björling, Erik. 2017. *Rättstillämpningens tystnad: En rättsvetenskaplig narratologisk studie om argumentation och rättsliga uttryck inom civilprocessen*, Juridiska Institutionens Skriftserie, Gothenburg University

Blackstone, William, Sir. 1979. *Commentaries on the Laws of England*, Vol. II. para 1, Oxford University Press [originally published 1765–9]

Bogue, Roland. 1989. *Deleuze and Guattari*, Routledge

Borch, Christian and Kornberger, Martin. 2015. *Urban Commons, Rethinking the City*, Routledge

Bourdieu, Pierre. 1991. *Language and Symbolic Power*, (trans.) Gino Raymond and Matthew Adamson, (ed.) John B. Thompson, Cambridge: Polity

Bourdieu, Pierre. 1993. *The Field of Cultural Production: Essays on Art and Literature*, (ed. and intro.) Randal Johnson (various translators), Cambridge: Polity

Boyle, James. 1997–98. "A Politics of Intellectual Property; Environmentalism on the Net?", in *Duke Law Journal*, 47, 87

Boyle, James. 2003. "The Second Enclosure Movement and the Construction of The Public Domain", in *Law and Contemporary Problems*, 66, 1/2 (Winter/Spring): 33–34

Braidotti, Rosi. 2011. *Nomadic Subjects: Embodiment and Sexual Difference in Contemporary Feminist Theory*, Columbia University Press [originally published 1994]

Braidotti, Rosi. 2013. *Metamorphoses: Towards a Materialist Theory of Becoming*, John Wiley & Sons [originally published 2002]

Braidotti, Rosi. 2013b. *The Posthuman*. John Wiley & Sons

Braidotti, Rosi, Colebrook, Claire and Hanafin, Patrick (eds). 2009. *Deleuze and Law: Forensic Futures*, Basingstoke: Palgrave Macmillan

Bring, Ove. 2015. *Parthenonsyndromet: kampen om kulturskatterna*, Atlantis

Bruncevic, Merima. 2011. "The Lost Mural of Bruno Schulz: A Critical Legal, Perspective on Control, Access to and Ownership of Art", in *Law and Critique*, 22, 1

Bruncevic, Merima. 2014. *Fixing the Shadows: Access to Art and the Legal Concept of Cultural Commons*, Juridiska Institutionens Skriftserie, Gothenburg University

Bruncevic, Merima. 2017. "Subjektets död: en postapokalyptisk livvaka" in *Ord & Bild*, March

Burdon, Peter. 2015. *Earth Jurisprudence: Private Property and the Environment*, Routledge

Butler, Judith. 2011. "Who Owns Kafka"', in *London Review of Books*, 33, 5(3) March

Calhoun, Craig. (ed.) 1992. *Habermas and the Public Sphere*, Cambridge, MA: London: MIT Press

Connolly, William E. 2012. "Habermas, Deleuze and Capitalism", in *Theory & Event*, 11, 4, 28 November

Cornish, William. 2004. *Intellectual Property*, Oxford University Press

Craig, Carys J. 2011. *Copyright, Communication and Culture: Towards a Relational Theory of Copyright Law*, Cheltenham UK; Northampton, MA: Edward Elgar

Dahlberg, Leif. 2011. "Pirates, Partisans and Politico-Judicial Space", in *Law & Literature*, 23, 2: 262–281

Debord, Guy. 1956. *Theory of the Dérive*, Les Lèvres Nues #9 (November 1956) reprinted in Internationale Situationniste #2 (December 1958) (trans.) Ken Knabb

DeBriyn, James. 2012. "Shedding Light on Copyright Trolls: An Analysis of Mass Copyright Litigation in the Age of Statutory Damages" in *UCLA Entertainment Law Review*, 19: 79

Deleuze, Gilles. 1988. *Spinoza: Practical Philosophy*, (trans.) Robert Hurley, City Lights Books, San Francisco

Deleuze, Gilles. 1990. *The Logic of Sense* (trans. and eds.) Mark Lester with Charles Stivale, Constantin V. Boundas, New York: Columbia University Press [originally published in 1969]

Deleuze, Gilles. 1992. "Postscript on the Societies of Control", in *The MIT Press*, 59, Winter: 3–7

Deleuze, Gilles. 1994. *L'Abécédaire de Gilles Deleuze*, avec Claire Parnet, Paris: DVD Editions Montparnasse

Deleuze, Gilles. 1999. *Masochism: Coldness and Cruelty*, (trans.) Jean McNeil, Zone Books [originally published in 1967]

Deleuze, Gilles. 2000. *Proust and Signs: The Complete Text*, (trans.) Richard Howard, The Athlone Press [originally published in 1972]

Deleuze, Gilles. 2003. *Francis Bacon: The Logic of Sensation*, (trans.) Daniel W. Smith, Continuum [originally published in 1981]

Deleuze, Gilles. 2009. *Cinema 1: The Movement-Image*, (trans.) Hugh Tomlinson and Barbara Habberjam, University of Minnesota Press [originally published in 1983]

Deleuze, Gilles. 2010. *Cinema 2: The Time Image*, (trans.) Hugh Tomlinson and Robert Galeta, Continuum [originally published in 1985]

Deleuze, Gilles and Guattari, Félix. 1986. *Kafka: Towards a Minor Literature*, (trans.) Dana Polan, University of Minnesota Press [originally published in 1975]

Deleuze, Gilles and Guattari, Félix. 2004. *Anti-Oedipus: Capitalism and Schizophrenia*, (trans.) Robert Hurley, Mark Seem, and Helen R. Lane, foreword by Michel Foucault, Continuum [originally published in 1972]

Deleuze, Gilles and Guattari, Félix. 2011. *A Thousand Plateaus: Capitalism and Schizophrenia*, (trans. and foreword) Brian Massumi, London: Athlone [originally published in 1988]

Dusollier, Séverine. 2006. "The Master's Tools v. The Master's House: Creative Commons v. Copyright", in *Columbia Journal of Law & Arts*, 29, 271

Elkin-Koren, Niva. 2005. "What Contracts Cannot Do: The Limits of Private Ordering in Facilitating a Creative Commons", in *Fordham Law Review*, 74, 375

Engel, Antk. 2009. Workshop presentation. "Deterritorialization, Reterritorialization, and Lines of Flight", *COST Action IS0803: Remaking Eastern Borders in Europe: A Network Exploring Social, Moral and Material Relocations of Europe's Eastern Peripheries*, Work Group 1: Borders Nicosia (Cyprus)

Esposito, Roberto. 2010. *Communitas: The Origin and Destiny of Community*, Stanford University Press

Finchett-Maddock, Lucy. 2016. *Protest, Property and the Commons: Performances of Law and Resistance*, Routledge

Flood, Alison. 2012. "Huge Franz Kafka Archive to be Made Public, Israeli Judge Rules that Disputed Cache of Papers Belonging to Max Brod Should be Published", *Guardian Online*: www.guardian.co.uk/books/2012/oct/15/franz-kafka-archive-public

Floridi, Luciano. 2014. *The Fourth Revolution: How the Infosphere is Reshaping Human Reality*, Oxford University Press

Foucault, Michel. 1986. "Of Other Spaces", (trans.) J. Miskowiec, *Diacritics* 16: 22–27

Foucault, Michel. 1991. *Discipline and Punish: The Birth of the Prison*, (trans.) Alan Sheridan, Penguin Books [originally published in 1975]

Foucault, Michel. 1998. "What is an Author", (trans.) Robert Hurley and others, in *Aesthetics, Method, and Epistomology*, The New York Press [originally published 1967]

Freyfogle, Eric T. 2013. Keynote address, *Common Core Europe*, University of Torino, 15–16 November

Geissler, Benjamin. 2002. *Finding Pictures*, documentary film, Benjamin Geissler Filmproduction

Geissler, Benjamin. 2012. *Die Bilderkammer des Bruno Schulz – das letzte Werk eines Genies – Mobile Installation von Benjamin Geissler*, (exhibition catalogue) Umweltbibliothek, Grosshennersdorf

Goldfarb, David. Conference Paper. 2013. "Schulz the Pre-Raphaelites and an encounter with Dante", Colloque international interuniversitaire *Schulz lu et interprété en Europe Centrale: entre modernisme et modernité. Poétique, réception, regards croisés*, INALCO, Sorbonne, Paris, 21–23 March

Goodchild, Philip. 1996. *Deleuze and Guattari: An Introduction to the Politics of Desire*, Sage Publications

Gordon, Wendy J. 1988–1989. "An Inquiry into the Merits of Copyright: The Challenges of Consistency, Consent, and Encouragement Theory", in *Stanford Law Review*, 41: 1343

Grotius, Hugo. 1925. *On the Law of War and Peace*, Book 2. Ch. 2 (trans.) Kelsey, Oxford, Clarendon Press, 1925 [originally published in 1625]

Guattari, Félix. 1995. *Chaosmosis: An Ethico-aesthetic Paradigm*, Indiana University Press

Guattari, Félix. 2003. *Essais d'analyse institutionnelle*, Editions La Découverte [originally published 1972]

Guattari, Félix. 2005. "The Three Ecologies", Continuum [originally published 1989]

Guattari, Félix. 2012. *La révolution moléculaire*, Les Prairies Ordinaires [originally published 1977]

Guattari, Félix and Negri, Antonio, 1990. *Communists Like Us: New Spaces of Liberty, New Lines of Alliance*, (trans.) M. Ryan, J. Becker, A. Bove, and N. Le Blanc, (ed.) S. Shukaitis, Semiotext(e)/Foreign Agents

Guattari, Félix and Rolink, Suely. 2008. *Molecular Revolution in Brazil*, (trans.) Karel Clapshow and Brian Holmes, Semiotext(e)/Foreign Agents [originally published 1986]

Grossman, Sanford J. and Stiglitz, Joseph E. 1980. "On the Impossibility of Informationally Efficient Markets", in *American Economic Review*, 70: 393, 405

Guilbault, Lucie. 2011. "Darfurnica, Miffy and the right to parody!" in *JIPITEC*, 3, 236: para 1

Gustafsson, Håkan. 2002. *Rättens Polyvalens: En rättsvetenskaplig Studie av Sociala Rättigheter och Rättssäkerhet*, Lund Studies in Sociology of Law

Gustafsson, Håkan. 2003. "Begärets Dunkla Mål", in *Retfaerd*, 3: 102

Gustafsson, Håkan. 2010. "Fiction of Law", in *Rechtstheorie* 3: 319–363

Gustafsson, Håkan. 2014. *Dissens: Om Det Rättsliga Vetandet*, Jure

Habermas, Jürgen. 1974. "The Public Sphere and Encyclopedia Article", in *New German Critique*, 3: 49–55, (trans.) Sara and Frank Lennox [originally published in 1964]

Habermas, Jürgen. 1985. *The Theory of Communicative Action: Vol. II, Lifeworld and System: A Critique of Functionalist Reason*, (trans.) Thomas McCarthy, Boston, MA: Beacon Press

Habermas, Jürgen. 1992. *The Structural Transformation of the Public Sphere: An Inquiry into a Category of Bourgeois Society*, (trans.) Thomas Burger with the assistance of Fredrick Lawrence, Cambridge, MA: Polity, MIT Press, [originally published in 1962]

Hanafin, Patrick. 2014. Keynote address, *Fictions of Law, Law and Literature Conference*, University of Verona, November

Haraway, Donna. 1991. *Simians, Cyborgs and Women: The Reinvention of Nature*, Free Association Books [originally published 1984]

Hardin, Garrett. 2009. "The Tragedy of the Commons", in *Journal of Natural Resources Policy Research*, 1, 3: 243–253, [originally published in 1968]

Hardt, Michael and Negri, Antonio. 2004. *Multitude: War and Democracy In the Age of Empire*, New York: The Penguin Express

Hardt, Michael and Negri, Antonio. 2009. *Commonwealth*, Cambridge, MA: Harvard University Press

Hardt, Michael. 2010. "The Common in Communism", in *Rethinking Marxism: A Journal of Economics, Culture & Society*, 22, 3: 346–356

Harvey, David. 1973. *Social Justice and the City*, Oxford: Blackwell

Harvey, David. 2000. *Spaces of Hope*, Edinburgh: Edinburgh University Press

Harvey, David. 2001. *Spaces of Capital: Towards a Critical Geography*, London: Routledge

Harvey, David. 2004. "The Right to the City", in (ed.) L. Lees, *The Emancipatory City: Paradoxes and Possibilities*, London: Sage

Hassan, Ihab. 1977. "Prometheus as Performer: Toward a Postmodern Culture?" in (eds.) Benamou, Michel and Caramello, Charles, *Performance in Postmodern Culture*, Wis.: Coda Press

Helfer, L. R. 2004. "Regime Shifting: The TRIPS Agreement and New Dynamics of International Intellectual Property Lawmaking", in *Yale Journal of International Law* 29: 1

Hemmungs-Wirtén, Eva. 2004. *No Trespassing: Authorship, Intellectual Property Rights, and the Boundaries of Globalization*, University of Toronto Press

Hemmungs-Wirtén, Eva. 2008. *Terms of Use: Negotiating the Jungle of the Intellectual Commons*, University of Toronto Press

Hjelm, Mats. 1998. "Kring, konst och intelligenta maskiner – Humanistisk kritik i informationssamhället" in (ed.) Sven-Olov Wallenstein *Nomadologin*, Skriftserien Kairos, nummer 4, Kungliga Konsthögskolan, Raster Förlag

Hyde, Lewis. 2012. *Common as Air, Revolution: Art and Ownership*, Union Books

Iljadica, Marta. 2017. "Copyright and the Right to the City" in *Northern Ireland Legal Quarterly*, 68(1): 59–78

Käll, Jannice, 2017. *Converging Digital and Human Bodies: Posthumanism, Property, Law*, Juridiska Institutionens Skriftserie, Gothenburg University

Keenan, Sarah. 2014. *Subversive Property: Law and the Production of Spaces of Belonging*, Routledge

Kellogg, Catherine. 2005. "Love and Communism: Jean-Luc Nancy's Shattered Community", in *Law and Critique*, 16: 339–355

Krikorian, Gaëlle and Kapczynski, Amy (eds). 2010. *Access to Knowledge in the Age of Intellectual Property*, Zone Books

Lefebvre, Alexandre. 2005. "A New Image of Law: Deleuze and Jurisprudence", in *Telos*, 130: 103–126

Lefebvre, Alexandre. 2006. "Habermas And Deleuze On Law and Adjudication", in *Law and Critique*, 17: 389–414

Lefebvre, Alexandre. 2006b. "We Do Not Yet Know What the Law Can Do", in *Contemporary Political Theory*, 5: 52–67

Lefebvre, Alexandre. 2007. "Critique of Teleology in Kant and Dworkin: The Law Without Organs (LwO)", in *Philosophy Social Criticism*, 33: 179

Lefebvre, Alexandre. 2008. *The Image of Law: Deleuze, Bergson, Spinoza*, Stanford University Press

Lefebvre, Henri. 1991. *The Production of Space*, (trans.) D. Nicholson-Smith, Oxford: Blackwell

Lessig, Lawrence. 1999. *Code and Other Laws of Cyberspace*, New York: Basic Books

Lessig, Lawrence. 2001. *The Future of Ideas: The Fate of the Commons in a Connected World*, New York: Random House

Lessig, Lawrence. 2006. *Code Version 2.0*, New York: Basic Books

Lippard, Lucy. 1997. *Six Years: The Dematerialisation of the Art Object*, University of California Press, California

Litman, Jessica. 1996. "Revising Copyright Law for the Information Age", in *Oregon Law Review*, 75: 19

Locke, John. 1690. *Two Treatises of Government*, available at: http://mlr.com/DigitalCollections/products/ModernWorld/find.htm

Maclean, Ruth. 2017. "Desecrated but Still Majestic: Inside Palmyra After Second Isis Occupation", in *Guardian Online*, 9 March

Macmillan, Fiona. 2013. "The Protection of Cultural Heritage: Common Heritage of Humankind, National Cultural Patrimony or Private Property?" in *Northern Ireland Legal Quarterly*, 64(3)

Madero, Marta. 2010. *Tabula Picta: Painting and Writing in Medieval Law*, University of Pennsylvania Press

Marcussen, Lars. n.d. *Deleuze and Space: The Smooth and the Striated*, available at: www.architectureandspace.com/sider/deleuze-and-space-the-smooth-and-the-striated_89.aspx

Massey, Doreen. 2005. *For Space*, London: Sage

Massey, Doreen. 2007. *World City*, Cambridge: Polity

Matteo, Perin. 2005. "The Sense of Freedom. The Surprise of Being-In-Common", in *Law and Critique*, 16: 315–338

Menahem Shohet, David. 1931. *The Jewish Court in the Middle Ages: Studies in Jewish Jurisprudence According to the Talmud, Geonic and Medieval German Responsa*, New York: Commanday-Roth Co

Minkkinen, Panu. 1998. "Law, Science and Truth", in (ed.) Ari Hirvonen, *Policentricity: The Multiple Scenes of Law*, Pluto Press

Moore, Nathan. 2000. "A Distant Hand Fell From His Shoulder", in *Law and Critique*, 11: 185–200

Moore, Nathan. 2004. "So You Love Me", in *Law and Critique*, 15: 45–64

Moore, Nathan. 2007. "Icons of Control: Deleuze, Signs, Law", in *International Journal for the Semiotics of Law*, 20: 33–54

Morton, Timothy. 2007. *Ecology without Nature: Rethinking Environmental Aesthetics*, Harvard University Press

Morton, Timothy. 2013. *Hyperobjects: Philosophy and Ecology After the End of the World*, University of Minnesota Press

Murray, Jamie. 2007. "Deleuze and Guattari's Intensive and Pragmatic Semiotic of Emergent Law", in *International Journal for the Semiotics of Law*, 20: 7–32

Murray, Jamie. 2013. *Deleuze and Guattari: Emergent Law*, Routledge

Mussawir, Edward. 2011. *Jurisdiction in Deleuze: The Expression and Representation of Law*, Routledge

Mussawir, Edward. 2011b. "The Activity of Judgment: Deleuze, Jurisdiction and the Procedural Genre of Jurisprudence", in *Law, Culture and the Humanities*, 7: 463

Nancy, Jean-Luc. 1991. *The Inoperative Community*, (trans.) P. Connor, (ed.) C. Fynsk, Minneapolis: University of Minnesota Press

Nancy, Jean-Luc. 2000. *Being Singular Plural*, (trans.) R. D. Richardson and A. E. O'Byrne, (eds.) W. Hamacher and D. E. Wellbery, Stanford University Press

Okediji, Ruth. 2008. "WIPO-WTO Relations and the Future of Global Intellectual Property Norms", in *Netherlands Yearbook of International Law*, 39: 4

Ostrom, Elinor. 1990. *Governing the Commons: The Evolution of Institutions for Collective Action*, Cambridge University Press, edition from 2011

Ostrom, Elinor and Hess, Charlotte. (eds.). 2007. *Understanding Knowledge as a Commons: From Theory to Practice*, MIT Press

Pallas Loren, Lydia. 2007. "Building a Reliable Semicommons of Creative Works: Enforcement of Creative Commons Licenses and Limited Abandonment of Copyright", in *George Mason Law Review*, 14: 271

Paloff, Benjamin. 2004/2005. "Who Owns Bruno Schulz? Poland stumbles over its Jewish past", in *Boston Review*, available at: http://bostonreview.net/BR29.6/paloff.html

Peczenik, Alexander. 1995. *Vad är rätt?: Om Demokrati, Rättssäkerhet, Etik och Juridisk Argumentation*, Stockholm: Fritze

Philippopuolos-Mihalopoulos, Andreas. 2009. *Niklas Luhmann: Law, Justice, Society, Nomikoi, Critical Legal Thinkers*, Routledge

Philippopoulos-Mihalopoulos, Andreas. 2013. "The Autopoietic Fold: Critical Autopoiesis Between Luhmann and Deleuze", in Philippopoulos-Mihalopoulos,

A. and La Cour, A. (eds.) *Luhmann Observed: Radical Theoretical Encounters*, Basingstoke: Palgrave Macmillan, pp. 60–84

Philippopoulos-Mihalopoulos, Andreas. 2014. *Spatial Justice, Body, Lawscape, Atmosphere*, Routledge

Pottage, Alain and Sherman, Brad. 2010. *Figures of Invention: A History of Modern Patent Law*, Oxford University Press

Prestidge-King, Charles. 2005. "A Sketch For a New Community: The Inoperative Community and Modern Politics", in *Cross-Section*, 1, available at: https://digitised-collections.unimelb.edu.au/handle/11343/141

Pufendorf, Samuel. 1703. *Of the Law of Nature and Nations*, available at: https://archive.org/details/oflawofnaturenat00pufe

Purdy, Jedediah. 2015. *After Nature: A Politics for the Anthropocene*, Harvard University Press

Radin, Margaret, J. 2009. *Reinterpreting Property*, University of Chicago Press [originally published 1993]

Ross, Alex. 2016. "The Frankfurt School Knew Trump Was Coming", in *New Yorker Online*, 5 December

Savigny, Friedrich Carl von. 1840. *System des heutigen römischen Rechts*, available at http://dlib-pr.mpier.mpg.de/m/kleioc/0010/exec/books/%22199236%22

Ramond, Charles. 2010. "Deleuze, Schizophrénie et Mondialisation", in *Capitalismes: en sortir?*, Dossier de la revue Cités 41, coordinated and presented by Gilles Campagnolo, Charles Ramond and Jacques de Saint-Victor, pp. 99–113

Rose, Carol, M. 2003. "Romans, Roads, and Romantic Creators: Traditions of Public Property in the Information Age", in *Law & Contemporary Problems*, 6: 89

Safi, Michael. 2017. "Ganges and Yamuna rivers Granted Same Legal Rights as Human Beings", in *Guardian Online*, 21 March available at: www.theguardian.com/world/2017/mar/21/ganges-and-yamuna-rivers-granted-same-legal-rights-as-human-beings

Schaeffer, Maritza. 2008-2009. "Contemporary Issues in the Visual Art Realm: How Useful are Creative Commons Licenses?" in *Journal of Law & Policy*, 17: 360

Sloterdijk, Peter. 1998. *Sphären I: Blasen: Mikrosphärologie*, Frankfurt-am-Main: Suhrkamp

Sloterdijk, Peter. 1999. *Sphären II: Globen: Makrosphärologie*, Frankfurt-am-Main: Suhrkamp

Sloterdijk, Peter. 2004. *Sphären III: Schäume: Plurale Sphärologie*, Frankfurt-am-Main: Suhrkamp

Soja, Edward. 1996. *Thirdspace: Journeys to Los Angeles and Other Real-and-Imagined Places*. Oxford: Basil Blackwell

Sousa Santos de, Boaventura. 1987. "Law: A Map of Misreading. Toward a Postmodern Conception of Law", in *Journal of Law & Society*, 14: 279

Stapleton, Jamie. 2002. *Art, Intellectual Property and The Knowledge Economy*, unpublished thesis, Goldsmiths College, University of London

Stivale, Charles J. 2005. *Gilles Deleuze: Key Concepts*, (ed.) Stivale, Charles, Acumen

Sutter de, Laurent and McGee, Kyle (eds.). 2012. "Introduction", in *Deleuze and Law*, Edinburgh University Press

Toffler, Alvin. 1980. *The Third Wave: The Classic Study of Tomorrow*, New York: Bantam

Tuori, Kaarlo. 2002. *Critical Legal Positivism*, Aldershot

Vandenberghe, Frédéric. 2008. "Deleuzian capitalism", in *Philosophy Social Criticism*, 34: 877

Wadstein MacLeod, Katarina. 2016. Interview for Swedish Radio, P4 *Det motsägelsefulla svenska kulturarvet – ett reportage*, 1 March 2016, available at: http://sverigesradio.se/sida/avsnitt/697597?programid=767

Wallenstein, Sven-Olov. (ed.) 1998. *Nomadologin*, Skriftserien Kairos, nummer 4, Kungliga Konsthögskolan, Raster Förlag

Waxman, Sharon. 2010. *Loot: Tomb Robbers, Treasure and The Great Museum Debate*, London: Old Street Publishing

Zizek, Slavoj. 2009. *In Defence of Lost Causes*, Verso

Zizek, Slavoj. 2011. *Living in the End of Times*, Verso

Directives

Directive 93/98/EEC of 29 October 1 993 harmonizing the term of protection of copyright and certain related rights

Directive 2001/29/EC of the European Parliament and of the Council of 22 May 2001 on the harmonisation of certain aspects of copyright and related rights in the information society, (Infosoc)

Directive 2004/48/EC of the European Parliament and of the Council of 29 April 2004 on the enforcement of intellectual property rights (IPR Enforcement Directive or IPRED)

Case law

International Criminal Court

Prosecutor v. Dario Kordic and Mario Cerkez, IT-95-14/2-T, 26 February 2001, p. 206

Prosecutor v. Ahmad Al Faqi Al Mahdi, ICC-01/12–01/15, 27 September 2016

Australian courts

Mabo v. Queensland (No. 2) (1992) *Australian Law Journal Review* 66: 408

European Court of Justice

C/128-11 *UsedSoft*

C-419/13 *Art & Allposters International*

Swedish courts

The Wikimedia Commons Case (Supreme Court), Högsta Domstolen, case number NJA 2016 s. 212 (NJA 2016:20), delivered on 4 April 2016

The Wikimedia Commons case (First Instance Court) Stockholms Tingsrätt, Patent- och marknandsdomstolen in Stockholm. case number PMT 8448–14, delivered on 6 July 2017. The Turkish Collection Kammarrätten in Stockholm, case number 2069-13, delivered on 29 May 2013

US courts

Cariou v. Prince, 714 F. 3d 694 (2d Cir. 2013)
Pierson v. Post 3 Caines. R.175 (NY Sup. Ct 1805)
Capitol Records, LLC v. ReDigi Inc. (No. 12-0095, 2012 US Dist.)

Conventions and other international law instruments

1949 Convention (I-IV) for the Amelioration of the Condition of the Wounded and Sick in Armed Forces in the Field. Geneva, 12 August and their Additional Protocols
1954 Protection of Cultural Property in the Event of Armed Conflict with Regulations for the Execution of the Convention (Hague Convention)
1972 UNESCO Convention Concerning the Protection of the World Cultural and Natural Heritage (World Heritage Convention)
1994 Annex 1C of the Marrakesh Agreement Establishing the World Trade Organization, signed in Marrakesh, Morocco on 15 April 1994 (TRIPS)
2001 UN High Commissioner for Human Rights: The Impact of the Agreement on Trade-Related Aspects of Intellectual Property Rights on Human Rights, Report of the High Commissioner, UN ESCOR, 52nd Sess., UN Doc. E/CN.4/Sub.2/2001/13
2002 European Convention on Transfrontier Television
2007 UN Declaration on the Rights of Indigenous Peoples (DRIPS)

Index

For Product Safety Concerns and Information please contact our EU representative GPSR@taylorandfrancis.com
Taylor & Francis Verlag GmbH, Kaufingerstraße 24, 80331 München, Germany

www.ingramcontent.com/pod-product-compliance
Ingram Content Group UK Ltd.
Pitfield, Milton Keynes, MK11 3LW, UK
UKHW011002180926
475701UK00004B/524
* 9 7 8 0 3 6 7 2 3 2 4 9 8 *